W9-BVC-573

The

COAST

GUARD

EXPANDS

1865–1915

The
COAST
GUARD
EXPANDS
1865–1915

New Roles, New Frontiers

Irving H. King

NAVAL INSTITUTE PRESS • ANNAPOLIS, MARYLAND

Library of Congress Cataloging-in-Publication Data
King, Irving H.
  The Coast Guard expands, 1865–1915 : new roles, new frontiers / Irving H. King.
       p.   cm.
  Includes bibliographical references and index.
  ISBN 1-55750-458-X (alk. paper)
  1. United States. Revenue-Cutter Service — History. 2. United States. Life-Saving Service — History. 3. United States. Coast Guard — History. I. Title.
HJ6645. K489   1996
359.9'7'0973—dc20   95-38786

Printed in the United States of America on acid-free paper ∞

03 02 01 00 99 98 97 96   9 8 7 6 5 4 3 2
First printing

All photographs courtesy of the U.S. Coast Guard unless indicated otherwise.

To thirty graduating classes of cadets,
who have taught me as much
as I have taught them.

Contents

Preface   ix

Introduction   1

CHAPTER ONE
The Reforms of Sumner I. Kimball   4

CHAPTER TWO
Cutters on the Alaskan Frontier, 1867–1889   22

CHAPTER THREE
A Struggle to Survive   54

CHAPTER FOUR
Cutter Operations during the 1880s   62

CHAPTER FIVE
Return to a Military Chief   72

CHAPTER SIX
The Bear *and the Overland Expedition*   82

CHAPTER SEVEN
The Spanish-American War   109

CHAPTER EIGHT
Operational Highlights, 1898–1914   126

CHAPTER NINE
The Revenue Cutter School of Instruction   154

CHAPTER TEN
The U.S. Life-Saving Service   192

CHAPTER ELEVEN
The Birth of the U. S. Coast Guard   223

Epilogue   243

APPENDIX A:
Summary of Cutter Operations, 1880–1914   246

APPENDIX B:
Equipment in Stations of the Life-Saving Service   248

Notes   251

Bibliography of Works Cited   273

Index   283

Preface

This book is the third in a series that, upon completion, will cover the history of the U.S. Coast Guard and its forerunners. The first book, *George Washington's Coast Guard,* formed the basis for chapters 1 and 2 of the second book, *The Coast Guard under Sail,* which thus stands as a complete account of what we know as the Coast Guard from its inception in 1790 as the U.S. Revenue Cutter Service until the end of the Civil War. This book picks up the story at that point and carries the history of the Revenue Cutter Service forward to 1915, when Congress united it with the U.S. Life-Saving Service. This union gave birth to the U.S. Coast Guard.

Like its predecessors, this volume emphasizes the dual character of the Revenue Cutter Service: an adjunct to the naval establishment and a servant that met U.S. maritime needs. In the former capacity, it fought alongside the U.S. Navy during the Spanish-American War. The *McCulloch,* under the command of Capt. Daniel B. Hodgsdon, served with Commodore George Dewey's Asiatic Squadron at Manila Bay in the Philippines. Meanwhile, halfway around the world at Cárdenas Bay, Cuba, the *Hudson* saved the navy torpedo boat *Winslow* in a heroic rescue that earned Lt. Frank Newcomb, the *Hudson*'s commanding officer, the only gold medal awarded by Congress for service in the war.

The wartime exploits of the Revenue Cutter Service caused Congress to recognize the military value of the cutters, which helped cuttermen to gain retirement rights. The successful participation of revenue cutters in naval battles also made it possible for supporters in Congress to save the service from eradication when, in 1911, the Taft administration recommended its complete elimination.

In the role of meeting maritime needs, the service developed its own special character during the years of expansion into new frontiers. It explored the Alaskan frontier for the United States, rescued whalers trapped in the Arctic ice, saved native Alaskans from starvation, and went to the aid of fur seals threatened with extinction. Continuing to give assistance to mariners in distress, the service improved its record in this regard by reforming its own operations and by using the newly invented radio and new, more powerful cutters. The sinking of the *Titanic* resulted in the service taking on the obligation to operate the international ice patrol for the world's merchant fleet. It performed a myriad of other duties, from destroying derelicts that threatened merchant shipping to serving the nation's interests on the Yukon River during the gold rush, preventing the spread of yellow fever in the Gulf of Mexico, assisting victims of the San Francisco earthquake, and taking medical care to deep-sea fishermen.

The Peace of Appomattox brought to an end the tragic American Civil War and left the Revenue Cutter Service and the Life-Saving Service, like the rest of the nation, crying for reconstruction. Sumner Increase Kimball stepped forward and reformed both organizations. He ran the Revenue Cutter Service and the Life-Saving Service together from 1871 to 1878, then chose to lead the Life-Saving Service alone, which he did until 1915. Kimball's greatest contribution to each organization was the elimination of political patronage in the selection, assignment, and promotion of personnel. Kimball eliminated political patronage in the Life-Saving Service and the Revenue Cutter Service before the national government reformed the civil service, thus setting a precedent for the nation to follow. His efforts allowed the Life-Saving Service to become the best organization of its kind in the world and the Revenue Cutter Service to establish an academy where capable young men trained for a life of service. Kimball's work also provided an opportunity for continued reform that, after 1889, took place under the leadership of a military chief.

My interest in Coast Guard history was inspired by the work of Stephen H. Evans, *The United States Coast Guard, 1790–1915*. When I first read his work, I thought that Evans was the father of Coast Guard history. I still do. Although I have developed some disagreements with Evans over how the service evolved and have drawn some different conclusions, I believe his work to be the foundation on which the rest of us must build and I happily acknowledge my debt to him. Since his book was published in 1949, no other work has provided a scholarly account of the Revenue Cutter Service's history for the years between the Civil War and 1915. This book is intended to fill that gap by presenting a comprehensive history of the service's struggle to survive as an independent agency during the era, its operations, its participation in the Spanish-American War, and its union with the Life-Saving Service to form the Coast Guard. In a chapter on the Coast Guard Academy, which, since its origin as the Revenue Cutter School of Instruction in 1876–77, has educated the vast majority of the service's officer corps, this work sheds new light on the service's development.

This work also presents new interpretations of the service's history. Basically, I like to fly the Coast Guard flag high, but I differ with Evans in some of my interpretations. Evans wrote that Ezra Clark, who succeeded Kimball as the head of the service, failed to retain cutter officers on his staff, with unfortunate results for the service that were turned around only when Capt. Leonard Shepard took over as the service's commandant. In fact, Clark saved the service from a naval takeover in spite of the officer corps. Evans wrote that Shepard saved the service from its tragic decline with many modernizing trends. Shepard was an important commandant, but real progress came under Shepard's successor, Capt. Charles Shoemaker, at a time that favored all naval establishments. It resulted from the initiatives of not only Leonard Shepard but of Ezra Clark and all of the treasury secretaries of that era.

I devote one chapter to the general history of the Life-Saving Service, which joined with the Revenue Cutter Service in 1915 to give birth to the Coast Guard. It is imperative, for the unity of the book, to provide this account, but I believe that the essential story of the Coast Guard is in the history of its seagoing establishment. That arm of the service has absorbed all other agencies, beginning with the Life-Saving Service, that have joined with it. In addition, Dennis L. Noble's *That Others Might Live: The U.S. Life-Saving Service, 1878–1915,* published by the Naval Institute Press in 1994, is now available.

Like the first two works of this series, the present volume is founded extensively on primary source materials, particularly public records of the relevant government agencies and cruise reports of the cutters. Many individuals have helped me to search the records, and I express my gratitude to them. The staff at Waesche Hall, the U.S. Coast Guard Academy Library, especially Sheila Lamb, Pamela McNulty, and Jean Huyek, gave much needed and continued assistance. The staff of the Connecticut State Library in Hartford helped me to find federal documents that were invaluable to this work. Robert M. Browning and Scott T. Price, historians at Coast Guard Headquarters, and Cindee Herrick at the Coast Guard Academy Museum assisted me in locating photographs. Angie Spicer VanDereedt at the National Archives helped me to use Record Group 26, the Records of the United States Coast Guard.

Thanks also go to the staffs of the Naval Historical Center, Washington, D.C.; the Louisiana State Museum, New Orleans; the Mariners Museum, Newport News, Virginia; the G. W. Blunt White Library at Mystic Seaport; the Fogler Library, University of Maine; the Earl K. Long Library, University of New Orleans; the University Library, University of Massachusetts; the Washington State Library, Olympia; the Portland Public Library, Portland, Maine; and the Filson Club, Louisville, Kentucky.

In addition, I am grateful to Elizabeth Junkins for typing several drafts of the book; to my wife, Ann E. King, for her encouragement while I was writing and for her many helpful suggestions after she read the final draft; and to Terry Belanger for her invaluable editing of the book.

The

COAST

GUARD

EXPANDS

1865–1915

Introduction

Congress established the Revenue Cutter Service on 4 August 1790 in an effort to prevent smuggling. Alexander Hamilton, the nation's first secretary of the treasury, convinced Congress of the need for a service to help U.S. customs collectors do their jobs. He was aware that the task would be difficult. The British customs service had found it impossible to collect tariffs in North America—it had not even been able to collect enough revenue to pay its own expenses. Calling upon the Royal Navy for assistance provoked a revolution, which led to the loss of part of Great Britain's empire. After the American colonies declared their independence, several tried to collect tariffs but found the task beyond their capabilities. By 1790, smuggling was not only a well-established national custom as a result of America's long years of colonial status, but it had become a meritorious enterprise.

Realizing the daunting task that faced the new U.S. Revenue Cutter Service, President George Washington insisted on the appointment of honorable men to command the nation's first revenue cutters. Then, he and Alexander Hamilton demanded that those captains treat the skippers of vessels that they stopped at sea with the respect due American freemen. It was the good fortune of the United States to have a man of Hamilton's brilliance, who recognized the need for tact in enforcing the nation's customs laws and who had the force of will to ensure compliance with his wishes. By combining a spirit of enterprise with a

1

proper respect for American citizens, the U.S. Revenue Cutter Service succeeded where the British customs service had failed. More important, it established respect for the new constitutional government and its laws.

Because of the cutter service's success in helping the customs service to collect tariffs, the government also turned to the Revenue Cutter Service to perform delicate tasks that were certain to generate strong opposition. In 1807, President Thomas Jefferson called on the service to enforce the embargo, which forbade American trade with foreign nations. President Andrew Jackson ordered cutters to uphold national sovereignty when South Carolina challenged U.S. tariff policies during the Nullification Controversy of 1832–33, and President Franklin Pierce ordered the service to return fugitive slaves to their masters under the Compromise of 1850.

From its beginning, the service performed a myriad of more mundane jobs for the new nation. It assisted mariners in distress by hauling them off of rocks and sandbars when they went aground, it pumped out their sinking ships and towed them into port, and it broke ice in the nation's harbors so that ships could go to sea during the winter months. In 1832–33, it added winter cruising to assist mariners in distress. Following the Mexican War, it extended its services to the Pacific Ocean.

The Revenue Cutter Service also served the public interest by enforcing quarantine laws, settling labor disputes on the nation's waterways, and charting America's coastal waters. It assisted the Lighthouse Service by scouting sites for new lighthouses. It transported men and supplies to the lights, put out stakes to mark channels in rivers and harbors, set buoys to warn mariners of navigational dangers, and inspected the nation's lighthouses.

For a brief time before the Mexican War, the first military commandant of the Revenue Cutter Service, Capt. Alexander V. Fraser, began attempts to combine the Revenue Cutter Service with the Lighthouse Service and the Life-Saving Service, but the sectionalism of the 1850s terminated the trend toward unity and saw the ouster of the service's military leadership. Not until the twentieth century would Congress take action to join these organizations into the U.S. Coast Guard.

In almost all government documents and correspondence before 1843, the organization was referred to as the Revenue Cutter Service or the Revenue Service, the cutters as revenue cutters or cutters. Moreover, the 1843 law did not establish an official name for the service but, rather, added to the old ones the names Revenue Marine Service and Revenue

Marine. Finally, in 1863, Congress officially sanctioned the designation Revenue Cutter Service. But that did not solve the problem, for Revenue Marine Service continued to be used along with Revenue Cutter Service until the mid-1890s, when Revenue Cutter Service began to hold sway. For convenience, I use Revenue Cutter Service in this book.

From 1790 on, the secretary of the treasury ran the Revenue Cutter Service through local customs collectors, who played a major role in the selection, appointment, and promotion of all officers. The customs collectors exercised power over officer assignments and determined the duration of their tenure. When an officer was charged with wrongdoing, a collector arranged for an investigation. Collectors contracted for the construction, repair, and maintenance of the cutters; assigned their cruising grounds; and regulated their movements. They paid the service's bills and kept the books, and they maintained a voluminous correspondence with the secretary of the treasury about all aspects of the service. For a brief time during the 1840s, Fraser took over those functions as the captain commandant of the service, but the sectionalism of the next decade terminated the military commandant's tenure. Congress would not restore that tenure until the late nineteenth century.

In addition to the many duties that the service performed in meeting the nation's maritime needs, it served as an adjunct to the U.S. Navy. In the latter capacity, it helped to build the navy and then fought alongside it in the Quasi-War with France, the War of 1812, the war against piracy in U.S. waters, the Seminole War, the Mexican War, and the Civil War.

Until the Civil War, the service operated a fleet of small armed sailing cutters. It built a few disappointing steamers while Fraser was commandant but then returned to sail until just before the Civil War, when it built the steam cutter *Harriet Lane*. As a result of the Civil War, more than two thirds of the service's cutters were steam powered by 1865, and the trend toward steam would continue after the war. The Revenue Cutter Service would also undergo considerable changes in other areas during the postwar period.

CHAPTER ONE

The Reforms of Sumner I. Kimball

T he amount of the nation's foreign commerce carried in U.S. ships fell off precipitously between the Civil War and World War I. Before 1860, U.S. ships had carried two thirds of the nation's foreign trade; by 1865, they carried less than one third and, by 1900, less than one tenth.

Congress was partly responsible for this deplorable situation. Favoring shipbuilders over shipping companies, it prohibited the return to the U.S. flag of ships that had fled to foreign registration during the Civil War, and it imposed high protective tariffs on copper, iron, hemp, canvas, and other shipbuilding materials. These policies combined with a shortage of skilled labor to drive up shipbuilding costs by 50 percent. Operating more expensive ships than their competitors proved difficult for domestic firms.

Having wrested both freight cargoes and passenger service from the United States during the Civil War, Great Britain fought to retain that trade. She increased her advantages over U.S. shipping companies by aggressively developing iron-hulled steamships. The opening of the Suez Canal in 1869 added to steamers' advantages over sailing ships, and the British government heavily subsidized the Cunnard Line, tough competition indeed for U.S. companies.

The nation's maritime tradition was kept alive during the late nineteenth century by a flourishing coastal trade and a rejuvenated United States Navy. The Navigation Act of 1817 excluded foreign ships from the coastal trade, which was therefore dominated by U.S. firms. As the century passed, those firms turned more and more to the use of efficient fore and aft-rigged schooners, often built in the state of Maine where labor costs were low and shipbuilding timber still existed. Their schooners increased in size and carrying capacity until each represented a considerable investment.

The booming coastal trade had a significant impact on the development of the U.S. Revenue Cutter Service. As the ever-larger schooners wrecked on the coast with spectacular losses in lives and property, the American public began to demand improvements in cutters, lifesaving stations, and aids to navigation. Such demands, combined with expanding revenue cutter operations in Alaskan waters following the purchase of Alaska Territory from Russia in 1867, led to a reorganization of the service.

George S. Boutwell, secretary of the treasury under President Ulysses S. Grant, led the reorganization. He appointed N. Broughton Devereux chief of an interim Revenue Marine Bureau consisting of the Revenue Cutter Service, the Steamboat Inspection Service, the Marine Hospital Service, and the Life-Saving Service. Devereux took charge of the bureau on 1 July 1869 and set to work by establishing two boards to overhaul the Revenue Cutter Service. One board, under Capt. John Faunce, was charged with investigating personnel matters, and the other, under Capt. Carlisle T. Patterson of the Coast Survey, was directed to analyze the cutter fleet.[1]

Devereux appointed eleven men with diverse backgrounds to Patterson's board because he believed that analysis of the service's cutters was most important, but he apparently was not motivated by any general criticism of the fleet. He simply wanted a study done by a board of experts who would provide him with basic information so that he could begin to address the service's needs. Representing the Revenue Cutter Service on the board were four captains (Faunce, Douglass Ottinger, John McGowan, and George R. Slicer) and two chief engineers (Charles S. Wheeler and Frank H. Pulsifer). A chief engineer and two constructors from the navy served with the cutter officers, and eminent engineer and constructor Charles W. Copeland from New York provided a civilian perspective.[2]

Patterson's board started work immediately and produced information for Devereux to use in his 1869 report to Congress. Subsequently, Captains Ottinger and James H. Merryman of the Revenue Cutter Service joined Patterson on a special commission that prepared a report on the type of vessels best suited for revenue cutter work. Boutwell received their report on 1 May 1870 and presented it to Congress on 26 May. The report provided the Treasury Department and Revenue Cutter Service with guidance for more than a decade.[3]

Twenty-four steamers and twelve sailing cutters made up the cutter fleet in 1869. This was the same ratio of steam to sail existing at the end of the Civil War. (The Revenue Cutter Service had entered the war with a fleet of twenty-four cutters; only one, the 180-foot side-wheel cutter *Harriet Lane*, had been steam powered.) In the 1869 fleet, four of the steamers were small tugs stationed at New York, Boston, and Baltimore; six were stationed on the Great Lakes; and the remaining fourteen steamers were on the Atlantic and Pacific coasts. Six of the cutters on the Atlantic Coast had been built toward the end of the Civil War.

Because Devereux was most interested in knowing what the board members thought of the steamers on the lakes, they traveled there first. After an inspection tour, the board declared the cutters to be good vessels for service (on the lakes) and recommended putting them into full service in 1870. It would cost $10,000 to repair the cutters and another $95,000 to reactivate them, but the board thought they were worth these expenditures. With one exception, the board recommended stationing the lake steamers at their 1869 locations: the *Perry* at Erie, Pennsylvania; the *John A. Dix* and *William P. Fessenden* at Detroit, Michigan; the *Sherman* at Cleveland, Ohio; and the *Andrew Johnson* at Milwaukee, Wisconsin. The board said that the *Salmon P. Chase*, which was at Ogdenberg, New York, should be moved to Oswego, New York. The board then turned its attention to the propeller-driven steamers built during the Civil War. Four of the six already had been sold by the service, which had retained the two considered best. The board recommended keeping only the *Mahoning*, the better of the two, and replacing the *Wayanda* with a fast 390-ton side-wheeler.[4]

With regard to the sailing cutters, Devereux reported that the service had recently sold three schooners (the *Joseph Lane, Toucey,* and *Crawford*) as unfit for duty. Of the twelve remaining schooners, he recommended selling seven and keeping five. He wanted to replace the *Jacob Thompson, Rescue, Relief, Petrel, Resolute, Antietam,* and *Racer* with steamers. He evaluated the *James C. Dobbin, James Campbell, Vigilant, Reliance,* and *Active* as "superior vessels of their class" that should be retained as cutters.[5]

Finally, in his 1869 report, Devereux expressed a desire to build four new steamers: a large propeller-driven ship, a large side-wheeler, and two small side-wheelers.[6] His request makes it clear that he had not yet settled on an appropriate type of vessel for the service and that the board of experts had not yet tackled the difficult issue of a proper cutter type. All that is clear from Devereux's report is that the Revenue Cutter Service had unequivocally accepted steam as the proper mode of power for a cutter.

In the subsequent 1870 report, the special commission investigating the proper vessel for a cutter did specify that "the engines for the steamers should be of the simplest and most approved types . . . in actual use in the merchant marine." For propeller-driven craft, it recommended "the latest improved patterns of the inverted single direct-acting engine"; for side-wheelers, it preferred the walking-beam engine. The commission believed that first-class cutters should be able to run at 13 knots, second-class cutters at 11 knots, and third-class cutters at 10 knots.[7]

The commission expected the service to equip its cutters with sails in order to contain operating costs, when possible. During normal cruising under steam, the cutters were to run at half-speed to save on coal consumption.[8]

Devereux asked the Congress for $125,000 to cover the unexpected cost of operating three cutters, the *Lincoln, Wayanda,* and *Reliance,* in Alaskan waters in 1869. The cutters had been dispatched into the Bering Sea following the acquisition of Alaska Territory, and no provision previously had been made for those operations.[9]

Also, Devereux considered the classes of cutters that should be assigned to the nation's coasts, the ports from which they should sail, and the waters they should cruise to provide the best protection for the revenue. When he made his recommendations, he was conscious of the Revenue Cutter Service's obligation to protect U.S. shipping by cruising coastal waters in the winter season, and he believed that the service should be able to provide twenty steamers to act as dispatch boats for the navy on either the Atlantic or Pacific coast. Thus, he believed that new cutters should be built for speed and have the capacity to carry large quantities of fuel and provisions.

Devereux classified the cutters as follows: first class, 400 tons or more; second class, 250–399 tons; third class, 150–249 tons; and fourth class, 75–149 tons.[10] He recommended stationing steamers of those classes at the locations shown in Table 1-1.

TABLE 1-1 *Recommended Locations for Cutters, 1869*

STATION	FIRST CLASS	SECOND CLASS	THIRD CLASS	FOURTH CLASS
Eastport, Maine	1			
Castine, Maine			1	
Portland, Maine		1		
Portsmouth, New Hampshire			1	
Boston, Massachusetts	1			
New Bedford, Massachusetts			1	
Newport, Rhode Island			1	
New London, Connecticut		1		
New Haven, Connecticut			1	
New York, New York	1		1	
Wilmington, Delaware		1		
Philadelphia, Pennsylvania			1	
Norfolk, Virginia		1		
Cherrystone, Virginia			1	
Baltimore, Maryland			1	
New Bern, North Carolina			1	
Beaufort, South Carolina		1		
Charleston, South Carolina		1		
Savannah, Georgia			1	
Key West, Florida			1	
Cedar Keys, Florida			1	
Mobile, Alabama		1		
New Orleans, Louisiana		1	1	
Galveston, Texas		1		
San Francisco, California	1			
Astoria, Oregon		1		
Washington Territory (port of entry)		1		
Alaska (headquarters at Sitka)	1	1		
Erie, Pennsylvania		1*		
Cleveland, Ohio		1*		
Detroit, Michigan		1*		
Milwaukee, Wisconsin		1*		
Marquette, Michigan		1*		
Oswego, New York				1

* *Light-draft vessel.*

Source: *N. Broughton Devereux*, Report of the Chief of Revenue Marine, of the Steamboat Inspection, Marine Hospitals, and Life-Saving Stations, *Washington, D.C.: Government Printing Office, 1869.*

At various times before completion of the commission's study and the reform of the Revenue Cutter Service, the nation's press had considered the cutters a pleasure fleet. Customs collectors were largely responsible for this perception, for they used the cutters under their control as their own private yachts. An officer's ability to provide a fine cuisine and to cater pleasure cruises was often more important to his advancement than his navigation and seamanship skills. Some officers entered the service at very high rank without any prior experience at sea. They received promotions for political reasons and were retained indefinitely at desirable locations, whereas other officers suffered at hardship posts. According to Kimball, such use of the cutters was "the most pernicious practice that ever cursed the service," and at one time "threatened its ruin."[11] The service was demoralized by such political abuses, incompetence, and lax administration.

In its report to Congress of 26 May 1870, the commission proposed several solutions to problems uncovered by the two boards. During the Civil War, the Revenue Cutter Service had increased the size of its officer corps and fleet to meet expanding obligations. It had accepted officers without adequate checks of their character and professional competence. Ships not suited to the service's peacetime roles had been added to the fleet; as a result, operations had been impaired and costs had increased. The commission recommended centralizing administrative control for economy and efficiency, eliminating political influence in personnel decisions, selling old vessels, and building new ones designed to meet the needs of the service. At the time of the commission's report, the aggregate tonnage of all cutters stood at 9,208. On active duty were 200 commissioned officers and a total of 1,046 petty officers, seamen, firemen, cooks, stewards, and boys. The commission recommended reducing the cutter fleet to 7,175 tons, by assigning to particular stations the smallest cutters that could perform the duties required, and reducing the officer corps to 183 men and enlisted ranks to 878 men and boys.[12]

Boutwell responded to these recommendations by placing authority over both the Revenue Cutter Service and the Life-Saving Service in a newly created Revenue Marine Bureau within the Treasury Department and selecting Kimball, then a chief clerk in the department, to head the bureau. Kimball assumed his responsibilities on 1 February 1871, but Congress did not formalize the organization through legislation until 3 March 1875. Kimball continued to head the bureau until the end of fiscal year 1878, when he volunteered to lead the U.S. Life-Saving Service.[13]

Sumner I. Kimball

Born in Lebanon, Maine, on 2 September 1834, Kimball attended a number of academies in southern Maine and was graduated from Bowdoin College in 1855. He taught school while still a student, studied law in his father's office, and gained admission to the bar in 1858. After serving as a commission clerk for the state of Maine, he opened his own law practice in North Berwick. In 1859, his fellow citizens elected him to the state legislature, where he served as its youngest member. During the Civil War, he moved to Washington and accepted a job as a clerk in the office of the second auditor of the treasury. He became a chief clerk in 1870, and, the following year, Secretary Boutwell offered him the position of chief of the Revenue Marine Bureau. Kimball's integrity, force of will, and administrative experience recommended him for the job.[14]

Six months after taking office, Kimball revised the service's regulations in order to reform the system. The most important of the new regulations implemented a merit system of appointment and promotion for the officer corps, provided for economy of operations, and centralized control in headquarters. To gain admission to the officer corps candidates now had to pass both physical and professional examinations. A successful candidate had to enter the service at one of the lowest officer grades, either third lieutenant or second assistant engineer. Thereafter, he earned promotions on the basis of professional qualifications without regard to seniority. The use of political influence to acquire an assignment or to revoke a set of orders was prohibited. Kimball set the normal tour of duty at a station at two years. To reduce the cost of operations, the new regulations encouraged the use of sails in ordinary cruising, established tables of allowances for stores and equipment, and forbade repair of cutters without the approval of headquarters. The regulations held officers accountable for all property and its care and forbade the use of cutters for any purpose other than public business. Each cutter was required to submit a weekly transcript of her log to the Treasury Department. Compliance with the wishes of headquarters was assured by a systematic inspection of all units by officers from the Treasury Department.[15]

While Kimball was working on his new regulations, Captain Faunce was taking drastic action to raise the professional standards of the officer corps. His personnel board, consisting of Captains Slicer and Patterson and Dr. E. H. Stein of the navy (detailed as physical examiner), first met on 22 October 1869. During the next two years, the board reviewed the qualifications of every officer in the service and found some of them totally unfit for duty. For example, a second lieutenant appointed in 1864 had no knowledge of instruments or charts, another officer was chronically drunk, and a third was evaluated as amounting to nothing. Faunce's board removed 7 of 19 captains and 33 of 103 lieutenants from the service. Those retained were given rank commensurate with their abilities. In addition, the board implemented Kimball's new regulations.[16]

According to Kimball, the service benefited greatly from the actions of Faunce's board. In 1872, he said that the Revenue Cutter Service had "the best corps of junior officers it ever possessed," and they were motivated to do their best to gain promotion. He added that the officers generally accepted the reforms, as did the collectors in charge of the vessels, once it

Capt. John Faunce, oil painting by George Sottung. Claire White-Peterson photo, courtesy of U.S. Coast Guard Academy Library.

was made clear to them that the department meant to enforce the regulations. Abuse of the cutters as a personal perquisite of office had ended.[17]

Before the conclusion of fiscal year 1873, the Revenue Cutter Service gave two examinations for admission into the service and for promotions, one in September for engineers and the other in November for line officers. Both were conducted in accordance with the new regulations. In addition to the written and oral examinations, all candidates had to demonstrate practical ability with the instruments and tools of their respective professions. The engineers, Kimball noted, were taken to the shop for the purpose. Following the examinations, those who qualified were promoted without regard to seniority and new candidates were ranked according to the results of their examinations. Kimball reported that the officers admitted and promoted "constitute[d] an able and efficient corps."[18]

The initial reforms in the Revenue Cutter Service predated general reforms in the Treasury Department, which was notoriously corrupt and generally riddled by patronage during the last half of the nineteenth century. Reform did not take place within the department as a whole until the administration of President Rutherford B. Hayes, and the department established general standards of qualifications for positions only after passage of the Civil Service Act of 1883. In contrast, the Revenue Cutter Service was rid of its incompetent personnel early in President Grant's administration,[19] and it set standards for appointments and promotions in 1871.

After implementing his personnel policies, Kimball persuaded Congress to pass legislation authorizing the establishment of a training school to ensure a continuous supply of competent new officers. Chief Inspector George W. Moore, Superintendent of Construction Merryman, and Capt. John A. Henriques, three senior officers who appreciated the benefits to be derived from such an institution, had encouraged Kimball to found the school. The authorization was tucked away in a few sentences of a lengthy piece of legislation dated 31 July 1876. Although little noticed at the time, it has had lasting importance, for it laid the foundation for the U.S. Coast Guard Academy.[20]

While Kimball, Faunce, and Henriques were implementing a merit system of promotion for revenue cutter officers, Kimball took quick action to reduce the total tonnage of the cutter fleet, the number of men on the payroll, and operating costs. At the same time, the cutters sailed more miles each year and provided improved services to the nation's maritime community. Kimball resisted the commission's findings in only one area. He strongly opposed its recommendation to cut the officer corps but called instead for a compensated retirement system for revenue cutter officers.

Reacting to the commission's recommendation to reduce aggregate tonnage by 2,033 tons, Kimball sold the big, old cutters that were poorly suited to revenue work and replaced them with smaller, more efficient ones. By 30 June 1872, he had already reduced the aggregate tonnage by 657 tons. In addition, vessels on the stocks and proposed for construction totaled 1,565 tons versus the total tonnage of 2,797 for those vessels to be replaced, the *Wayanda, Chase, Lincoln, Nansemond, McCulloch, Reliance, Petrel,* and *Relief* or *Racer.* These changes would reduce the aggregate tonnage of the fleet by 1,889 tons, close to the total amount recommended by the commission.[21]

At the beginning of 1872, the Revenue Cutter Service had a fleet of twenty-five steamers (including two steam launches) and ten sailing vessels. By November, twenty-seven steamers, two steam launches, and eight sailing vessels were in the fleet. The steam cutters included both side-wheelers and propeller-driven vessels. There were three new ships, the *Grant* at New York City; the *Hamilton* at Philadelphia, Pennsylvania; and the *Colfax* at Baltimore, Maryland. The largest cutter, the 550-ton *Lincoln,* was propeller driven. Excluding the two 15-ton steam launches, the 80-ton, propeller-driven *Hamlin* was the smallest cutter.[22]

Kimball was most pleased with the 350-ton, propeller-driven iron steamer *Grant,* built by Patsey, Jones and Company of Wilmington, Delaware; the 250-ton side-wheel steamer *Colfax,* built by Dialogue and Wood of Camden, New Jersey; and the 250-ton *Hamilton,* built by David Bell of Buffalo, New York. The 250-ton *Gallatin,* a vessel like the *Hamilton* under construction in the same yard, had a propeller problem on her trial run, but Kimball believed that she would be a good cutter once her propeller was replaced. He described the three successful new cutters as "well built, of fine model, commodious, and of great strength and speed." They were, he said, the best cutters ever employed by the service.[23]

Captains Merryman and John W. White, two most capable and experienced officers, according to Kimball, supervised all new construction. They were assisted by First Lieutenants Henry P. Hamlin and Thomas B. Mullett. Consulting engineer Charles E. Emery of New York built and installed the ships' engines and boilers, which were designed for economy, efficiency, and speed. The replaced cutters had small boilers requiring great quantities of fuel or complicated machinery requiring great quantities of lubricants. Thus, the new, more efficient cutters resulted in savings for the service.[24]

During 1872, Merryman, White, and Emery supervised the construction of three additional steamers: a 250-ton iron-hulled cutter with twin screws, a 150-ton iron-hulled cutter with a single screw, and a 250-ton wooden cutter with a single screw. Although iron was superior to wood for cutter construction, there were only a few builders of iron vessels in the United States. This lack of competition resulted in high costs for iron ships, and the price of iron itself contributed to the impossibility of building all of the new cutters of that material. The service had an urgent need for several new expensive ships to replace worn-out cutters, and the cost of iron increased 20 percent between the time of writing proposals for the new cutters and the time of issuing the bids.[25] The constant increases in both labor and material costs complicated efforts to replace the old fleet, but progress was made. On 30 June 1873, the service had a fleet of twenty-eight steamers and six sailing cutters. These figures included three excellent new steamers, the 250-ton, twin-screw *George S. Boutwell,* the 235-ton, single-screw *Oliver Wolcott,* and the 147-ton, single-screw *Manhattan.* Congress had appropriated an additional $200,000 for vessels, and the service was building three 250-ton propeller-driven steamers with the money. The new steamers replaced cutters that were both unsuited to the service and difficult to maintain.[26]

Trends in cutter construction begun by Kimball during the early 1870s continued throughout the decade. Merryman and Emery were still supervising new construction in 1881. With few exceptions, the service continued to build propeller-driven steamships specifically designed for designated stations. Three new cutters joined the fleet in 1874 (the *Richard Rush, Alexander J. Dallas,* and *Samuel Dexter*), one in 1875 (the *John F. Hartley*), two in 1876 (the *Tench Coxe* and *Thomas Corwin*), one in 1877 (the *Alert*), and one in 1878 (the *Salmon P. Chase*). All except the small sloop *Alert,* built for special duty in assisting the Life-Saving Service, and the bark *Salmon P. Chase,* built as a schoolship for the new academy, were propeller-driven steamers. The *Rush* had a compound engine, and the small steamer *Hartley* was built for harbor duty at San Francisco. But all of the new cutters were more economical to operate than previous cutters and were considered to be admirably suited to the duties required of them. Ezra Clark, Kimball's longtime assistant who succeeded him as bureau chief in 1878, claimed that they were superior vessels that had attracted the attention of naval architects both at home and abroad.[27]

The service continued to sell the worst of its cutters. It disposed of five old schooners needing extensive repairs: the *Rescue* in 1874; the *Reliance, Active,* and *James Campbell,* 1875; and the *James C. Dobbin,* 1881. The first three had been built in 1867, the *Campbell* in 1856, and the *Dobbin* in 1853. Three big steamers of 500 tons or more, all built in 1865, were sold: the propeller-driven *Lincoln* in 1874 and the side-wheelers *Salmon P. Chase* and *Hugh McCulloch* in 1875 and 1876, respectively. Proceeds of $83,413 realized from the sales were applied toward the cost of a new vessel for the service.[28]

Unfortunately, only one new cutter was under construction in 1881. Congress had appropriated $75,000 for an additional cutter, even though Clark had asked for funds to replace four vessels that he considered unsafe and too far gone to be repaired.[29] No new cutter had joined the fleet since the *Chase* in 1878, and no new steamer had joined the fleet since 1876. This disturbing trend seems to have overlapped the administrations of Kimball and Clark. Although new cutters continued to join the fleet through 1878, when Kimball assumed full-time duties as superintendent of the Life-Saving Service, no new vessels were funded by Congress from 23 June 1874 to 3 March 1881. Between 1869 and 1874, Kimball had succeeded in raising $925,000 for new construction; the next appropriation was for Clark's cutter in 1881. The trend of the era is made clear by appropriations of $175,000 for rebuilding cutters in 1881 and 1882, while only $86,000 was appropriated for new construction.[30]

Between 1873 and 1880, the Revenue Cutter Service repaired twelve cutters. Only four of the twelve, the *Andrew Johnson, Schuyler Colfax, Levi Woodbury* (formerly *Mahoning*), and *Manhattan,* had been built for the service. The *E. A. Stevens,* also known as the *Naugatuck,* had been accepted as a gift during the Civil War. The remaining seven cutters, the *Peter G. Washington, William E. Chandler, Hugh McCulloch* (formerly *Mosswood*), *Albert Gallatin, Louis McLane* (formerly *Delaware*), *John A. Dix* (formerly the *Wilderness*), and *William H. Seward,* had been purchased for the service at the end of the war. Clark claimed that it was departmental policy to repair only those vessels that would be as good as new when the work was completed, but he also wrote that repairing existing cutters had "enabled the Department to maintain its small fleet in efficient condition, at an expense far below the cost of replacing the old vessels with new, and within the appropriations annually made by Congress to meet the expenses of the service."[31]

An unfortunate policy had been established. The combination of rising costs and limited resources had led the service to repair old cutters, in some cases as old as twenty years, rather than build new ones. Four old steamers were extensively repaired, according to Clark, and the hull of the side-wheeler *Andrew Jackson* was almost completely rebuilt. In addition, she received a new boiler and had her engine and machinery over-hauled.[32]

In 1881, the fleet consisted of thirty-six cutters, with an aggregate tonnage of 6,956, plus two small steam launches. There were thirty-one steamers, four sloops, and one bark. Twenty of the steamers had propellers, eight were side-wheelers, and one was a peculiar vessel with a side propeller. The four small sloops all served on special duty with the Life-Saving Service, and the bark served as a schoolship. The thirty-six cutters mounted fifty-eight guns and had a complement of 183 officers and 720 crewmen. Twenty-one of them had been built since the reforms of 1869. Thus, the fleet still benefited from the new construction of the 1870s, but the troublesome trend of repairing old cutters would have very negative consequences as time passed.

The special commission had estimated the service's operating costs at $943,639 per year, much less than actual operating costs in previous years, yet the service spent only $930,250 on operations for the fiscal year ending 30 June 1872. This was $13,000 less than the commission's estimate and $190,776 less than the cost of operations for 1871. This figure was much less than the cost for each fiscal year between 1865 and 1871, as can be seen in the following figures taken from Kimball's 1872 annual report:[33]

FISCAL YEAR ENDED	OPERATING COSTS
30 June 1865	$1,229,434
30 June 1866	1,777,231
30 June 1867	1,167,125
30 June 1868	1,293,662
30 June 1869	1,185,702
30 June 1870	1,133,670
30 June 1871	1,121,026
30 June 1872	930,250

The costs of operating the Revenue Cutter Service had not been kept separate on the Treasury Department's books before 1864. As the figures above show, the cost of operations had declined in most years from the end of the Civil War to 1871, and the decline from 1871 to 1872 brought the cost below $1 million.[34]

Operating costs increased slightly in 1873, but the impact of Kimball's reforms was to reduce operating expenses, not only under Kimball but also under his successor, Ezra Clark. Figures for fiscal years 1873 through 1881 were as follows:

FISCAL YEAR ENDED	OPERATING COSTS
30 June 1873	$995,308
30 June 1874	903,601
30 June 1875	897,899
30 June 1876	842,912
30 June 1877	841,176
30 June 1878	844,061
30 June 1879	844,527
30 June 1880	845,333
30 June 1881	846,791

Costs reached their lowest point in 1877, at the depths of the panic, but expenditures were kept close to the 1877 figure for the remainder of the five-year period ending in 1881.

The commission had recommended reducing the number of enlisted men and boys in the service to 878. During the first five months of 1871, a total of 1,046 petty officers, seamen, firemen, cooks, stewards, and boys still manned the cutters. In May, Kimball took steps to comply with the commission's wishes by having headquarters prepare a chart specifying the authorized enlisted complement for the cutters, and he ordered cutter captains to reduce their crews to those numbers by 1 July 1871. The chart indicated a crew of 37 for a first-class steamer; 31, a second-class steamer; 19, a third-class steamer; 9, a fourth-class steamer; 29, a 250-ton schooner; 24, a 189-ton schooner; and 21, a 120-ton schooner.

Kimball's initiative greatly reduced the size of the cutters' crews. In 1869, a first-class cutter had gone to sea with a total complement (officers and enlisted) of 73; a second-class cutter, 55; a third-class cutter, 32; and a fourth-class cutter (identified as one of 75–150 tons with a 4-foot draft), 20. By June 1873, Kimball could boast that the cutter crews had been reduced to a total of 860, which was 18 fewer than the number recommended by the commission just three years before.[35]

At the same time that Kimball was complying with the commission's recommendations to cut the aggregate tonnage of the fleet, reduce the cost of operations, and cut the size of the crews, the cutters were improving their performance. In the fiscal year ending 30 June 1872, revenue cutters sailed 166,098 miles, assisted 219 vessels in distress, seized or reported for violation of the nation's laws 1,594 vessels, boarded and examined 24,932 vessels, and saved thirty-seven lives. Such statistics are important only in comparison with those of other years. When compared with the figures for the years from 1860 through 1870, they demonstrate that the performance of the Revenue Cutter Service was improving under Kimball's leadership; however, statistics were listed by calendar year during the 1860s and Kimball listed them by fiscal year. During each calendar year from 1860 through 1870, the cutters sailed an average of 147,599 miles, assisted 119 vessels, seized or reported for violation of the nation's laws 114 vessels, boarded and examined 13,098 vessels, and saved seventeen lives. The total number of vessels seized or reported for violation of the nation's laws in 1872 included 1,104 reported by two New York harbor boats whose reportings were not kept in the statistics during the 1860s. Subtracting this figure from the total number for 1872 allows for more meaningful comparisons: more than three times as many vessels were seized or reported for violating the law in 1872 than in any one year during the 1860s and more than four times as many as the annual average during the 1860s.[36]

Kimball attributed the service's improved performance and reduced operating costs to implementation of the special commission's recommendations and the "strict enforcement of the revised regulations," which had, as he said, "effected a thorough reorganization of the service."[37] The service continued to improve its performance under both Kimball and his successor, Ezra Clark, as can be demonstrated by comparing statistics in Tables 1–2 and 1–3. Table 1–2 lists those for the period 1860–70, the years before implementation of the new regulations and reorganization, and Table 1–3 lists those for the period 1872–81, the years following these changes.

"It is a noteworthy fact," Clark observed in his 1881 report to Congress, that during the four years after completion of the reorganization (1878 through 1881), "the work performed by revenue vessels nearly equals, indeed, in some particulars exceeds, that for the ten years ended with 1870."[38]

Kimball did not implement the commission's recommendation to reduce the commissioned officer corps to 183 men; neither did his successor. There were 198 officers on the rolls in 1872, 1873, and 1881. In his reports to Congress for 1872 and 1873, Kimball argued that he could not reduce the number further. Several officers had to work with the expanding Life-Saving Service. Three or four captains were usually assigned to inspection duty or to supervise new cutter construction or repairs. More than 5 percent of the officer corps was unable to serve on active duty because of some "permanent disability incurred in the service," either during the

TABLE 1-2 *Performance Statistics, Revenue Cutter Service, 1860–70*

YEAR	MILES SAILED	BOARDED AND EXAMINED	SEIZED OR REPORTED FOR VIOLATION OF LAW	ASSISTED IN DISTRESS	LIVES SAVED
1860	112,939	11,095	96	88	5
1861	159,574	12,991	111	129	20
1862	147,455	9,728	143	134	23
1863	174,111	9,386	118	117	19
1864	99,326	38,815	103	61	3
1865	126,552	17,375	90	116	7
1866	192,597	8,607	133	143	33
1867	192,313	10,850	154	126	14
1868	155,910	7,923	83	108	25
1869	156,910	7,927	79	109	25
1870	105,903	9,386	149	175	18
Total	1,623,590	144,083	1,259	1,306	192
Average per year	147,599	13,098	114	119	17

Source: author

Civil War or in dangerous peacetime duties. Since the number of officers had been limited by law, on 25 July 1861, to one of each grade for each ship, Kimble argued that "the exigencies of the service demanded either the removal of the limitation . . ., the establishment of a retirement list, or the dismissal of a large number of unfortunate men, who have devoted the best years of their lives, in war and in peace to the faithful service of their Government, at a meager compensation, and who have been therein overtaken by infirmity and decrepitude, that their places may be filled with men capable of active duty. The practicable, as well as the humane measure is to establish a retired list similar to that of the Navy."[39]

Revenue cutter personnel could receive a pension only if wounded while serving in cooperation with the U.S. Navy in time of war, and then they received a pension at a rate set by Congress on 18 April 1814. Since then, pensions for naval personnel had been increased considerably and had been extended to their heirs, without regard to whether they were disabled in peace or war. No such provisions covered revenue cuttermen. Nevertheless, they still had to cruise the coast in winter, which put them in greater danger than naval personnel normally faced in peacetime, and their work protecting the nation's revenue was vital to the country's well-being.

TABLE 1-3 *Performance Statistics, Revenue Cutter Service, 1872–81*

YEAR	MILES SAILED	BOARDED AND EXAMINED	SEIZED OR REPORTED FOR VIOLATION OF LAW	ASSISTED IN DISTRESS	LIVES SAVED
1872	166,198	24,932	1,594	219	37
1873	185,668	30,543	1,605	210	109
1874	169,882	27,748	1,810	153	4
1875	198,117	22,225	1,245	195	81
1876	194,261	23,686	1,225	195	45
1877	196,036	25,396	1,260	204	60
1878	238,505	31,096	2,009	192	76
1879	252,112	32,853	3,444	210	123
1880	265,763	36,318	3,556	114	65
1881	282,027	29,101	3,163	148	141
Total	2,148,569	283,898	20,911	1,840	741
Average per year	214,857	28,390	2,091	184	74

Source: author

Surely, Kimball argued, they deserved a pension plan similar to the navy's. Such a plan, he continued, would ensure continued progress in the Revenue Cutter Service.[40] His refusal to reduce the officer corps and his call for a retirement system for revenue cutter officers similar to the navy's would be repeated by him, as well as by Clark in 1872, 1873, 1876, and 1881.[41]

In arguing for pensions for cutter officers in 1881, Clark stressed that they deserved a pension. In addition to repeating all the old arguments, with new statistics added to bring the material up to date, he listed the valuable services that they performed for the nation. They guarded the coast against smugglers; enforced the nation's neutrality laws; enforced laws governing merchant shipping; rendered assistance to those in peril on the sea at all times, especially in inclement weather; maintained peace among Alaskan natives; protected the seal herds in Alaskan waters; assisted many other branches of government, especially the Life-Saving Service; and served with the navy in time of war. By putting all services in proper perspective, Clark argued, with justice, that the work of saving lives by the Revenue Cutter Service, the Life-Saving Service, the Lighthouse Service, and the Signal Service gave "our country a just preeminence amongst the nations of the world for humane governmental institutions."[42]

CHAPTER TWO

Cutters on the Alaskan Frontier, 1867–1889

O n 29 March 1867 at 0400, Secretary of State William H. Seward and Russian Minister to the United States Edward de Stoeckl signed a treaty transferring Alaska to the United States for $7,200,000. Americans reacted most critically. Pundits claimed that the sophisticated Russian had sold a totally worthless territory to a gullible Seward. Outbursts of derision characterized the purchase as "Seward's Folly," "Seward's Ice Box," and "Walrussia." It required a supreme effort by supporters of the treaty to push it through the Senate and to convince the House of Representatives to pass the necessary appropriations bill. Subsequently, the cruise reports of the Revenue Cutter Service revealed the true value of Alaska.

The Revenue Cutter Service quickly became the nation's principal agent in Alaska. Its cutters transported government officials, scientists, and doctors to the territory and carried stranded Americans, including whalers trapped in the ice, from the territory to the United States. Its officers explored Alaska and evaluated the area's natural resources, peoples, and problems. They communicated their findings to the government and thus played a significant role in the formulation of government policy. As the principal law enforcement agency in the territory, the service protected the people of Alaska and the resources on which they depended for their livelihood.

The Bear *with Inuits on board in Kotzebue Sound.*

Within four months of the purchase, the Treasury Department dispatched the revenue steamer *Lincoln* (Capt. William A. Howard) to the territory. Departing San Francisco, California, in July, the cutter carried her usual complement of officers and men plus several government officials and scientists. At Sitka, she left Lt. George W. Moore, who established a provincial headquarters there. The cutter then dropped off a party of Coast Survey men, headed by George Davidson, who began to gather information for new charts. She transported a surgeon who collected specimens for the Smithsonian Institution, while she herself carried out a general reconnaissance north and west of Sitka. Her crew made surveys, investigated sites for lighthouses and other aids to navigation, decided that Unalaska was an ideal location for a coaling station, and located fishing banks across the North Pacific. In a single seine haul off Unalaska, the *Lincoln*'s crew caught 2,500 salmon and herring. When the *Lincoln* returned to San Francisco in November, she and her crew had accomplished much that they had set out to do and had laid the foundation for future cutter operations in Alaskan waters.[1]

The USRC Lincoln

During the first year of U.S. ownership of Alaska, Capt. John W. White sailed the *Wayanda* north on a long exploratory cruise. His cruise report provided evidence of coal, gold, and silver in Alaska; of rich cod and salmon stocks; of fertile grasslands; and of the need for further exploration.

On Cook's Inlet northwest of Sitka, White discovered vast veins of good-quality coal that came out of the ground in bright, clear blocks. According to White, geographers who had written that the inlet was of little value were wrong. It was instead a big body of water, surrounded by mountains, plains, valleys, and forests, with shores rich in natural resources.[2]

White reported the discovery of gold on mainland streams that emptied into Steven's Passage. He had seen "rich specimens of gold-bearing quartz and silver ore which had been obtained from lodes on Baranoff (Sitka) Island; also very rich specimens of copper-ore and galena found on other islands of the archipelago." With confidence, White predicted that additional mineral deposits would be found in the area.[3]

The waters of Alaska abounded in fish. It had been argued that the banks near the Aleutians were not good fishing grounds, but White answered that they were. He had found the entire length of the banks rich in both codfish and halibut. The best fishing, he reported, was in seventy or eighty fathoms. One day, needing a supply of fish while sounding south of Kodiak, he had the men back the sails and put out a line that had five hooks baited with Puget Sound clams. On some sets, he had caught as many as 5 fish, each weighing as much as forty pounds. With twenty lines out, the crew caught 250 fish in just two hours.[4]

White wrote that the grass on Unalaska and Kodiak was six to eight feet high and very thick. With no shelter but the ravines, small Russian cattle lived on this grass year-round and were as fat as seals.

A decade after White's cruise in the *Wayanda*, William Gouverneur Morris, a Treasury Department special agent, tried to counter false information that had been published about the new territory at the time of the purchase. In a 163-page report, he went to great lengths to convince the department that Alaska was rich in natural resources. He tried to introduce facts and reality into discussions about the territory and quoted extensively from Captain White's cruise report. In the appendix, he included a three-page account of Alaska by Gen. Oliver O. Howard of the U.S. Army that was based on information gathered by Howard from Captain White during a trip together up the Columbia River and an eight-page account

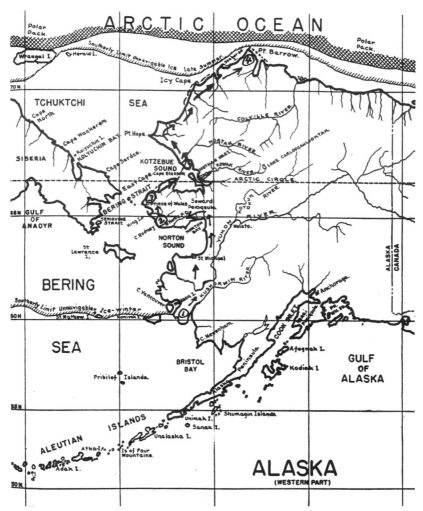

*Map of Alaska (western part). Includes route of the Overland Expedition,
1897–1898: (1) landing; (2) Charlie's deer; (3) Lopp's deer; (4) Point Barrow.*

of the revenue cutter *Walcott*'s 1875 cruise to Alaska. Within a few years,
cruise reports of other cutters' trips to Alaska would be published in the
Executive Documents of the House of Representatives.

Captain White did not have to tell Americans about the abundance of
fur seals in Alaskan waters. When the *Wayanda* sailed into the Bering Sea,
several companies, both American and foreign, were already killing seals

there, with Aleuts doing the work. Traditionally, native Alaskans had fished and stored food during the summer months for the long, hard winter. Working for the sealers kept them from that all-important task, and, worst of all, the sealers paid for their labor with whiskey, thus endangering the natives. Captain White wrote in his report that he "knew that when the ships were gone the Aleuts would be left without food, and that the great slaughter of the seals would soon destroy all."[5] Because White's job was to protect the territory, he broke all whiskey barrels that he found, stopped the killing of any but two-year-old male seals, and required the sealers to pay the Aleuts in clothing and provisions.

In 1870, the U.S. government followed White's advice and designated the Pribilof Islands, located in the Bering Sea about 250 miles north of Unalaska, as a federal reserve. The most important locations in the group were Saint George and Saint Paul islands. The government leased the privilege of killing male seals on those islands to the Alaska Commercial Company. At the same time, it assigned the task of trying to protect the females to the Revenue Cutter Service, which did a creditable job within the three-mile limit around the islands. But the policy was woefully inadequate, for the seals were fair game outside of this limit.[6]

Protection of the seals was complicated by the fact that seals, like salmon, are far-ranging creatures. If the herds were to survive, the females would have to be protected both on shore and while fishing at sea. This was a difficult diplomatic problem that would be settled only after years of tough negotiations with Great Britain, Canada, Russia, and Japan.[7] The problem of protecting the native Alaskans would also take years of hard work.

Captain White's concerns about the impact of liquor on native Alaskans might have played a role in the government's ban of its importation into Alaska. In section 1955 of the Revised Statutes, Congress gave the president authority to restrict the importation of firearms, ammunition, and distilled spirits into Alaska Territory. Under the law, an individual who violated any of these restrictions was punished by forfeiture of the forbidden products. If the value of the products exceeded $400, punishment could include forfeiture of the vessel. That individual also could be fined up to $500 and imprisoned for up to six months. To ensure compliance with the law, officials could demand a bond from the owner or master of any vessel bound for Alaska with restricted products on board. On 4 February 1870, the year following the *Wayanda*'s cruise, President

Grant proclaimed the importation of liquor into Alaska Territory illegal and banned the importation of firearms and ammunition into Saint Paul and Saint George Islands.[8]

Treasury Secretary Boutwell implemented the president's wishes by ordering customs officials to refuse clearance to vessels bound for Alaska with liquor on board. Any vessel, clearing for any other port, that would pass through Alaskan waters with liquor, firearms, or ammunition on board was required to post a bond worth twice the value of the restricted products. The bond was returned upon proof of having landed liquor somewhere other than in Alaska or firearms and ammunition somewhere other than on Saint Paul and Saint George islands. Subsequently, on 3 July 1875, Acting Secretary of the Treasury Charles F. Conant informed customs collectors that importation of breech-loading rifles and fixed ammunition into Alaska was forbidden, and he ordered collectors to refuse clearance to vessels bound for Alaska with such cargo on board. Any vessel, bound elsewhere, that would pass through Alaskan waters with these products on board, had to post a bond worth twice the value of the banned products. Proof that the products had been landed somewhere other than in Alaska was required to recover the bond.[9]

Some of the restrictions on arms shipments to Alaska were obviously the result of concern for the survival of fur seals because the first prohibition was on shipments to Saint Paul and Saint George islands, the most important of the seal islands. Extension of the ban to importation of breech-loading weapons into the entire territory, however, suggests fear of Alaska's native population as a motive. The correspondence of special agent Morris and of Maj. M. P. Berry, the customs collector at Sitka, certainly could have raised such fears.

From the time they arrived in Alaska, those officials expressed concerns about the possibility of violence by native Alaskans, but their fears were alleviated somewhat by the presence of a garrison of soldiers at Sitka. They agreed that there was a danger of conflict between the whites and native Alaskans, and they believed that, if violence occurred, it probably would be started by bad whites as a result of excessive drinking by both the whites and the native Alaskans.[10]

After the government withdrew the garrison on 14 June 1877, Morris's correspondence with the Treasury Department took on an hysterical quality. On 23 July, he wrote to Secretary John Sherman and quoted collector Berry: "I have the best reasons for believing that if there is not a vessel dispatched at a very early date to this port [Sitka], that this people have been handed over bodily for slaughter to the Indians."[11]

Morris undoubtedly agreed with Berry. He reported that Sitka Jack, a chief of the Kolosh tribe, had told him that when one thousand of his tribe, who were off hunting and fishing, returned, he intended to seize all of the valuable property in Sitka because everything in the country belonged to his tribe. Capt. Charles Thorne, master of the steamer *California*, had told Morris that the Indians thronged his ship at the dock and were arrogant and insolent, in total contrast to their behavior while the army garrison was in Sitka. Morris added that bloodshed was inevitable unless a gunboat was sent to Sitka.[12]

Morris's fears led him to write to Capt. James M. Selden, skipper of the revenue steamer *Wolcott*, then undergoing repairs at Seattle. He asked Selden when the cutter would be ready to go to sea, what her complement was, and what arms she carried. Selden responded that the *Wolcott* would be repaired by mid-August but she was not a suitable vessel for service against native Alaskans. She had too few men and inadequate housing for an expanded complement. She carried just one 24-pound howitzer. In addition to her Dahlgren howitzer, the *Wolcott* carried fifteen rifles (nine Ballards and six Spencers), seventeen Colt navy revolvers, and nine cutlasses. The cutter had no bulwarks, which would leave her crew exposed to ambush, and she carried just sixty tons of coal, not enough for extended cruising. A cutter stationed at Sitka, Selden argued, should carry a steam launch, a Gatling gun, and a medical officer, none of which the *Wolcott* had.

In August, the revenue steamer *Corwin* (Capt. John W. White) arrived in Alaskan waters. While she was there, the Alaskans were peaceful, which convinced Morris that the *Corwin*'s presence had prevented the violence expected by Major Berry. But the department must bear in mind, Morris added in his report, that the Alaskans were not going to cause trouble while a gunboat lay at anchor before their villages. They would claim to have peaceful intentions, even if they planned to shed blood the minute the cutter was out of sight.

In fact, the expected violence did not occur after the garrison was removed, and even Morris was impressed by the Alaskans. Their behavior, he wrote, was commendable and prudent. There had been periods of danger, of course, and he was still convinced that only the strong arm of the government could prevent some grotesque horror that would shock the civilized world, for he thought it the nature of things that the two races should clash.

The special agent concluded this part of his correspondence with reports from Captain White of the *Corwin* and Captain Selden of the *Wolcott*. The Treasury Department had dispatched the *Corwin* to Sitka after the army garrison was withdrawn, in response to the concerns expressed by Morris and Berry. After arriving at Sitka, on 10 August 1877, Captain White reported that native Alaskans greeted him in their canoes and wanted to trade fish and game for other products. Most of the men were off fishing, which was normal for that time of year, and none of those left behind expected any trouble. He, himself, had seen no signs of danger but recommended sending an armed ship to Sitka every two or three months to assure the Alaskans that the government had not deserted the place and to serve as a restraining influence.[13]

Subsequent to the *Corwin*'s departure, the *Wolcott* visited Sitka to attend a potlatch (celebration) given by Sitka Jack. On 18 October, Captain Selden reported that the situation had not changed since the *Corwin* had left. The chiefs had assured him that there would be no disturbance. He believed that the Alaskans were guilty of only petty thievery. The whites had punished them severely when the army was in town, but they were now hesitant to do so. Selden thought that the whites were more afraid of what could happen than of any immediate threat and that the Alaskans wanted to get along with the whites and posed no serious danger. He planned to stay through the celebration, he wrote, and, if nothing happened after that, to return to Port Townsend.[14]

Morris added to his correspondence a story from the *San Francisco Chronicle* about a British subject, William Rath, who had drunk excessively with a native Alaskan. After they became intoxicated, Rath collapsed in his bed, and the Alaskan died. The latter's family subsequently threatened to kill Rath in retaliation and demanded a tribute of $2,000 from Sam Goldstein, whose home had been the site of the debauch. Ultimately, a compromise was worked out. Rath and Goldstein paid the family $250 and a supply of "hoochenoo," a cheap rum drink made by the Indians. Morris concluded this story by asking who would be next.[15]

I. C. Dennis, deputy collector at Wrangel, wrote: "A gunboat or revenue cutter has a pacifying effect upon whites and Indians, and the presence of one in these waters occasionally would have more effect toward suppressing the liquor traffic and preserving order and quiet than forty regiments of troops without means of transportation.[16] Morris had written earlier that the cutters had "been the safeguard and life of the Territory," and they were still necessary, he said, "for the protection of the lives, liberty, and property of its inhabitants."[17]

Most cutters were deemed inadequate for the job of peacekeeping in Alaska. As an example, Morris reported that the revenue steamer *Richard Rush* had a complement of just six officers and thirty crewmen and was armed with two 20-pound bronze Dalghren rifled howitzers, twelve breechloading rifles, twelve revolvers, and twelve cutlasses. Although she could shell a village, Morris wrote, she could not land enough men to destroy it or burn the canoes, which was the greatest punishment that one could inflict upon the coastal Alaskans, for they were completely dependent on fishing, hunting, and trading. They had been chastised in the past but by gunboats with larger crews and more powerful batteries than those of the *Rush*. The *Corwin*, then nearing completion in Oregon, Morris noted, was a staunch vessel. She would make a fine Alaskan cutter.[18]

And indeed she did. The *Corwin* established the pattern of regular arctic cruising by cutters. Between 1880 and 1885, she left San Francisco in April or May of each year with the objective of reaching Point Barrow, seven hundred miles north of the Bering Strait. She always stopped at Unalaska for coal and went on to the Pribiloff Islands, Saint George and Saint Paul, before continuing to Point Barrow. On her return trip, she stopped again at Unalaska and arrived back in San Francisco in October or November.[19]

Built in 1876 by the Oregon Iron Works at Portland, the steamer *Corwin* had auxiliary sails and measured 145 feet in length, 24 feet in beam, and nearly 11 feet in draft. According to her skipper, Capt. Calvin L. Hooper, she was a sturdy vessel, and John Muir, the famous naturalist, wrote that she was built "of the finest Oregon fir, fastened with copper, galvanized iron, and locust-tree nails." She was sheathed with Oregon oak and sailed as a cutter for a quarter of a century before the service sold her on 14 February 1900.[20]

The *Corwin* began systematic cruising north of the Arctic Circle under the command of Captain Hooper, described by Capt. Robley D. Evans, USN, as "an able, fearless man who would carry out orders and accomplish his mission."[21] Within the Treasury Department, Hooper was known as an able officer with a great knowledge of the Arctic.[22] The *Corwin*'s primary objectives on her 1880 cruise to the frozen reaches of the north were to search for two overdue whalers, the *Mount Wollaston* and the *Vigilant*, which had failed to return from their 1879 trip to the pack

The USRC Corwin

ice, and to find out what had happened to a polar expedition under the command of Navy Lt. Comdr. George Washington DeLong.

DeLong had led a polar expedition via the Bering Straits to determine whether an open sea route reached the pole or if there was a major continent above Siberia. James Gordon Bennett, publisher of the *New York Herald*, financed the expedition, which was sponsored by the U.S. Congress. DeLong had sailed from San Francisco in the steam bark *Jeannette* in the summer of 1879 and made for Wrangel Island, where he had planned to establish a base camp before striking out for the pole.

On the 1880 cruise, Hooper found no credible evidence of the *Jeannette* but learned that the captain of the whaling bark *Helen Mar* of New Bedford had seen the two missing whalers under way during the previous fall in clear water about forty miles southeast of Herald Island. Hooper drove his cutter through fog and ice toward the island and reached a point fifty to one hundred miles farther north than any vessel had reported reaching during the previous year. Then, pack ice forced him to retreat. When he returned to San Francisco, he shared with the captain of the *Helen Mar* the belief that the two whalers had been crushed in the ice.[23] He still held out hope that the *Jeannette*, which was equipped for exploration, had survived even if she had been caught in the ice.

During his second year's cruise in the Arctic, on 22 May 1881, Hooper heard from the captain of the whaling bark *Rainbow* that a sealing party of Tchuktchis from Cape Serdze in Siberia had discovered a wreck that was almost certainly one of the lost whalers. Believing this information of great importance and unable to drive the cutter farther north at the time, Hooper decided to dispatch a sled party to investigate. At Marcus Bay, he engaged a dog team, driver, and interpreter. He put First Lt. William J. Herring in charge of a party of five that included 3d Lt. William E. Reynolds, a coxswain, and two Tchuktchis. The men set out with twenty-five dogs, four sleds, one skin boat, one tent, and a stove. They found the Tchuktchis who had discovered the wreck and received from them a number of articles recovered from the ship. Later, the *Corwin* reached the village of Wankerem and bought still more recovered articles, including a pair of silver bowed spectacles belonging to Capt. Ebenezer F. Nye of the *Mount Wollaston* and a pair of deer horns. Upon returning to San Francisco, Hooper learned that the antlers were a well-known trademark of the *Vigilant*.[24] All evidence pointed to both the *Mount Wollaston* and the *Vigilant* having been crushed in the ice. Before the former sank, Captain

Nye had gone on board the *Vigilant,* which later met the same fate as the *Mount Wollaston.*

Because the winter of 1880–1881 was unusually mild, Hooper was able to explore new ground on his 1881 cruise but searched in vain for the *Jeannette.* When he reached Herald Island, he put a party ashore to look for signs of DeLong's expedition. Later, on 12 August, after many frustrating attempts to push through the ice, the *Corwin* reached Wrangel Island and Hooper put another search party ashore. Although they failed again to find the *Jeannette* or DeLong, Hooper and the *Corwin's* crew became the first U.S. explorers to reach Wrangel Island. Before leaving the island, Hooper raised the U.S. flag and claimed it for the United States.[25]

Lest the *Corwin's* achievements seem to have been accomplished too easily, Hooper reported the perils posed by ice on this trip. The wind increased to a moderate gale, and the snow fell so thick that the crew could not see beyond the length of the ship. Shortly after midnight, they found themselves "entirely surrounded by heavy ice, and were compelled to use the engine to work out of it: in doing so the rudder was broken and unshipped, every pintle being carried away. The situation was anything but pleasant, caught in the end of a rapidly closing lead, 120 miles from open water, in a howling gale and driving snow storm and without a rudder. It at first appeared as if the destruction of the vessel was inevitable. However, after several hours of hard work, steering as best [they] could by means of the sails, and giving the vessel a great many hard bumps and nips, [they] succeeded in getting into the open lead again, and by six o'clock had prepared a jury rudder."[26]

From survivors of the DeLong expedition, it was later learned that the *Jeannette* had been locked in the ice about forty miles from Wrangel Island. After drifting in the Arctic Ocean for twenty-one months, she was finally crushed by the ice. She sank north of the 77th parallel. Her crew had retreated to the Siberian mainland by boat and sled. DeLong and twenty others died in the effort; thirteen of the crew survived to tell the story.[27] According to Allard, DeLong's expedition ended in tragedy, but it "helped disprove facile theories of an open polar sea and of the presumed Arctic landmass near Russia, and provided valuable insight into the polar basin's hydrography."[28]

During her first Alaskan cruise in 1880, the *Corwin* also had enforced laws against selling liquor and breech-loading weapons to the native

Alaskans. Hooper seized the American schooner *Leo* for violating those laws on 13 July. He put 2d Lt. William H. Hand in charge of a prize crew and ordered Hand to take the vessel to San Francisco and report to the Treasury Department. On 29 August, Hooper seized the schooner *Loleta* for selling breech-loading arms to the Alaskans and dispatched her to San Francisco with a prize crew under Lt. Paul Wyck. This was the second year in a row that the Revenue Cutter Service had seized the *Loleta* for selling liquor to the Alaskans but it would be the last—the *Schooner* was wrecked on Saint Lawrence Island en route to San Francisco that fall.[29]

Hooper not only supported the government's policy of prohibiting liquor sales to the native Alaskans, but he advocated strengthening the ban. On both the 1880 and 1881 cruises, he visited Saint Lawrence Island, where he saw evidence of wholesale starvation that was a result of excessive liquor consumption. During visits to four villages in 1880, he counted sixty-one adult male corpses, estimated that two hundred deaths had occurred in three villages, and learned from survivors at a fourth village that they had lost another two hundred persons. To survive, the living had eaten their dogs and walrus hides that covered their boats and homes. In 1881, Hooper noted in his report that, because of a lack of time and fear of exaggeration, he had fallen short of the truth. At one of the villages where he had estimated the loss of seventy-five persons, Muir did a careful examination of both homes and grounds and placed the number at two hundred.[30]

Hooper believed that the natives of Saint Lawrence Island would become extinct if the government did not stop alcohol from reaching them. He recommended taking strong action to prevent such a disaster. He wanted collectors at San Francisco authorized to stop all ships from sailing to the Arctic with liquor on board. Hooper reported that vessels typically cleared port after posting a bond guaranteeing that they would not sell alcohol to native Alaskans, then returned home with papers falsely claiming to have sold their alcohol in Siberia. Too often, they had sold the liquor in Alaska; even when they had sold it in Siberia, it was often ultimately traded to Alaskan natives. Hooper recommended sending a cutter to the Arctic each year before the whalers left port and giving the cutter authority to search any vessels for liquor, even those found in Russian waters.[31] He held out little hope for the survival of the Arctic natives unless such actions were taken.[32]

In contrast to his support for the nation's liquor laws, Hooper opposed laws banning the sale of breech-loading weapons to the native Alaskans. Many of them had legally acquired such weapons and had become used to hunting with them. Consequently, they had lost some of their ability with bow and arrow, which made it essential to their survival that they be allowed to acquire firearms. If the government would not allow them to have breech-loading rifles, he recommended that, at least, it should authorize them to possess double-barreled shotguns.[33]

Hooper also recommended dropping the use of the name Eskimo for Arctic Alaskans. They called themselves *Inuits*, a term which should be used by whites, he wrote. The term *Eskimo*, meaning raw fish eater, had been given in derision by the natives of Northern Labrador to the natives of Southern Labrador.[34]

While in the Arctic, Hooper collected samples of marine life, birds, animals, and fossils for the Smithsonian Institution. He made anthropologic and zoologic observations, took hydrographic readings, discovered coal deposits, corrected mistakes on the American Hydrographic Chart, reported ice conditions, investigated murders, observed the activities of whalers and sealers, and seized a number of vessels for violating the nation's sealing laws.[35] And, most important, he set the pattern for regular Arctic cruising by the Revenue Cutter Service.

On her 1881 cruise, the *Corwin* took on the job of transporting scientists to the Arctic. In addition to Muir, Irving C. Rosse, M.D., and Edward W. Nelson, U.S. Signal Service, accompanied the crew that summer. Doctor Rosse served as the ship's surgeon, provided medical care for the native Alaskans, studied the effects of cold and exposure on the *Corwin*'s crew, and studied native diseases. Nelson took notes on the natural history of Alaska, made ethnologic observations, and studied the birds of the Arctic. Muir took notes on the region's fauna and studied the glaciation of the area.

On their return to the United States, each passenger wrote up his findings. Rosse's "Medical and Anthropological Notes on Alaska," Muir's "Botanical Notes on Alaska," and Nelson's "Birds of Bering Sea and the Arctic Ocean" were published in the *Executive Documents of the House of Representatives.* Muir's "On the Glaciation of the Arctic and Subarctic Regions Visited by the United States Steamer *Corwin* in the Year 1881" was published in Hooper's *Cruise of the Corwin, 1881.* Muir published separately his account of the cruise in his own *The Cruise of the Corwin.* His work demonstrated that the Aleutians were almost wholly the product of glaciation and not exclusively the result of volcanic activity.[36]

In 1882, the rugged and personable Capt. Michael A. ("Mike") Healy replaced Hooper as the *Corwin's* commanding officer. Thanks to Father Albert S. Foley's book, *Bishop Healy: Beloved Outcast*, about one of Captain Healy's brothers, it is known that the captain was born in Georgia to Mary Eliza Smith, a slave, and Mike Healy, an Irish American plantation owner. Because Healy and his four brothers would have been slaves under Georgia law, their father sent them to New York, where they attended a Quaker school. His brothers matriculated at Holy Cross College, Worcester, Massachusetts. His oldest brother, James Augustine, became the first black Catholic bishop in the United States, at Portland, Maine. Another brother, Patrick Francis, became the president of Georgetown University. Mike Healy, who preferred a life of action, joined the Revenue Cutter Service.

Healy had made his first cruise to the north as a young officer on board the *Rush* (Capt. John A. Henriques) in 1868. While Hooper patrolled the Arctic Ocean in the *Corwin*, First Lt. Mike Healy was patrolling Alaska's Pacific Coast in the *Rush*. By 1881, he was known as a brilliant seaman; by 1894, he would become a legend in his own time and the best-known American in Alaska.[37]

An 1894 article in the *New York Sun* stated that he was better known in the waters of the North Pacific and Arctic Ocean than any president of the United States or statesman of Europe. In the Arctic, if one asked who was the greatest American, the answer came back, "Why, Mike Healy." He *was* the United States to the natives of the Northwest, the article claimed, "the sole representative of legal authority in much of the territory north of Port Townsend." A saving angel and a nemesis of the whalers in the Arctic, he was "the ideal commander of the old school, bluff, prompt, fearless, just. He knew Bering Sea, the Straits, and even the Arctic as no other man" knew them.[38]

On her 1882 cruise under Healy, the *Corwin* participated in a case of nineteenth-century gunboat diplomacy. The results were tragic and might have been an indirect consequence of the fear of native Alaskans expressed earlier by special agent Morris and customs collector Berry. The Revenue Cutter Service, as mentioned earlier, had played an important law enforcement role in Alaska before 1882. In 1877, the U.S. government had withdrawn the few, scattered army garrisons from the territory. During the

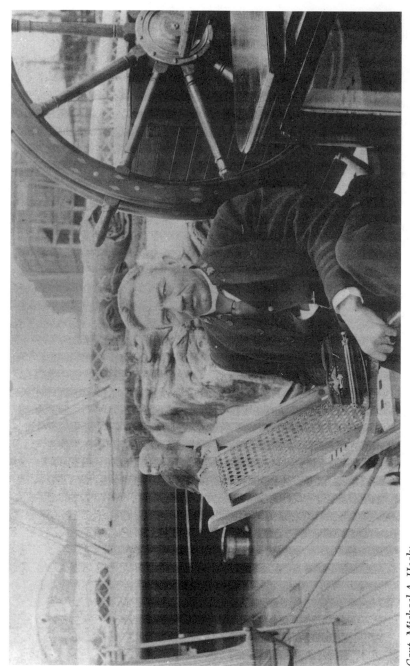

Capt. Michael A. Healy

next two years, the cutters had been the only law enforcement agents left in Alaska. In 1879, a small detachment of marines, commanded by a naval officer, had been assigned to Sitka to protect that community, but even the marines were dependent on the cutters for transportation. Deputy Collector Dennis at Wrangel praised the Revenue Cutter Service for its "pacifying effect upon both whites and Indians." The cutter, he noted, was more effective in "suppressing the liquor traffic and preserving order and quiet than forty regiments of troops, without means of transportation."[39]

Most of the service's peacekeeping assignments had amounted to nothing more than stopping individuals from fighting, but a most unusual case developed in October 1882. On the 22nd, at Killisnoo near Sitka, a whaling party from the Northwest Trading Company was chasing a whale through the inlet when an accidental explosion in the whale gun killed Tith Klane, a Tlingit shaman. Other Indians on board took the boat and two white whalers, E. H. Bayne and S. S. Stulzman, ashore and held them for ransom. When the Indians threatened to kill the whalers and burn the company buildings unless they were given two hundred blankets, the company appealed to E. C. Merriman, the naval officer at Sitka, for help. With about one hundred marines, he in turn boarded the *Corwin*, under the command of Captain Healy. The cutter arrived at Killisnoo on 25 October; the next day, Merriman put the marines ashore with orders to free the whalers and recapture the company's property. He said that he was not going to give the Indians two hundred blankets. In fact, he was going to fine them four hundred blankets, and, if they did not respond favorably, he was going "to burn their village and destroy their canoes and fishing tackle."[40]

Indeed the government's representatives did just that, but the conditions under which this destruction took place are in dispute. Basing their accounts on government documents, both Evans and Reed claim that when the natives appeared menacing, forty of their canoes were destroyed and the guns of the cutter leveled their summer village on Kootznahoo Inlet. Both authors report that it seemed no lives were lost, a lesson was learned, and peace returned to the area.[41]

In contrast to these accounts, Wilkinson bases his account on native Alaskan sources and claims that the Alaskans gave up their hostages and the boat when the *Corwin* arrived at Kootznahoo Inlet. Merriman demanded a fine of four hundred blankets, and, when the fine was refused, had the canoes and village destroyed. Wilkinson describes Americans shooting into the canoes with a new Gatling gun, then boring holes in them with an auger and sinking them in Chatham Strait. The marines, he notes, landed on the beach, poured kerosene on what was left of the houses after the *Corwin*'s guns had done their work, and burned them to the ground. Wilkinson claims that six children who were left in the village suffocated in the fire, that the marines stole possessions from the houses before setting them on fire, and that the village residents suffered terribly through the next winter and, to a lesser degree, for years thereafter.[42]

It is certainly true that a tragic incident of gunboat diplomacy occurred in Alaska, probably as a result of cultural differences between nineteenth-century government officials and the Alaskans of Kootznahoo Inlet. One hundred years after the event, in October 1982, the Alaskans still remembered the destruction of their village with bitterness. That year, the U.S. government paid them $90,000 in damages for the property destroyed in 1882.

Healy continued the routine of Arctic cruising established by his predecessor. Like Hooper, and in contrast to the impression left by the destruction of the Indian village at Kootznahoo Inlet in 1882, Healy was most anxious to protect native Alaskans, and he shared Hooper's belief that liquor and rifles were the key to their survival. In 1884, Healy found very little whiskey on the Alaskan side of the Bering Strait, although there was evidence of it at all the villages he visited on the Russian side, and the results were most positive. The native Alaskans appeared better fed, clothed, and cared for and healthier than in previous years. Fear of their extinction had passed, if liquor could be kept from them.[43] Healy was convinced that the cutters were having a positive impact.

By 1884, the Inuits referred to the *Corwin* as "do-mi-ak-puck pe-chuck ton-i-ka," which meant "no whiskey ship." That summer, he found evidence of whalers having sold whiskey in just one Alaskan village, on Kruzenstern Island, where he sent First Lt. David A. Hall ashore with an armed boat's crew to confiscate the liquor from a crowd of half-drunken Alaskans. Although Hall was successful in his mission, the Alaskans would not tell him or Healy who had sold them the liquor. In contrast to that experience, Healy noted that the Alaskan women, who usually bore the brunt of abuse caused by excessive liquor consumption, welcomed the crew of the *Corwin* and helped them to find liquor hidden in their villages.

Healy found twenty-five gallons of liquor on board the bark *Northern*

Light (Capt. James McKenney) in 1884. He would have seized the vessel, but McKenney insisted that the liquor was for his crew. Since the quantity was not great enough to prove otherwise, Healy sealed some of the liquor and left the rest to be used. Later that summer, he met the *Northern Light* again and unsealed the rest of the ship's liquor. Healy visited many other whalers that summer, and some of the captains admitted that they had had whisky on board for trading purposes and had thrown it overboard when they learned that a revenue cutter was in the area.

Also sharing Hooper's belief that the government should let the Inuits have breech-loading rifles, Healy was convinced that no evil would come of such a policy. The Inuits were a peaceable people who rarely gathered in large numbers, so they posed no threat to U.S. control in Alaska. The whalers had reduced the supply of animals on which the natives depended for their livelihood, he wrote, and this made it harder for them to gather food and provide shelter for themselves. It was his belief that allowing them to have rifles would just help them to make a living.

On 1 June 1884, Healy put 3d Lt. John E. Lutz ashore on Otter Island to protect the sea herd there. Lutz chased one suspicious vessel away from Saint Paul Island and took fifteen prisoners, nine of them Japanese sealers. On 9 September, en route south, Healy picked up Lutz and his prisoners and continued on to Unalaska.

At the end of the summer, Healy advocated fostering both the cod and salmon fisheries in Alaskan waters. He did what he could to help captains of fishing vessels by sharing his charts and extensive personal knowledge of the Arctic.

The *Corwin*'s law enforcement operations that summer had included returning deserters to their ships. At Port Clarence, Healy took four deserters from the whaler *Dawn* on board the cutter and returned them to their ship.

When she arrived at Unalaska on 11 September on her voyage south, the *Corwin* was carrying ninety-eight passengers for San Francisco. Most of them were whalers who had suffered from a severe season in the Arctic. Twenty-two were from the steamer *Bowhead* (Capt. Everett E. Smith), which had been crushed in the ice north of Icy Cape. Smith and his crew had been rescued by the steamer *Narwhal* and the *Baelena,* which took them to Cape Sabine. Then the *Narwhal* carried word to Point Hope that the *Corwin*'s help was needed. Healy picked up crewmen from the *Bowhead* and deserters from *Dawn* at Cape Sabine and three more whalers, two from the wrecked schooner *Caleb Eaton* and one from the steamer *Beda*, at Indian Point. Other wrecked whalers were taken from the *Wanderer, Orca,* and *Thrasher.* The *Corwin* also transported miners from Saint Michaels and a U.S. Army scout. Most of these men had no supplies and no other way to get back to the States.

Bowhead whales were often found along the edge of the ice pack in the Arctic. They even ventured into the pack for food if they could find openings through which they could surface to breathe. Looking for their quarry, the whalers ran their ships close to the ice and followed promising leads into the pack, a dangerous practice. The ice was bad in 1884, and many whaling ships were caught in the ice pack and crushed. Healy reported that most whalers were wrecked near Point Barrow and recommended establishing a life saving station there. The station, he noted, could also serve as a law enforcement center and a base for gathering meteorologic data and scientific information. Whalers had told him that they would be happy to transport all necessary supplies for the station free of charge.

On the trip to San Francisco, the *Corwin* was unbelievably overcrowded. A total of two hours and three sets of messes were needed to feed everybody at each meal. Men slept everywhere—in lockers, shaft-alley, steam-drum room, and paint locker; on coils of rope in the forecastle; and on deck. Two men shared Healy's cabin with him. In spite of the crowded living conditions, everybody on board the *Corwin* got along well. The rescued whalers were happy to be going home, and revenue cutter personnel were generous, as usual, to fellow mariners in need. Healy reported that the whalers, as a whole, were greatly appreciative of the *Corwin*'s services to them: "The former distrust and professional jealousy of the service, due to the natural dislike men have of being kept under surveillance, have almost entirely disappeared."[44]

In addition to rescuing many of the whalers that summer, Healy provided them with medical care. The *Corwin*'s surgeon treated one man on the *Dawn* and three each on the *Fleetwing* and *Hunter.*

As a result of his busy summer, Healy called upon the Treasury Department to send two cutters to the Arctic each summer, one to cruise between Unalaska and the Seal Islands and the other between the Seal Islands and Point Barrow. There was just too much work for one cutter, he wrote, to the detriment of the services provided, especially in the southern area. (Healy's recommendation would bear fruit in the late 1880s when the *Rush* joined the *Bear*, the *Corwin*'s replacement, in cruising Arctic waters.)

On both his 1884 and 1885 cruises, Healy continued the service's work of exploring Alaska by sending men from the mouths of the Kowak and Noatak rivers hundreds of miles into the hinterland. Third Lt. John C. Cantwell led two parties on difficult missions before finally reaching the headwaters of the rivers, the ultimate objective of both missions. He mapped a large tract of unknown wilderness, collected natural history materials for the Smithsonian Institution, and discovered great quantities of salmon in the rivers. He found the entire area rich in fur-bearing animals and discovered coal, silver, and gold in the valley of the Kowak River (actually, the Kobuk River, but it was referred to as the Kowak in many official documents of that era). Within a few years, prospectors would follow his route to the gold fields.[45]

On 8 July 1884, Healy sent a boat's crew, with Cantwell in charge and Second Assistant Engineer Samuel B. McLenegan as second in command, to explore the Kowak. Others in the party were quartermaster Horace Wilbur; fireman Frank Lewis; James Miller, a miner; and a native interpreter. Cantwell provided the expedition with enthusiasm; McLenegan offered technical ability and a realistic assessment of accomplishments. In contrast to the typical conflict between line and engineering officers of the day, the two men worked well together.[46]

The expedition faced many problems, the most serious being difficulties with the *Corwin*'s steam launch. It drew too much water for the river, lacked adequate power to make progress against the river's 4–5-knot current, and had a balky, unreliable engine. Cantwell finally left McLenegan behind with the launch and forged ahead in two small skin boats.

Whenever the air was calm, mosquitoes plagued the explorers. In his account of the adventure, Cantwell wrote that the party plunged into a pine forest and was attacked by mosquitoes and sand flies with a persistence beyond belief. When his hands were occupied, the mosquitoes attacked his face, neck, and head with "venomous force." After two hours of this, the party finally emerged into the open tundra, where a breeze sprang up. The men threw themselves onto the ground and buried their "heads in the yielding moss and grass until the wind had blown the mosquitoes away."[47]

Navigation of the unknown river was also difficult. At the first rapids, the men approached what appeared to be a calm area in the river. Just as

Capt. John C. Cantwell

the steam launch reached the center of the area, its boilers lost all steam and the river rolled the launch onto its beam ends. Both men and supplies were thrown into the water. To make progress against the current, everyone except Cantwell and Lewis entered the water to pull on a towline. At the end of 10½ hours of this grueling work, the party had gone just 6 miles upstream.

The 1884 expedition explored the Kowak River valley from its mouth on Hotham Inlet to a point 370 miles upstream. Cantwell's last hope of accomplishing his mission was dashed when McLenegan informed him on 2 August that the launch's leaky boilers made it impossible to keep up steam, and that he was not sure the launch could even make it back downstream to Hotham Inlet. The party had to rejoin the *Corwin* at the inlet by 20 August. The river level was dropping, and the men had to pass shoals and rapids below. Reluctantly, Cantwell decided that they must head south while there was still time to return to the inlet.

Yet, Cantwell was not defeated by the river. He had explored and mapped 370 miles of it and another 205 miles of Selawik Lake. He had established good relations with the natives of the river valley and had studied their numbers, customs, and habits. He was sure that they would be helpful in the future. The majestic beauty of the area had impressed him, and, most significantly, he was sure that he had laid the foundation for future successful exploration.

Thanks to Healy, Cantwell would have another chance to explore the Kowak River during the summer of 1885, and he spent the winter at San Francisco planning for the effort. He would take coal in the launch to eliminate cutting firewood for the vessel. McLenegan installed a preheater on the boiler intake in order to solve the problem of inadequate steam pressure. When summer arrived, Healy gave McLenegan the opportunity to explore the Noatak River while Cantwell again sought the headwaters of the Kowak.[48]

Cantwell made quick progress in 1885, in stark contrast to the grueling fight upstream the year before. The steam launch worked well; time was not wasted in cutting wood on the lower river, which was free of obstructions; and there was little current. Healy put the steam launch into the waters off Hotham Inlet on 2 July. Cantwell arrived at the mouth of the river the next day and, two days later, reached a point that had taken ten days to reach the year before.[49] In six days, he had ascended 370 miles upstream, the highest point achieved in 1884 and on 16 July, just twelve days from the river's mouth, he reached Lake Carloogahlooktah, the principal source of the Kowak.

Cantwell's report was effusive:

At 6:30 the Indians stopped as if at a signal, and Tah-tah-rok called my attention to a low rumbling noise ahead. I thought at first it was thunder, but its steady sound, and the fact that thunder is seldom heard in these latitudes, convinced me that it was falling water. We pushed ahead, and my feelings can scarcely be imagined when, at 8 o'clock, we rounded a high, rocky bluff and came suddenly in sight of a seething

mass of white water bursting its way through a gorge composed of per-
pendicular masses of slaty rock two hundred to three hundred feet
high, surmounted by a forest of spruce and birch. The channel was
completely choked with sharp-pointed rocks, past which the water flew
with delightful velocity, breaking itself into mimic cascades of foam
and spray.[50]

After Cantwell regained the mouth of the Kowak, he was rejoined by
McLenegan, fresh from exploring the Noatak River. McLenegan revealed
that the Noatak was a barren river with few resources of any value and
thinly populated by very poor Indians. He had seen little game, and the
river, which he had ascended in a skin canoe, was almost impassable in
summer. At its source, or more accurately, its many sources, the Noatak
was a mere shadow of the stately river that flowed into the sea and had
"degenerated into a mere rambling creek," without enough water to float
even a light canoe. Not a vestige of life was to be seen. McLenegan continued, "Even the hardy water-foul, that seek the solitude's [sic] of the far
north, seemed to have forsaken the region. . . ."[51]

Despite his disappointment, McLenegan had achieved his objective,
and Healy reported on the success of both expeditions in his 1885 cruise
report. They had reached the headwaters of the rivers: "a feat which was
never before achieved, and one which has hitherto been considered impossible of accomplishment in the time given." Detailed reports of the expeditions were prepared, along with Healy's own report of the cruise, and
forwarded to the department. Assistant U.S. Fish Commissioner Charles
H. Townsend had accompanied Cantwell on his ascent of the Kowak
River. His "Notes of the Natural History and Ethnology of Northern
Alaska" also accompanied those reports. The whole package, with wonderful illustrations, was published by the House of Representatives at
Washington in 1887. The Treasury Department's satisfaction is revealed
in its request that Congress make provisions to furnish the department
three thousand copies of the published report.[52]

On 23 May 1889, the *Rush* received orders to sail to the Pribiloff Islands and cruise the southern Alaskan waters. The *Rush* had been built in
1885 by Hall Brothers of San Francisco. The yard repaired the engine and
boiler of the old *Rush*, built by the Atlantic Works of East Boston eleven
years earlier, and used them in the new cutter. Completed in November,
the *Rush* then cruised the Bering Sea in an unsuccessful search for the

whaling bark *Amethyst.* Upon her return to the States, she was assigned to the port of San Francisco and cruised along the coast of California. Each spring, the Rush sailed to the Pribiloff Islands, with orders to remain there until late September or until relieved by the *Bear.*[53]

When the *Rush* got under way on 1 June 1889, the cruise was enlivened by the presence of Isabel S. Shepard, the wife of Capt. Leonard G. Shepard, and their two children. Although it was not common for the wives of revenue cutter captains to sail with their husbands, they did accompany them on occasion, and the service accepted the practice as long as permission was obtained from headquarters before sailing. Healy's wife accompanied him on a few Arctic cruises without any negative consequences; however, John Cantwell took his wife along on a short passage without notifying headquarters of her presence, and the fact was understandably retained as a negative mark on his permanent record.

History is indebted to revenue cutter officials for allowing Isabel Shepard to accompany her husband in 1889, for she wrote a delightful, valuable account of her trip.[54]

Although Mrs. Shepard had made the cruise before, and would do so again, she was so seasick during the first three days at sea that she wondered why she had set sail. After she recovered from her seasickness, the sea and the ship's food must have agreed with her, for she gained six pounds during the first four weeks. The ship's crew ate a lot of fish. In addition, the cutter left San Francisco with enough provisions for five months, including four sheep that Captain Shepard put ashore on an island in Unalaska harbor to provide fresh mutton throughout the summer. The *Rush* also carried one hundred tons of coal and a pet goat. Captain Shepard stored twenty tons of the coal on the aft section of the main deck to keep the cutter's propeller in the water because her stern tended to buck up out of the water.

The cutter sailed with about fifty persons on board. In addition to the Shepards, there were eight officers (four lieutenants, three engineers, and a doctor), the crew, stewards, and cabin boys. Some of the crew, who had shipped just before leaving for the Bering Sea, were unfamiliar with the cutter's guns. The crew also included foreign nationals from Scotland and the Netherlands.

The officers and crew probably liked the captain's wife. She was conscious of being a guest on the ship and tried to stay out of the way and not

The USRC Rush

interfere with the ship's routine. She organized a dance on the *Rush* at Unalaska and invited Russian women from the village and men from a visiting ship. An Aleut played a cabinet organ and accordion. The dance provided a unique, lively evening on board the *Rush*. Mrs. Shepard also explored mountains ashore and never seemed to have difficulty finding officers willing to hike with her. At one time, she tried to convince the captain to take her hunting for polar bear, but he refused. To do so would have taken the cutter away from her assigned mission.

An observant, inquisitive woman, Mrs. Shepard frequently commented on the flowers and the natural beauty of both land and sea. The geology of Alaska did not escape her notice. Reading her account of the cruise, one is also reminded of the presence of a Russian church at the center of each Alaskan village and island. In the Alaska Commercial Company's library at Unalaska, she was delighted to find copies of Dickens, Thackeray, Hawthorne, Irving, Cooper, Prescott, and Motley.

Of course, the *Rush* and the Revenue Cutter Service were in Alaskan waters to do a job, not to entertain the captain's wife, but her comments on the cutter's operations are informative and often more illuminating than the typically terse ships' logs.

When the *Rush* went into Unalaska to take on coal, Mrs. Shepard found the *Bear* and *Thetis* there for the same purpose. The *Bear* (Captain Healy) had had a rough, wet passage from the United States, she noted, because her deck was weighted down with lumber being transported to Point Barrow. In 1888, the *Bear* had rescued 110 men whose ships had been wrecked in a vicious storm off Point Barrow, and Healy had intensified his long-standing campaign to have a house of refuge constructed at Barrow for shipwrecked sailors. The materials on board the *Bear* were for a prefabricated house to serve that purpose. At the end of the summer, when Mrs. Shepard saw the *Bear* again, she learned that the project had gone very well indeed. With the help of sailors at Point Barrow, the *Bear*'s crew had put up a habitable house in just three weeks.

On the return trip from Barrow, the *Bear* had transported "the maimed, the halt and the blind." According to Mrs. Shepard, her passengers included invalids from whalers, paralytics, epileptics, and the insane.[55]

Before heading for the Pribiloff Islands in July, the *Rush* performed a number of traditional cutter assignments—transporting a sick woman from an isolated location to a town with medical facilities, towing the disabled ship *Stamboul* into Unalaska for water and provisions, and firing a twenty-one-gun salute to celebrate the Fourth of July. Her doctor cared for both whites and native Alaskans.

The *Rush*'s assignment on the Pribiloff Islands of Saint Paul and Saint George was to enforce the nation's sealing laws. She had already seized the British sealer *Minnie* for taking 418 sealskins in violation of those laws. The *Minnie*'s captain was unusual in that he admitted he was guilty of pelagic sealing.

After arriving at the islands, Shepard destroyed a quantity of liquor. The native Alaskans viewed this as a disaster, but, of course, Shepard's actions were in keeping with U.S. policy.

According to Mrs. Shepard, her husband took no pleasure in seizing sealers, but he was dedicated to doing his duty. During the summer of 1889, he and the *Rush* confiscated about two thousand illegal sealskins and several schooners. They took the skins to Unalaska and the ships to Sitka. Everything was sold at auction for the benefit of the U.S. government.

The *Rush*'s normal routine was to order the sealers to heave to. If they obeyed the order, the captain sent a boat with two officers and a crew armed with pistols to board. If the sealers did not comply, the captain ordered the *Rush*'s guns run out. That summer, British vessels forced the issue and stopped for inspection only after the *Rush* displayed her guns. There was talk of British men-of-war heading for the Arctic to rescue British and Canadian sealers, but none showed up.

Early in July, the *Rush*'s crew boarded the British schooner *Black Diamond* and found twenty-eight sealskins on board. She was sent into Sitka under the "control" of one officer from the *Rush*. Later, Shepard learned that the *Black Diamond* simply defied the orders of the lone cutterman on board and went into Victoria, British Columbia, instead of Sitka. Shepard anticipated this, but, with a small crew, he could not put more than one man on any single vessel. Subsequently, the Treasury Department ordered cutter captains to confiscate all food except what would be needed by her crew before an illegal sealer could reach port.

By 27 July, the *Rush* had boarded seven or eight sealers in the Bering Sea and had seized two of them for illegal sealing. One had freshly killed seals on board, and the captain of the second sealer admitted having taken seals at sea in violation of the law. That same day, 27 July, the *Rush*'s crew boarded the *Maggie Mac* after a chase near the Pribiloff Islands. The *Maggie Mac* had 561 sealskins on board, but the captain insisted that he had not taken any of the seals at sea. Although Shepard did not believe his story, he let the *Maggie Mac* go.

Two days later, Shepard seized the British schooner *Pathfinder* with 850 sealskins taken in the Bering Sea. On 30 July, he captured another British schooner, the *Juanita*, with 619 sealskins, and caught the American schooner *James G. Swan* with hunters in the water and 171 skins on board the schooner. He seized the *Swan* and sent her into Sitka, but she sailed into Port Townsend instead.

During the month of August, the *Rush* continued to board sealers. She seized some of them and allowed others to go on their way, according to circumstances. On 1 September, when the *Bear* replaced her at the Pribiloff Islands, the *Rush* took on board native Alaskan sealers who had been left at sea by the schooners and other persons who had been stranded and sailed for Sitka.

The night before the *Rush* set sail for home, her complement attended a concert for the benefit of two of the cutter's pilots at Yakutat. Mrs. Shepard commented: "After the concert there was dancing. It varied the monotony of the rainy days and nights. In walking up the street we almost needed our small boat to reach the building in which it was given, but we arrived undissolved and in a fairly good condition, considering all things."[56]

The highlight of the evening was a comical song written by a resident of Sitka and sung by First Lt. Francis Tuttle to the music of Nat Goodwin's "That's All." The song was about the *Black Diamond* overpowering the sole cutterman who was assigned to take her into Sitka. According to Mrs. Shepard, meaningful glances were directed at her husband while the song was sung:

> The "Shepard" came into our bay with a *Rush*,
>> That's all, that's all.
> He had swept Behring [*sic*] Sea with a revenue brush,
>> That's all, that's all.
> And our Johnny Bull cousins who live in B.C.
> Are shaking their fists at the flag of the free
>> That's all, that's all.
>
> The *Black Diamond* was captured, but she ran away,
>> That's all, that's all.
> Mistaking Victoria for Sitka's fair bay,
>> That's all, that's all.

> And vain was the talk of the gallant prize crew,
> He was one against many, so what could he do?
> He did what he had to—so would I, so would you.
>   That's all, that's all.[57]

The *Rush* arrived in Puget Sound in early October. The crew beached the cutter outside of Olympia, Washington, and cleaned her copper bottom, thus avoiding drydock bills. On 3 October, she sailed into Port Townsend and ended her Bering Sea cruise at San Francisco eleven days later.

An extension of efforts to stop pelagic sealing beyond the nation's territorial waters had threatened to cause conflict with Great Britain, but, in 1891, each nation agreed to send its naval vessels to the Bering Sea to check illegal poaching by its own nationals. Revenue cutters assisted U.S. Navy vessels on this assignment. In 1895, the commandant of the Revenue Cutter Service formed the Bering Sea Patrol to enforce laws against pelagic sealing in Bering Sea and the Aleutians. Thereafter, the patrol became most important to the cutter service, and naval participation fell off after 1900.[58]

Under the command of Captain Hooper, who made his headquarters at Unalaska, cutters on the Bering Sea Patrol sailed north in May 1895 and cruised the sealing grounds until that November. The routine was repeated by six cutters in 1896 and four in 1897. In a narrow sense, the patrols had thoroughly successful seasons. They sailed over 221,000 miles, boarded 447 different vessels a total of 805 times, inspected 98,246 sealskins, and seized 11 vessels for violating the sealing laws.[59] In a broader sense, however, the Bering Sea Patrol failed to give adequate protection to the seal herds until 1911, when an international agreement signed by the United States, Canada, Russia, and Japan ensured the international cooperation that was required to save the seals from extinction.

Capt. Godfrey Carden had commanded the *Manning* on the 1910 Bering Sea Patrol, when she sailed nearly 15,000 miles and boarded 14 Japanese sealers. Japan had 816 men on 25 vessels with 201 hunting boats in the Bering Sea that season, and they took an estimated 5,000 skins. Carden reported that he was sure that they took many of them illegally; the great enemy of the sea, he wrote, was the Japanese sealer, who lay outside the three-mile limit and killed the female between the rookeries and the squid feeding grounds. Such practices caused the loss of three seals for each one taken, the mother, her pup on shore, and the pup she was carrying. On 22 June 1910, Carden reported that the general opinion was that there would be no seals in a few years if pelagic sealing was not stopped. Some cutter personnel believed that their complete decimation could come within five years.[60]

The four significant sealing nations that signed the 1911 North Pacific Sealing Convention agreed to prohibit pelagic sealing north of the thirtieth parallel, to close their ports to pelagic sealers, and to share the seals taken legally. By 1912, the seal herd had doubled to 215,738. Within a decade it had increased to more than 600,000 and, by the end of the third decade, had grown to nearly two million.[61]

The Bering Sea Patrol also marked a type of cutter operations from which the Revenue Cutter Service excluded the usually dominant collector of customs. Cutters participating in the patrol reported directly to the commandant in Washington, D.C. In other operations, the collector retained his long-held control over the cutters.

CHAPTER THREE

A Struggle to Survive

K imball's reforms of the 1870s caused problems for the Revenue Cutter Service during the 1880s. When Secretary of the Navy William Chandler looked at the cutters after a decade of reform, he saw a fleet of thirty-six vessels, including twenty-three steamers that he said could "be classed as gunboats, are good vessels of their class, and must always be regarded as part of the available naval force." He was looking for ships because the nation had refused to fund enough naval vessels to employ all of the active-duty naval officers and new Naval Academy graduates. Chandler believed that a competent officer corps large enough to meet the nation's needs in wartime must be maintained. Because there were too few ships to employ an adequate number of officers in the naval establishment, other duties must be found for them. "A highly trained corps of officers, such as modern naval warfare demands," he wrote, "cannot be created in a day. If the personnel of the Navy is to be kept at its present standard of quality and numbers, it must be utilized in every form of government employment for which it is adapted." He stated that naval personnel were adapted to serve on U.S. revenue cutters.[1]

In his 1882 annual report, Chandler started his comments on the Revenue Cutter Service by stressing its naval character: "The Revenue Cutter Service affords a proper field for the employment of naval officers. The duty is directly in the line of their profession. They are fitted for it, both by training and experience; and if they could be so employed without detriment to the interests of the exist-ing corps of officers, a great and permanent benefit to the government and to the Navy would result."[2]

Chandler went on to argue that the work of cruising cutters was strictly naval, that the duties of revenue cutter officers were the same as those of naval officers, and that their discipline was naval. Employing young naval officers on cutters that cruised along the U.S. coast to assist vessels in distress would afford them outstanding seagoing experience. They would learn more about piloting and become more familiar with the coast than they could while serving on naval vessels. As young men, they would easily learn the profession of a revenue cutter officer.[3]

Arguing that the change suggested would save the taxpayer money, Chandler said that the government was reducing the navy while main-taining an officer corps of 185 in the Revenue Cutter Service and a school at New Bedford, Massachusetts, for their training. The Naval Academy at Annapolis had excellent facilities and enough instructors to train 335 cadets. It could provide all of the naval officers needed by the nation. Re-cent legislation had dictated that only a portion of the Annapolis gradu-ates could enter the navy; the rest would be given a year's pay and released from the service. By placing them in the Revenue Cutter Service, according to Chandler, the government would save the cost of a duplicate establishment with imperfect facilities.

Chandler intended to take over more than the academy. His report rec-ommended that the administration of the naval service and the Revenue Cutter Service be combined under the Navy Department. The small rev-enue cutters on harbor duty, the report suggested, should be left under the control of the Treasury Department, but the cruising cutters should be transferred to the Navy Department. They could continue to perform their Treasury Department duties, with their movements directed, "for the time being," by the collectors of customs, Chandler said.

To make his proposal attractive to the officers of the Revenue Cutter Service, Chandler recommended that they be made permanent commis-sioned naval officers with all the benefits of the naval corps, including placement on the retired list of the navy in case of extreme age or disabil-ity. (Of course, chiefs of the cutter service had been trying unsuccessfully to gain retirement benefits for more than a decade.) Chandler did not threaten the standing of revenue officers on board the cutters. Both line and engineering officers would continue to be promoted to higher positions and to command of the cutters. Naval Academy graduates would fill only the openings at the entry level of the cutter establishment.

Chandler's proposal challenged Ezra Clark, who had taken over as head of the Revenue Marine Bureau in 1878, by threatening the independent existence of the Revenue Cutter Service, but Clark proved to be a worthy champion of the service. He sent a stinging twelve-page rebuttal to Congress on 27 January 1883.[4]

Clark started his report with a brief history of the Revenue Cutter Service and explained that Congress had created it to protect the nation's revenue, which was still its principal duty. The secretary of the treasury controlled the management of the service and assigned all officers and cutters, an arrangement, Clark asserted, that existed without confusion, to the great advantage of the public. He claimed that admiration of their work was almost universal.

At the end of his simple but forceful opening, Clark recalled when naval officers had served on board cutters. At only one time in the service's history, he wrote, had strained relations existed between customs collectors and the captains of the cutters; this occurred when naval officers were assigned to command revenue cutters between 1821 and 1832, and, because of the strained relations, the practice was discontinued.

Clark's report acknowledged that the cutters' effectiveness in preventing smuggling was not always apparent, but he claimed that smuggling increased whenever a cutter was removed from its station. He emphasized that the Revenue Marine Division had received calls for the deployment of more cutters and many letters expressing public gratitude for services provided, but it had received no calls to end any of the services rendered. The report included statistical accounts of operations for two periods: (1) the years 1861–70 and (2) the years 1871–81. A comparison of the two accounts illustrated obvious improvement in the service's operations during the second period.

In addition, the report presented a chart of the service's expenses for the years 1868–82. It demonstrated that expenses had been reduced, while operations had improved. The most impressive results, Clark asserted, had occurred during the years 1872–82, when cutters had assisted vessels in distress with an average annual value of $2,696,923 and had saved 642 persons (not counting those on the assisted vessels) from drowning during that period.

Clark pointed out that most of the cutters were then serving on stations for which they had been designed. They were commanded by officers of good character who were prompt, attentive to duty, and zealous in carrying out their assignments. To perform their duties successfully, revenue cutter officers had to know in detail the legislation that had created their many duties. Such knowledge, Clark declared, was the work of a lifetime in the service, not two or three years. Cruising along the coast, especially during the winter months, he asserted, was much more dangerous than midocean cruising. Revenue cutter officers had learned to cope with that danger over a lifetime. "The officers of the Revenue Marine," Clark boasted, "now constitute one of the best fitted, most thoroughly trained, most industrious, intelligent, active, and efficient bodies of public servants under the Government."[5]

The proposed transfer, the report continued, would be improper. The Revenue Cutter Service had been an important part of the customs service for nearly a century. Under these conditions, Congress should not change the status of this service without "grave and important reasons." The proposed change could not improve the service, Clark claimed. The only reason for it was to benefit the navy, specifically the younger officers of the navy. The people of the nation would disapprove of the move, the report continued. They were impatient with aristocratic rule and opposed the use of military force in civil affairs. Although the Revenue Cutter Service had been organized as a military force, it functioned in subordination to civilians in the Treasury Department and was a national police force, rather than a naval force.

The report argued, correctly, that the real motive for the proposal was to find employment for naval officers. It came, Clark noted, at a time when the navy was in deplorable condition, but was paying a total of $1,944,500 a year to 880 naval officers whom it did not need. The four to six annual vacancies in the Revenue Marine could not absorb enough of these officers to afford appreciable relief to the naval corps. Clark also asserted that applying the navy's system to the cutters would simply add to their expense.

Regarding the cost of running the Revenue Cutter School of Instruction, the report indicated that the school actually saved money for the government. Congress made no appropriations for the school. Cadets were appointed to fill vacancies at the third lieutenant rank, and while they were in school, third lieutenant billets were held open for them. Because they earned only three quarters of a third lieutenant's pay, cadets were less expensive to maintain than lieutenants. The *Chase* was used as a schoolship to train cadets while she performed her regular duties as a cutter. The only real problem with the program, the report said, was that it was too short—it should be a four-year program. As for educating revenue cutter officers at the Naval Academy, that would be a mistake, the report indicated, because the course of study and its instruction methods were not suited to the needs of the Revenue Marine Service. According to his report, Clark believed that if the cutter school were closed, the service would be better off returning to the system of recruiting officers by competitive examination from the merchant marine, rather than accepting Naval Academy graduates.

Reminding Congress that previous attempts at such a transfer had failed, Clark used arguments made during the debate over an 1843 proposal to bolster his case. He quoted from Secretary of the Treasury Walter Forward, who had claimed that the change was designed to embarrass the department in carrying out its obligation to the revenue. Forward had added, significantly according to Clark: "Without intending any disparagement of the officers of the Navy, it is not believed that the habits and discipline of that meritorious class of men are calculated to suit the character of service to which it is proposed to assign them, especially when they must be subject to the orders and directions of the collector of the customs . . . which subjection is deemed highly essential, both for the efficiency of the duties to be discharged and the better security of the interests of the revenue." Forward had concluded his case by reminding Congress that it had been necessary to stop using naval officers in the Revenue Cutter Service because of "difficulties and objections which occurred in the practical operations of the measure."[6]

Clark also quoted from the conclusions of an adverse report prepared by Jabez W. Huntington for the Senate Commerce Committee in 1843 and reminded Congress that the Senate had voted in agreement with the committee that year. Clark stated that he was just the last in a long line of Treasury Department officials, including Secretaries Hamilton, Louis McLane, and Forward, who confirmed the advantages of the existing system. It was, he asserted in his report, the obligation of the secretary of the navy, who had made the proposal, to show how the current system did not work.

In his report, Clark included materials from previous inquiries into using naval vessels and personnel to perform revenue work, including a response by Secretary of the Navy Isaac Toucey to an 1859 Senate proposal to transfer the Revenue Cutter Service to the Navy Department. He reported having asked the heads of the Bureaus of Yards and Docks and Ordnance and Hydrography if the Navy Department could accept a transfer of the Revenue Cutter Service from the Treasury Department, carry out the work of the revenue cutters, and protect the coast. His bureau heads had concluded that the transfer "would be inexpedient." Toucey had agreed with them.[7]

The 1883 bill proposing to move the Revenue Cutter Service to the Navy Department never left the committee room.[8] But the issue lingered until 1889, when a new secretary of the navy, Benjamin Tracy, renewed the proposal. Although there was little new in Tracy's report (most of it was quoted from Chandler's 1882 report), the renewed effort got farther than its predecessor. A bill transferring the Revenue Cutter Service from the Treasury Department to the Navy Department passed the House in 1890, but it failed in the Senate.[9]

Tracy's proposal was more successful than Chandler's because revenue cutter officers, as well as the new secretary of the treasury, William Windom, supported it. Of 206 revenue cutter officers, 198 had signed a petition urging Windom to endorse the transfer. Their motive was economic self-interest. Numerous secretaries of the treasury had repeatedly asked Congress to grant revenue cutter officers the same pay and perquisites given to naval officers. Revenue cutter officers believed that they deserved such benefits, for they were essentially naval officers who served on naval vessels with all the discomforts and personal problems associated with such service. They had given up all hope of Congress passing legislation granting civil servants a retirement system or of the secretary of the treasury convincing Congress to grant them a retirement system. They therefore concluded, as they said in their petition, that their best chance of getting what they wanted was by transfer to the navy. Revenue cutter officers, the peers of all other services, they wrote, were "the poorest paid, least provided for, and hardest working organization of commissioned officers in the service of the Nation. Notwithstanding the withering disadvantages under which our service has always labored, we point with just pride to its record for efficiency and devotion to duty, whether it be amid the ice floes of Arctic seas, the winter tempest upon the rockbound coast of New England, or in the fever-infested ports of our coasts bordering the Gulf of Mexico."[10]

On 9 January 1890, Windom endorsed the officers' petition in a letter to Congress, in which he recommended approval of the proposal for transfer of the Revenue Cutter Service to the Navy Department. Windom's letter repeated most of Chandler's and Tracy's arguments for the transfer, and Windom added a few arguments of his own. Most important of the latter was Windom's claim that consolidation with the navy would relieve him of "duties regarding the personnel and material of the service, for which he has neither the time nor the technical knowledge to direct in person, and which in consequence demands a separate department for its management instead of coming under one individual naval head." Windom earnestly endorsed the desire of revenue officers for equality with officers of the other services. He credited naval and army officers with outstanding service when they worked with civil authorities, as for example when army officers cooperated with the Lighthouse Service and naval officers cooperated with the Coast Survey.[11] And he recommended approval of the proposal for the transfer of the Revenue Cutter Service to the Navy Department. As reported above, the bill, with such support, passed in the House, but failed in the Senate.

Tracy's proposal was revived in 1891, 1892, and 1902. By the time the Senate received the renewed proposal in 1891, Charles Foster was the new secretary of the treasury, and he opposed the transfer. The new discussions added nothing of substance to previous debates on similar bills. Each proposal failed to pass in either branch of Congress, and efforts to unite the Revenue Cutter Service and the navy were not revived with any vigor until 1911.[12] When they surfaced then, they would take on a new and different character.

One serious consequence of the support given to Secretary Tracy's proposal by revenue cutter officers and Secretary Windom occurred in 1890, however, when President Benjamin Harrison issued an executive order closing the Revenue Cutter School of Instruction. From May 1890 to May 1894, the *Chase* was laid up, and the Revenue Cutter Service took its new officers from graduates of the Naval Academy at Annapolis.[13] The navy had won a small reward for its persistence.

A second consequence was the appointment of Capt. Leonard G. Shepard to run the Revenue Cutter Service. Because he lacked the time and technical knowledge to direct the service in person, Secretary Windom assigned Captain Shepard to special duty in Washington on 14 December 1889. As noted in the *Register of the Revenue Cutter Service,*

Shepard's status underwent a change. The 1891 *Register* lists him as: "Special duty, Washington, D.C." In the 1892 register, he appears as: "Chief Division Revenue Marine."[14]

Two years later, on 31 July 1894, Congress officially established the position of Chief, Revenue Cutter Service, in legislation that ordered the secretary of the treasury to appoint a captain of the Revenue Cutter Service to that position.[15] No additional pay was allowed for the job. Not until 1908 would the captain commandant of the Revenue Cutter Service receive the same pay as a captain in the U.S. Navy. Shepard was the first military officer to run the service since the 1840s, when Capt. Alexander V. Fraser had been in charge, and he also became the first of the continuous line of officers who have held the position to the present day.

CHAPTER FOUR

Cutter Operations during the 1880s

Despite the navy's assault, the Revenue Cutter Service performed its duties successfully during most of the 1880s (see Appendix A). On average throughout the decade, 1,001 men sailed 38 cutters 305,582 miles annually at a cost of $870,024; they assisted 232 vessels with 2,775 persons on board and saved 78 persons from drowning. The value of vessels assisted each year averaged a total of $4,604,871. On average per year, the cutters' crews examined 27,411 ships' papers and seized or reported 1,882 ships for violating the nation's laws, for which those ships paid a total annual average of $558,577 in penalties.[1]

Revenue Marine Service Chief Ezra Clark reported the work done by the cutter service during the fiscal year that ended on 30 June 1881, beginning with a statistical analysis of the cutters' efforts to protect the nation's revenue and to assist vessels in distress. That year, 36 cutters, manned by 183 officers and 720 crewmen, sailed 282,027 miles, boarded and examined 29,101 ships, reported 3,163 of them for violating the country's laws, assisted 148 wrecked ships or ships in distress, and rescued 141 persons from drowning. There were 1,297 persons on board the vessels assisted, which had a total value, including cargoes, of $2,776,882. Cost to the United States was $846,791 for those services.[2]

Clark listed special services provided by each cutter that year. Several entries allow some insight into the work of the Revenue

Cutter Service. They clearly reveal that the service emphasized saving lives and property, and they state in simple terms the sometimes dull work that had to be done. Clark started and ended his account of the *Corwin* by listing the objectives and accomplishments of her 1880 and 1881 cruises to the Arctic Ocean. For the period between cruises, he mentioned her saving lives in San Francisco Harbor. His entry for the steamer *Stevens*, sailing out of New Bern, North Carolina, was typical for 1881. It listed many successful efforts to float and tow to safety grounded schooners and a few failed efforts to rescue stranded vessels; and it recorded the staking out of Wallace's channel and the entrance to Cedar Bay by the *Stevens*. Clark's entry on the steamer *Samuel Dexter*, sailing out of Newport, Rhode Island, was more thorough than most. It provided an account of the work of a cutter in the North throughout the four seasons of the year. In addition to towing many schooners to safety, the *Dexter* put down a mutiny on the sloop *Red Rover*; assisted vessels trapped in ice, including 32 frozen in Hyannis Harbor at the same time; and provided desperate ships' crews with provisions. Among these crews was that of the Italian bark *Machiavelli*, 131 days out of Alexandria, Egypt, off Montauk Point, New York.[3]

Clark concluded his report on the cutters with an account of services performed for the Life-Saving Service between 1 July 1878 and 30 June 1881. During those years, 22 cutters sailed 71,147 miles on life-saving duties. Four small sloops worked exclusively for the Life-Saving Service, as did five revenue cutter officers: Capt. John McGowan as superintendent of construction at New York; Capt. John W. White as superintendent and assistant inspector for the Twelfth District at East Oakland Station, California; First Lt. Walter Walton as assistant inspector for the Eleventh District at Milwaukee, Wisconsin; and First Lt. Charles F. Shoemaker and 2d Lt. Thomas D. Walker on special duty at Washington, D.C. In addition to their regular duties, six captains (James H. Merryman, Russell Glover, Daniel B. Hodgsdon, Leonard G. Shepard, John G. Baker, and George R. Slicer) and four second lieutenants (Charles H. McLellan, William C. DeHart, George E. McConnell, and Frank H. Newcomb) were detailed as superintendents of construction or assistant inspectors for various districts of the Life-Saving Service. The cutters transported superintendents, officers, boards of examiners, collectors of customs, boats, and supplies for the Life-Saving Service.[4]

Perhaps the best example of heroic services rendered to the nation's maritime community during the 1880s was the *Dexter's* rescue of survivors from the *City of Columbus* when she ran aground in 1884. During the early morning hours of 18 January, the iron-hulled steamer crashed into Devil's Bridge, an outcrop of rocks on the western end of Martha's Vineyard, Massachusetts. In spite of heroic efforts by the crew of the *Dexter* and volunteers from the Massachusetts Humane Society and the Gay Head Life-Saving Station, the disaster took the lives of 103 of 132 persons on board.

John Roach and Sons had built the *City of Columbus* at Chester, Pennsylvania, in 1878. She had run between New York and Savannah, Georgia, for a few years and was then purchased by the Boston and Savannah Steamship Company to continue the same run. At the time of the accident, she was worth $300,000 and was insured for $250,000. She measured 275 feet in length, 38 feet in beam, and 2,200 tons burden. Her compound engine, which generated 1,500 horsepower, was supported by fore and aft auxiliary sails on two masts. The *City of Columbus* could cruise at 12½ knots. She had space for 200 passengers in forty-two luxurious staterooms and simple quarters in steerage under the bow on the main deck. She could carry 2,500 tons of cargo, or as much as could a 122-car freight train.[5]

Her officers were experienced mariners with good records. Capt. Schuyler E. Wright, master of the *City of Columbus* on her last voyage, had gone to sea at the age of thirteen, had become the master of his first ship at thirty-eight, and at fifty-two held his fifth command. Captain Wright had a distinguished record and a reputation for devotion to duty. His first officer, Edwin Fuller, was a licensed master who had given up command of his own ship to join the officer corps of the *City of Columbus*. Augustus Harding, a twenty-seven-year-old mariner from Chatham on Cape Cod, was the second officer. Because he had no pilot's license, the captain was responsible for his actions as an officer. Experienced seamen made up the crew.[6]

The *City of Columbus* sailed from Nickerson's Wharf in Boston for Savannah on the afternoon of 17 January, rounded the tip of Cape Cod, and sailed through Nantucket and Vineyard sounds at a speed of 12 knots. As the moon rose at 2240, the ship left Pollock Rip behind. The sky was clear overhead, but a haze covered the land. At 0205, Second Officer Harding relieved the first officer in the pilothouse. Quartermaster Roderick A. McDonald had the wheel. When Nobska's light dropped astern, Captain Wright told the wheelsman to steer a course southwest by west. A few minutes later, with Tarpaulin Cove Light about a mile away, Captain Wright said he told Harding that when Tarpaulin Cove Light bore north, he was to go west-southwest. After giving his orders, the captain stepped into his quarters, located fifteen inches below and right behind the pilot-house. He sat down with his back against the steam radiator, next to the door to the pilothouse. Perhaps he dozed.[7]

Disaster followed shortly afterward. Watchman Edward Leary reported a buoy on the wrong bow, but he was not heard. He rushed to the pilothouse, and, after Second Officer Harding lowered the window, told him that there was a buoy on the port bow. Precious time had been wasted because of that closed window. Harding ordered "Port," followed by "Hard aport" from Captain Wright. At about 0315, the *City of Columbus* ran upon Devil's Bridge at the foot of Gay Head. Captain Wright tried unsuccessfully to back off the rocks. He sent Harding to set the jib and tried to swing the ship to seaward. Nothing worked; the ship was hard aground. Captain Wright ordered the lifeboats readied and told the passengers to put on life preservers.[8]

Conditions quickly worsened. The first launched boat cleared the *City of Columbus* with seven persons on board; only two were passengers. The ship then listed to port, plunging the lifeboats on the port side into the sea and making it impossible to control the launching of boats on the starboard side. A second lifeboat plunged into the sea and endangered everyone on deck. Clearly, no other boats could be launched. Water poured into the ship from the engine room. Combers broke over the deck, swept away the hatches, and threatened everything and anybody not firmly attached to the vessel. The only parts of the ship not pounded by the sea were the masts and rigging.[9]

Spray began to freeze, and the deck became slippery. A giant comber swept away the deckhouses. Only vigorous and healthy persons could make it into the rigging, and they showed no sign of consideration for women and children, who numbered about one third of the passengers. Not one woman reached the rigging, and no women were saved.

Capt. Thomas R. Hammond, a passenger from Goldsborough, Maine, condemned the officers and crew: "I do not think there was an attempt by the officers to save a life. They all looked after themselves and left the passengers to do the same; in fact I never saw a crew in such utter confusion and disorder." Thomas O'Leary, a ship's fireman, seemed to agree. "It was number one there about that time," he told a reporter in answer to a question about why most of the men who left in the first boat were officers and crewmen from the *City of Columbus*.[10]

A reporter from the *Daily Eastern Argus* (Portland, Maine) wrote that passenger John Cook "watched a man and woman who stood close together, hand in hand, unmoved by the turmoil about them. Spray was drenching them as the man leaned over and kissed the woman. They were embracing, Cook said, when a heavy sea washed them away." By 0410, less than an hour after the *City of Columbus* first went aground, the disaster was over except for those who clung to the masts and rigging and those in the lifeboats. When daylight broke, Captain Wright counted twenty-eight in the main rigging and five, including himself and Cook, in the fore rigging.[11]

Cook was awake when the ship ran aground. At first, he was unconcerned. Then, hearing the confusion and alarm in voices coming from the deck, he ran on deck, saw the predicament of the ship, and returned below to rouse his roommate. The latter refused to leave his berth; finally, Cook had to save himself. He went back on deck and climbed onto a deckhouse with Captain Wright and seaman John White. When the deckhouse went overboard, the three men survived by climbing into the fore rigging with two other men.[12]

Five persons survived in the lifeboats. Four exhausted men rowed one boat ashore and crawled onto the beach. A small naval tug, the *Speedwell*, picked up the second lifeboat containing a lone, unconscious survivor, Capt. Sherrington Vance. Fortunate enough to have been washed overboard alongside the waterlogged lifeboat, Vance had pulled himself into it before passing out.[13]

More than five hours passed before help appeared at Devil's Bridge. After sunup, the large screw steamer *Glaucus* had passed by along the Elizabeth Islands. Captain Maynard Bearse examined the wreck with his glass and recognized the *City of Columbus*, but he did not see the men in the rigging. He assumed that crew and passengers had been rescued by the Gay Head boatmen and continued on his way to Boston.[14]

The newspapers severely criticized Captain Bearse. Later, Forbes would write that Bearse "was neither heartless nor inhuman, nor was he a bad man . . .; he was simply a dull man with none of the inspiration of a true sailor, which should have made him put his helm up the instant he saw the wreck and make sure that not a single living soul remained to be helped."[15]

The first rescue vessel appeared between 0900 and 1000 that morning. A lifeboat of the Massachusetts Humane Society was manned by Gay Head American Indians. Fred Poole, on watch at the Gay Head light, had seen the ship's light on Devil's Bridge at 0500. Realizing it should not be there, he had called Horatio N. Pease, keeper of the light and the man in charge of the Humane Society's Gay Head lifeboat. Pease traveled five miles to get a volunteer crew of six men to man the boat. Joseph Peters, in charge of the boat, launched it at 0730. It took his crew more than an hour to reach the wreck; they were so exhausted that they had to rest before making a rescue attempt. Then, they convinced seven men on the ship to jump into the sea. They rescued all seven and reached shore at 1000.[16]

A second boat manned by another crew from Gay Head rowed out to the wreck. In three trips out, the six-man crew rescued twelve persons, whom they transferred to the revenue cutter *Dexter*. One died aboard the cutter.[17] The customs collector at the Vineyard had sent the navy tug *Speedwell* to the scene of the disaster, but when she arrived, the *Dexter* was already anchored at the scene. Grimly picking up bodies as she went, the *Speedwell* returned to port.[18]

The *Dexter* (Capt. Eric Gabrielson) had reached the scene at 1230. The cutter was returning from an offshore patrol when her crew spotted the *City of Columbus*. By then, Gabrielson reported that the wind was blowing hard, the sea "rolled mountain high." The *Dexter*, a wooden cutter (143 feet long, 23-foot beam, and 188 tons burden), took an awful pounding in the surf. The captain worried that the stove on the berth deck, although well secured, might break loose and set fire to the ship. In order to help the men in the masts of the wreck, the *Dexter* was anchored in an exposed location 200–300 yards off the starboard quarter of the *City of Columbus*. She "rolled rails under. A slip rope was fastened to the anchor and a seaman stationed to let go if need be."[19]

Captain Gabrielson ordered 2d Lt. John U. Rhodes to lower the *Dexter*'s boat; five volunteers joined him in a rescue effort. The seas heaved the small boat into the air and dropped it down again, making it difficult to pull away from the *Dexter*. Wreckage thick around the *City of Columbus* endangered all concerned. Rhodes yelled for the men in the masts to jump. Two brothers got up the courage to lead the way, and one was lost. On his first trip, Rhodes succeeded in rowing seven men to the *Dexter*.[20] Rhodes was the son of the master of the clipper ship *Golden Fleece*. Born at

Fair Haven, Connecticut, in 1850, he went to sea as a boy with his father. In 1873, he joined the Revenue Cutter Service. He served on the cutters *Campbell* and *Colfax* before joining the *Dexter* as a third lieutenant in 1880.

Lt. Charles D. Kennedy and four volunteers from the *Dexter* were lowered in the cutter's gig. Kennedy headed for the foremast where Captain Wright and four men had been clinging for twelve hours. One of the last two men to leave the foremast, the captain jumped to safety only after being assured that the men still in the mizzenmast were frozen.[21]

Lieutenant Rhodes volunteered to try to recover the bodies in the rigging, if he could get a good man to handle the boat. First Lt. Warrington D. Roath volunteered and tried unsuccessfully to position the boat properly. Rhodes transferred to the Gay Head lifeboat, which was better suited to the task, but it could not maneuver close enough to the *City of Columbus*. Rhodes tied a line around his waist and jumped into the water. His efforts to swim to the wreck were thwarted by debris and a nasty cut on the leg, so he was hauled back on board the *Dexter*. After getting into dry clothing and having his leg attended to, Rhodes made another rescue attempt. By this time, the seas had subsided. After several tries, the crewmen brought the *Dexter*'s dinghy alongside the *City of Columbus*, and Rhodes cut the two frozen figures out of the rigging.[22]

At 1615, Captain Gabrielson raised anchor and headed for his home port at New Bedford. The *Dexter* transported seventeen of the twenty-nine men who had been rescued and four corpses. The *City of Columbus* had departed from Boston with forty-five officers and crewmen and eighty-seven passengers. Twenty-eight of the ship's company and seventy-five passengers were lost. A Boston man lost his father, mother, brother, sister, and brother's child.[23]

A grateful nation honored the officers and crew of the *Dexter* and the Gay Head lifesavers. A joint resolution of Congress thanked them for their "brave and humane conduct," especially Lieutenant Rhodes, "who at the imminent peril of life, swam to the steamer, through heavy seas and floating wreckage, and rescued two men who were clinging to the rigging." The legislature of the State of Connecticut passed a resolution thanking Rhodes for his "gallant conduct." The citizens of Newport, Rhode Island, held a public meeting of appreciation for the *Dexter*'s crew. A reporter of *The Boston Sunday Globe* wrote: "The officers and crew, from the captain to the cabin boy, acted the part of heroes, both at the scene of the wreck and afterwards in caring for the survivors."[24] An "elegant" solid gold maltese cross was ordered for Rhodes by the German-Americans of Wilmington, North Carolina. Secretary of the Treasury Charles J. Folger ordered praise for the crew of the *Dexter* read on board every U.S. revenue cutter. The Massachusetts Humane Society presented a gold medal to Rhodes, silver medals to Captain Gabrielson and Lieutenant Kennedy, citations for humane efforts to the other officers, and $200 to the crew. Public subscriptions rewarded Rhodes with $2,053, and the Gay Head lifesavers with $3,500. From his reward, Rhodes gave each officer $150 and each crewman a uniform, mattress, and bedding.[25]

The U.S. Steamboat Inspection Service held an official inquiry into the conduct of the officers of the *City of Columbus* and the *Glaucus* in February 1884. It exonerated Captain Bearse of the *Glaucus*, but it punished Captain Wright of the *City of Columbus* and took both his pilot's license and certificate as a shipmaster. Because the second mate had no pilot's license, the starboard watch had been the captain's responsibility. He manfully accepted the blame for the neglect that had caused the disaster. Later, he became a stevedore in Savannah.[26]

In addition to the rescue of the survivors of the *City of Columbus*, the special work of the Revenue Cutter Service in 1884 was unusually important, according to secretary of the treasury. In the spring, four cutters cruised the waters of the Gulf of Mexico to prevent the violation of U.S. neutrality laws. The entire fleet maintained a sanitary patrol along the nation's coasts to prevent the introduction of cholera and yellow fever, and four cutters cooperated with the Marine Hospital Service to maintain a quarantine at the entrance to Delaware and Chesapeake bays and in the Gulf of Mexico.[27] The quarantine continued to be enforced in the Gulf and on the Great Lakes during 1885.[28]

In 1886, four cutters provided assistance to communities wracked by disasters. The *Dix* helped to extinguish a fire at Key West, sheltered and fed many people left homeless, guarded property, and preserved order. After an earthquake at Charleston, South Carolina, the *McCulloch* sheltered 170 persons. The *Penrose* rescued flood victims at Sabine Pass, Texas, and the *Woodbury* rendered assistance during a fire at Eastport, Maine.[29]

On 16 May 1888, Congress enacted legislation that established anchorage grounds for ships "in the bay and harbor of New York, and in the Hudson and East Rivers," effective immediately.[30] New York merchants had called for passage of an anchorage law to cut down on collisions between anchored vessels and those under way. Secretary of the Treasury William Windom assigned enforcement duty to the Revenue Cutter Service, which gave the job to the steamer *Manhattan,* commanded by Capt. Joseph W. Congdon. A down-easter with a maritime background and respected by the U.S. maritime community, Congdon had sailed on a number of America's finest clipper ships before entering the cutter service. No ship's captain enjoyed having anybody order him to move his anchored ship, but the captains so ordered by Congdon knew that he appreciated their situation. The cutter service or the local harbormaster gave each ship's captain a color-coded map that indicated where he could and could not anchor. When Congdon discovered a ship anchored outside of proper limits, he ordered the captain to move her. If the ship did not move under her own power, she was towed by the *Manhattan* or a private tugboat. Big schooners often required assistance in moving to a proper anchorage. During the first six months of 1889, the *Manhattan* discovered 1,328 vessels improperly anchored, towed 948 to proper anchorages, and removed the others.[31] The following year, the *Manhattan* discovered 1,750 ships improperly anchored, helped 1,365 to proper anchorages, and removed the rest.[32] Most important, collisions in the port declined considerably.

The Treasury Department's policy of repairing old cutters, established at the end of the 1870s, began to have a negative impact on the service in 1886. Secretary of the Treasury Daniel Manning's report on the Revenue Cutter Service, dated 1 November 1886, noted, "The performance of the regular duties of the Service has been continued with fidelity, energy, and freedom from disaster. . . . Several of the vessels of the revenue marine fleet are now worn-out by hard service, and should be replaced by new ones of improved construction. Suitable appropriations are needed, especially for a new vessel in place of the steamer *McLane,* lately withdrawn from Galveston as unseaworthy, and also for a steamer to replace one of those now on the New York Station."[33]

A year later, Manning's successor, Charles S. Fairchild, reported an increase in the work performed by the cutters, but he repeated Manning's call for new construction: "This service requires the immediate replacement of a considerable number of its vessels with new ones fully adapted to the requirements of the work to be performed." Only with new cutters could "proper efficiency be secured and real economy in expenditures be brought about." The steamer *McCulloch* on the Charleston station was "practically worn out, and should be disposed of." The *Stevens* on the

North Carolina coast was "no longer fit for regular duty." Cutters used in the nation's harbors were even less adequate for their assigned duties than the cruising cutters. Poorly designed in the first place, they had deteriorated with age and were required to handle an increase in traffic that was "carried on in vessels of remarkable size and speed."[34]

Fairchild reported that some progress had been made in 1887. A new steamer for boarding duty had been placed in service on the Mississippi River. Five additional steamers on harbor duty still had to be disposed of and replaced with proper vessels: the *Hamlin* at Boston, the *Washington* at New York, the *Tench Coxe* at Philadelphia, the *Penrose* at Galveston, and the *Hartley* at San Francisco. Fairchild estimated that the new cutters would cost $350,000, less any money realized from the sale of the old vessels.[35]

The condition of the fleet continued to deteriorate. In 1888, Fairchild reported that the service had "faithfully and successfully" carried out its assigned duties. He noted that the record would have been better except for the poor condition of some of the cutters that required replacement and more extensive repairs than available funds allowed.[36]

The following year, Secretary of the Treasury Windom reported that services had declined because of the condition of the cutter fleet. There was a decrease in the total number of miles cruised during fiscal year 1889, Windom noted, which was the result of withdrawing some completely worn-out vessels from the fleet and laying up others for repairs. The service had spent $67,000 to repair six cutters that year. Two new vessels were under construction, and six more were needed for service at Boston, New York, Philadelphia, Galveston, San Francisco, and Astoria.[37]

Windom could have made an even stronger case for the service's decline in 1889. In every category of activity for which records were kept, except one, the record of operations for 1889 fell below the average for the decade (see Appendix A). The cost of maintenance for the service was $965,000 in 1889, compared with an average cost of $870,024 per year throughout the entire decade, and the 1889 figure was $53,000 more than the cost for 1888, which was the second highest in the decade. Costs were going up, and services had begun to decline. Something had to be done.

CHAPTER FIVE

Return to a
Military Chief

Secretary of the Navy William Chandler wrote in 1882 that Ezra Clark ran the Revenue Cutter Service with an assistant chief, ten clerks, and a stenographer.[1] Peter Bonnett succeeded Clark in 1885; then, on 14 December 1889, Secretary of the Treasury William Windom appointed Capt. Leonard G. Shepard to special duty in Washington, D.C. Although the Treasury Department did not officially identify Shepard as chief of the Revenue Marine Division until 1892, it noted at that time that his appointment dated from 14 December 1889.[2]

Shepard was born in Dorchester, Massachusetts, on 10 November 1846. He entered the Revenue Cutter Service as a third lieutenant on 15 September 1865. He earned promotions to second lieutenant on 20 March 1869, to first lieutenant on 20 July 1870, and to captain on 14 March 1878. His first assignment as a new third lieutenant was to the *Moccasin* at Norfolk, Virginia. Following his promotion to first lieutenant, he took command of the *Guthrie* at Baltimore, commanded the *Washington* at New York, then served on board the *Grant* in the same city. As a captain, Shepard commanded the *McLane* at Galveston and the *Bibb* at Ogdensberg, New York, before taking command of the *Chase* and the Revenue Cutter School of Instruction at New Bedford, Massachusetts. During his tenure as superintendent of the school, from 15 June 1883 to 9 April 1887, the schoolship *Chase* made three cadet cruises to European waters.[3] From 1887 to 1889, Shepard commanded the *Rush* at San Francisco,

Capt. Leonard G. Shepard. Courtesy of U.S. Naval Institute.

whence he made three cruises to the Bering Sea (see chapter 2). Just before his appointment as chief of the division, Shepard received command of the *Bear.*

Soon after taking charge of the service, Shepard vigorously renewed his predecessors' calls for reform and emphasized, as they had done, that the service needed new ships and a retirement system for the officer corps. He stressed that the vessels in the fleet, as his predecessors had reported, were too small to perform their assigned duties, and new vessels were urgently needed. "The policy pursued for so many years past," he wrote in *1891,* "of making extensive repairs of old vessels is a mistaken one. Had the same amount of money, with a little more added, been judiciously expended in the building of new vessels of a modern type, the Service would now have a much more efficient force."[4]

The personnel situation, which Shepard believed as important as the material situation, had become a serious problem. With promotions practically stopped, the condition of the service was one of stagnation. There were captains on active duty over eighty years of age, who had served faithfully in every naval war since that of 1812. So many officers filled high-ranking billets that promotions were practically blocked. Shepard believed that, generally, an officer was well past his prime before he could reach the rank that entitled him to a command; this situation sapped the vitality of the corps.[5] Just how stagnant the officer corps had become was dramatized by the closing of the Revenue Cutter School of Instruction five months after Shepard took command. The last class of cadets at New Bedford graduated in May 1890. Following the school's closing, the *Chase* was laid up in ordinary.[6]

During Shepard's first full year as commandant, the service had thirty-six revenue cutters in commission. One new cutter, the 148-foot iron-hulled steamer *Winona*, joined the fleet in 1890, and two cutters were under construction that year. According to Secretary Windom, the service urgently needed two more cutters. The *Manhattan*, he argued, was unable to do the work assigned to her in New York, where a new larger and more powerful vessel was needed, and the increased workload in Alaskan waters urgently called for a new vessel on the Pacific coast.[7]

In 1891, the service constructed the 190-foot, 416-gross ton iron-hulled steamer *Galveston* and purchased the *Sperry*, a 31-foot sloop. Despite these acquisitions, Charles Foster, Windom's successor, described the service's need for cutters that year as urgent:

> The rapidly increasing commerce on the Great Lakes, the Pacific coast, and Puget Sound; the large number of Chinese subjects unlawfully landing on our shores, and the enormous quantities of opium believed to be smuggled into the United States from contiguous foreign territory; the additional service demanded of the revenue-cutter fleet in protecting government interests in Alaska, all require new and more efficient steamers."[8]

Foster believed that the Revenue Cutter Service urgently needed two new cruising steamers for the Pacific Coast and two for Lakes Michigan and Ontario; it also needed a new, bigger boarding vessel for San Francisco.[9]

The situation worsened in 1892. In addition to the new ships for which Foster had argued unsuccessfully during the previous year, the service now had to replace a cutter on the coast of New England. The *Gallatin* had wrecked in a blinding snowstorm near Gloucester, Massachusetts, on 6 January.[10]

In 1893, John G. Carlisle, who had replaced Foster as secretary of the treasury, reported the need for five cruising cutters and a boarding vessel. He also made an argument for purchasing new cutters instead of repairing old, worn-out ones.[11]

The service completed the steel-hulled harbor tugs *Hudson*, 96 feet long and 128 gross tons, and *Calumet*, 94 feet long and 123 gross tons, in 1893 and 1894, respectively.[12] Although both were modern tugboats and their addition to the fleet improved the service's ability to perform its duties in the nation's harbors, the basic situation remained desperate.

In 1894, Secretary Carlisle reported that new, bigger cutters were still urgently needed. Only the *Bear*, he argued, was able to perform the arduous duties required of the service in the waters of Alaska and the Bering Sea. He had been required to withdraw steamers from the coasts of California and Oregon to serve with the Bering Sea fleet during the summer. This had left the California and Oregon districts without cutters and had caused "serious embarrassment" to the Customs Service. New steamers were still needed on the Pacific Coast, in New York, and on the Great Lakes—the *Grant* had been moved from New York to Puget Sound, and the *Bibb* had been condemned as no longer seaworthy and sold.[13]

Carlisle's annual report for 1895 documented the continuing desperation of the cutter situation, but it also noted that a significant transition had begun. There were still thirty-six cutters in the fleet, the same number there had been during Shepard's first full year as commandant, and several new vessels were still urgently needed. Many of the cutters were old. Some had been in use more than thirty years; the *McLane, Crawford, Chandler*, and *Washington* had served with the navy during the Civil War. In addition to the earlier move of the *Grant* from New York, the *Perry* had been transferred from the Great Lakes to the Pacific Coast. The New York and Great Lakes stations were now practically abandoned, which seriously damaged the national interest. But, the report continued, Congress had authorized three new cruising cutters. Two, for service on the Great Lakes and the New England coast, were under construction. Plans for the third, for service on the Pacific Coast, were finished, and the Revenue Cutter Service had invited construction bids. It had also completed plans and invited bids for a harbor tug for San Francisco. The new vessels authorized by Congress, Carlisle wrote, would be modern, valuable additions to the service.[14]

Shepard also arranged to provide his office with knowledgeable technical advice. He hired two civilian naval constructors, James Lee and John Q. Walton, and, in 1891, appointed Capt. Russell Glover as superintendent of construction and repair and Chief Engineer John W. Collins as consulting engineer. Under the 1894 legislation that had ordered the secretary to appoint a captain to serve as the chief of the division, Congress had also authorized an engineer-in-chief for the Revenue Cutter Service. The organization appointed Collins, who had been an engineer in the navy before he entered the Revenue Cutter Service, to fill that position.[15]

The number of officers and enlisted men remained constant at around 1,000 during Shepard's tenure as commandant. There were 220 commissioned officers on the rolls when he took command in 1889 and during the following two years. In 1892, 2 officers were added, bringing the total to the authorized limit of 222, where it stayed through his tenure. Although the number of enlisted men fluctuated a bit more than the number of officers between 1889 and 1895, the service had 815 enlisted men, a full complement, during Shepard's first and last years as commandant.[16]

As noted above, the absence of a retirement system for the officer corps was the most significant personnel problem confronted by Shepard. In his annual report for 1894, Secretary Carlisle pointed out that, because of the absence of such a system, 33 percent of the senior officers were incapable of performing active service. "The higher grades contain so many of these superannuated officers," he wrote, "that the efficiency of the Service is seriously impaired." A bill (H.R. 6723) was then pending in Congress to correct what Carlisle described as "this evil," and he earnestly recommended its enactment.[17]

Shepard fought his last fight for passage of H.R. 6723. Congress enacted the law on 2 March 1895. Shepard died of pneumonia at his residence in Washington, D.C., just twelve days later. He had been working for passage of the bill when stricken, and the press attributed his illness to exertions on behalf of elderly officers in the service.[18]

H.R. 6723 improved the personnel situation for the Revenue Cutter Service, but it did not solve the problem. Under the bill, the president could authorize the convening of a board of three surgeons of the Marine Hospital Service for the purpose of examining officers who had been unable to perform their duties because of age or infirmity at the time the act was passed. Any officers whom the board declared permanently incapacitated would be placed on a waiting orders list and given one-half duty pay.[19] Before 1895 ended, thirty-nine officers had been examined under the law, found unfit for active service, and placed on a permanent waiting orders list. The immediate effect was to rid the service of those officers who, through no fault of their own, could not perform their duties. This opened the ranks to young, qualified officers and rejuvenated the officer corps and the service.

Unfortunately, the result was not permanent because the bill applied only to officers who were incapacitated and on active duty when the legislation was enacted. The service could not fill the positions of officers who became incapacitated after 2 March 1895. Thus, the problem was bound to return, for there were elderly nonincapacitated officers on the rolls when Congress passed the bill.[20]

Despite the shortcomings of the law, Shepard deserved credit for a temporary solution to the problem of an aged and infirm officer corps. He also reopened the school of instruction in the spring of 1894, a little less than one year before Congress passed the half-pay legislation.

Coast Guard historians have given Shepard credit for dramatically improving the cutter fleet and the officer corps.[21] He did fight for those causes, but he was merely continuing the effort made by his civilian predecessors (see chapters 1 and 4). The gains made during his tenure were modest indeed. Significant improvements were made under Shepard's successor, Charles F. Shoemaker, whose accomplishments came at a time favorable to all naval establishments.

Five days after Shepard's death, Shoemaker succeeded him as commandant. Shoemaker was born in Glendale, Iowa, on 27 March 1841. As a child, he traveled to various frontier army garrisons in Illinois and Kansas with his father, William, who was in the army ordinance department. In 1858, Congressman Miguel Otero of New Mexico gave young Shoemaker an appointment to the U.S. Naval Academy. After three years as a midshipman, he resigned from the academy and entered the Revenue Cutter Service. Commissioned a third lieutenant on 20 November 1860, Shoemaker was assigned to serve on board the *Lewis Cass* at Mobile, Alabama. When Capt. James J. Morrison turned that cutter over to state authorities in the spring of 1861, Shoemaker led the other officers and seamen back to Union lines. Between 1861 and April 1864, he served on several cutters, escorted vessels along the coast, and served on guard duty in the port of New York. He then resigned his commission and went into business in the west.

Shoemaker returned to the Revenue Cutter Service as a lieutenant in June 1868 and served at various stations on the Atlantic Coast until 1875. He was then appointed assistant inspector at the New York office. In 1876, he became assistant inspector of Life-Saving Stations in the Third District, which he reorganized and put into efficient working order. Transferred two years later to the office of the general superintendent in Washington, Shoemaker investigated the loss of life in wrecks and complaints against the keepers of lifesaving stations in all districts. In 1882, he became executive officer on the revenue steamer *Seward* in the Gulf of Mexico. He returned to the Life-Saving Service in 1885 as assistant inspector in the Third District and later as an inspector of all districts, except the twelfth on the Pacific Coast. Part of this time, he served under Inspector James H. Merryman, who was a paralytic, so much of the work devolved upon Shoemaker. He located sites for stations, conducted three hundred investigations, and brought serious charges against four assistant superintendents. In April 1891, he took command of the cutter *Washington* at the port of New York. Two years later, he took command of the cutter *Hudson* in Philadelphia and returned to New York, where he served until Secretary Carlisle ordered him to take command of the service in Washington.[22]

Building on the foundation laid by Shepard, Shoemaker dramatically improved the fleet of cutters. Between 1895 and the Spanish-American War in 1898, he increased the number, power, and speed of the cutters. He added several steel cutters to the fleet, as well as cutters needed for service on the Pacific Coast and Great Lakes and in the nation's harbors.

On 1 April 1895, the service had thirty-eight cutters, which it had obtained between 1864 and 1894. All but three, the sloops *Alert* and *Sperry* and the bark *Chase*, were steamers or steam launches. Fifteen cutters were constructed of iron, two of steel, and twenty-one of wood. All but six had been built since the Civil War, but only five since 1890. The only modern vessels, the steel-hulled harbor tugs *Hudson* and *Calumet*, had been built under Shepard. Only two cutters measured over 400 tons burden—the *Bear*, 703 gross tons, and the *Galveston*, 416 gross tons. The sloop *Sperry*, at 7 gross tons, was the smallest cutter. None of the cutters had a speed of more than 11 knots under ideal weather and sea conditions, and the average speed of the best of them did not exceed 9 knots.[23]

*Capt. Charles Shoemaker. Courtesy of Naval Historical
Foundation.*

In 1897, Shoemaker reported that the only modern vessels in the service, the *Windom*, *Hudson*, and *Calumet*, had been built under his immediate predecessor, Leonard Shepard. (The *Windom* was not completed until 1896, after Shepard's death.) Shoemaker also gave Shepard credit for having made plans for better vessels before he died.[24]

Forty cutters were in operation by 1 September 1897. Congress became more supportive of the service during the mid to late 1890s and authorized two new cutters in 1895, two in 1896, and three in 1897. The service constructed at least eleven new cutters under Shoemaker's directions between 1895 and 1898: the *Guthrie* and *Tybee*, 1895; the *Windom*, *Golden Gate*, *Scout*, and *Guard*, 1896; the *Gresham*, *McCulloch*, and *Manning*, 1897; and the *Algonquin* and *Onondaga* in 1898. Revenue cutter officers prepared the plans and specifications of these cutters and supervised their construction. All were steamers or steam launches. Seven were built of steel, two of composite construction, and two (both launches) of wood. Five of them (the *Manning, Gresham, McCulloch, Algonguin,* and *Onondaga*) were more than 200 feet in length, had a burden of more than 700 gross tons, and could steam at more than 17 knots. The *Gresham,* an all-steel cruiser of 724 tons, ran at a speed of 17½ knots on her trial run. The *Manning* and *McCulloch* were both of composite construction; the latter measured 869 tons burden and had a speed of 17½ knots. The *Golden Gate,* a steam tug of 171 tons burden, could make 13 knots. The *Algonquin* and *Onondoga* were similar to the *Gresham.*[25]

The *Manning* deserves special mention, for she served as the model for a new class of cutters that were the best ships operated by the Revenue Cutter Service until after World War I. The *Manning* was built of composite construction at Boston for $175,000. With frames placed at 2-foot intervals, she was covered with ⅜-inch steel plates and sheathed from her bottom to 2 feet above the waterline in 5-inch-thick Oregon fir planks. Below the waterline, she was sheathed in copper and had eleven watertight bulkheads. The *Manning* measured 205 feet 6 inches, overall length; 32 feet 10 inches, extreme beam; 17 feet, depth of hold; and 724 gross tons. She had a triple-expansion engine that generated 2,000 horsepower and a single screw that could push her along at more than 17 knots. The *Manning* had the first generators ever installed in a cutter to provide lights and bells. She had the lines of a clipper ship but the plumb bow of ships of her era. She and her sisters were the last cutters rigged for sail.[26]

Shoemaker benefited from Shepard's successful fight to retire aged and infirm revenue cutter officers. As a result of the 2 March 1895 legislation, Shoemaker was able to place 39 officers on a waiting orders list. All of them were disqualified for active duty because of age or ill health resulting from wounds suffered during the Civil War or injuries in the line of duty. Their retirement marked the culmination of a reform movement championed by secretaries of the treasury in their annual reports for 1872, 1873, 1881, and 1895. The interests of both the service and humanity called for the retirement of those aged men who had served faithfully for so long. Shoemaker was able to improve the officer corps (even though the corps remained at 222 officers) by appointing young, energetic, fully qualified men to junior ranks. At that time, 1,000 men served in the enlisted ranks.[27]

The USRC Manning

Neither Secretary Carlisle nor Shoemaker was satisfied with this reform. There was still work to be done to solve permanently the problem of
an aging officer corps. In 1895 and 1896, Carlisle (and in 1897, the new
secretary, Lyman J. Gage) called for the retirement, at three-quarters pay,
of any officer who reached the age of sixty-four years or who had served
for thirty years and was declared mentally or physically disqualified by a
medical officer. In his 1897 report, Shoemaker endorsed these recommendations, as well as Secretary Gage's call for placing enlisted men injured
in peacetime duty on a pension list.[28] The proposed reforms were reasonable, desirable, and fair, but it would take the triumphs of the 1897 overland expedition in the Arctic and the Spanish-American War to induce
Congress to accept the proposals of the secretary and the commandant.
To some degree, those triumphs were the result of the reforms already accomplished by Shepard and Shoemaker.

CHAPTER SIX

The *Bear* and the Overland Expedition

I n 1886, the revenue cutter *Bear* replaced the *Corwin* on the Pacific Coast, in part because the *Corwin* carried too little coal for extended cruising. The *Bear* would serve in Arctic waters for forty-one of her eighty-nine years as a cutter. She would make forty-two northern cruises and log an average of 16,000 miles per cruise.[1] Her captain, Michael A. Healy, wrote to Secretary of the Treasury Daniel Manning on 21 October 1886, about the *Bear*'s performance on her first Arctic voyage: "The *Bear* has been tried under all conditions of wind, weather and ice and has proven a very serviceable vessel. . . . For ice work alone she is understandably the best vessel in the Arctic Ocean, a fact attested by me and all who have seen her work in the ice in the past season."[2]

According to Albion, the "*Bear* was built at Dundee in Scotland in 1874, with oak frame and six-inch planking, sheathed with tough Australian ironwood, and braced in her bows to withstand the ice with which she would become all too well acquainted."[3]

The *Bear* measured 198 feet 6 inches in overall length, 190 feet 4 inches, at the waterline, and 29 feet 9 inches in the beam. With a draft of 18 feet 8 inches, she displaced 1,675 tons. She was rigged as a barkentine with two lesser masts of Norway pine and an iron mainmast. She could sail at 8 knots and steam at 9 knots. Her first nine years were spent as a sealer, sailing each March out of St. Johns, Newfoundland, for the Labrador sealing grounds.[4]

The USRC Bear *under way in the Arctic Ocean.*

The U.S. Navy purchased the *Bear* in 1884 for use in the Greely relief expedition. Lt. Adolpheus W. Greely, U.S. Army, had led twenty-four men into Baffin Bay, between Greenland and Canada, in 1881. They had left the United States in July and landed two months later at Discovery Harbor in Lady Franklin Sound, where they were trapped in the ice.[5]

On 17 December 1883, President Chester Arthur had convened a board to plan a relief expedition. After some interservice rivalry between the army and navy for the assignment, the navy was given the job. The first ship sent to the rescue was crushed in the ice, whereupon three ships were selected to make the rescue attempt: the *Thetis* (Comdr. Winfield Scott Schley), the *Bear* (Lt. William H. Emory), and the *Alert* (Comdr. George W. Coffin). The *Loch Garry* was taken along for logistical support. The *Thetis* had been built as an Arctic whaler at Dundee in 1881. She measured 188 feet 6 inches in length and 29 feet in the beam and drew 17 feet 10 inches of water. The British government offered the *Alert* for the expedition, which greatly increased international interest in the undertaking. The four vessels got under way for Baffin Bay in April 1884. Two months later the *Bear*, followed closely by the *Thetis*, found Greely and six other men near Cape Sabine in terrible condition. Eighteen of their associates had perished. One of those rescued, suffering from frostbite, lost both hands and feet and died en route to the United States. Following the rescue, the *Bear* put in at Portsmouth, New Hampshire, for full navy honors.[6]

The navy had no further use for a wooden vessel, such as the *Bear*. The Revenue Cutter Service, which had assumed responsibilities in the North Pacific, wanted the *Bear* and accepted her transfer in 1885. She was fitted out and sailed from New York to San Francisco in 106 days. After her arrival on 23 February 1886, she spent a great amount of her time cruising in Alaskan waters north of Norton Sound, up into Bering Strait, and on to Point Barrow.

During several years of the *Bear's* career as a cutter, her skipper was the rugged and effective Mike Healy. His personality accounts in part for the *Bear's* success as a cutter and for her lasting fame. As the *Bear's* skipper, he discovered salmon fishing grounds, rescued innumerable whalers from the ice, and fostered sobriety among the natives.

Healy had taken his own brand of law and order to the Arctic (see chapter 2). In the summer of 1886, he boarded the schooner *Cluea Light* and found twenty gallons of illegal whiskey and eight thousand Winchester cartridges on board. When the captain claimed no knowledge of the items, Healy gave the man a receipt for the ammunition, which he confiscated, and he ordered the whiskey thrown overboard.[7]

The following year, Healy confronted a mutinous crew on the American bark *Wanderer* off Umiak Island. The bark was adrift with her sails furled and her crew refusing to work the ship. Healy ordered his crew to man the *Bear's* guns and sent Lt. Albert Buhner and some of the cuttermen, armed with rifles, onto the *Wanderer*. When the bark's crew refused to obey the lieutenant's orders to return to work, Healy had the twenty-one offenders triced up. Each man's hands were shackled behind his back. A line was attached to the handcuffs, and, using a block for advantage, the cuttermen lifted each man off the deck until just his toes were touching. Each one was let down only when he agreed to return to work. Two of the men later required medical attention and were treated by the *Bear's* surgeon.[8]

The *Bear* continued her cruise and sailed into Unalaska to be met by another mutinous crew on the coal bark *Estella*. The bark's master approached Healy while he was coaling and watering his ship. He told Healy that, en route to Unalaska, three of the crew had beaten the mate and threatened to kill the bark's officers. Healy did not take action at that time, but, after several unpleasant exchanges with the surly mutineers, he had them triced up for fifteen minutes. Then he had them cut down. When they were still unrepentant, he chained them to a stanchion for 4½ hours. After that, Lt. David H. Jarvis returned them to the *Estella* and to work.[9]

Healy had not heard the last of these incidents. On 11 January 1890, a capacity crowd filled the Metropolitan Temple in San Francisco to hear charges of cruelty and drunkenness on duty brought against Healy. At the meeting, representatives of the Brewery Workers, the Coast Seamen's Union, and the Women's Christian Temperance Union, among others, including two of the *Bear*'s crewmen, voted unanimously against Healy. Secretary of the Treasury Windom appointed a board of inquiry, made up of T. G. Phelps, the customs collector at San Francisco; T. H. Bailhache of the Marine Hospital at San Francisco; and Capt. John W. White, former commanding officer of the revenue cutter *Wayanda*, to investigate the charges. When more than a score of witnesses appeared to refute the charges of drunkenness, they were dismissed. The charges of cruelty were more serious, and sworn affidavits confirmed that Healy had triced up civilian seamen. Appearing in his own defense, Healy argued that tricing up was a last resort on the Alaskan frontier. There were no jails there, and he had had the obligation to suppress the mutinies. So he had triced up the men to quell the mutinies. Tricing up had been illegal since 1863, but the board of inquiry agreed with Healy's arguments. It not only supported his actions but recommended that the Treasury Department recognize his "long and arduous service in the Arctic."[10]

Native Alaskans certainly expected the *Bear* and her officers to uphold law and order in the territory. The officers of the *Bear* intervened in family feuds and even murders. Because of the lack of secure lockups in the area, they usually took murderers on board when they sailed south.[11]

The *Bear*'s duties included enforcing the laws that were meant to protect the seal herds of the Arctic. On one trip, as the *Bear* approached Saint Paul Island, Healy sighted the American schooner *Allie Alger*. He brought the cutter alongside and ordered her skipper to heave to. The cutter's crew manned her guns while Lt. Oscar C. Hamlet boarded the sealer. Because her deck was freshly washed, she was marked as a possible poacher. Hamlet found 1,600 illegal sealskins in her hold. The *Bear*'s officers arrested the *Allie Alger's* officers and crew and threw them into jail to await trial. Then, they towed the schooner to Unalaska, where the skins were off-loaded, and sailed the schooner to Sitka. Healy meted out the same treatment to the British schooner *Ada* of Shanghai when he found 1,800 illegal sealskins in her hold.[12]

Healy was also the savior of mariners in the waters of the Pacific. When a whaler gave him a piece of wood with a message carved on it that had been given to the whaler by a Siberian native, Healy did not know if it was a legitimate call for help or a ruse to lure him away from the sealing grounds. Nevertheless, he acted quickly to try to save a life, if that was a possibility. On one side of the wood, the message read, "1887, J. B. V. Br. Nap. Tobacco Give." On the other side, it read, "S. W. C. Nav. M.10. Help. Come."

He decided that the message could be from J. B. Vincent of Martha's Vineyard, who was a boat steerer on the whaling bark *Napoleon* that had been lost in a gale on 5 May 1885. The *Bear* departed Port Clarence, Alaska, and steamed 150 miles to a location 10 miles southwest of Cape Navarin, Siberia, where Healy thought Vincent might be. In fact, Healy found Vincent fishing at the exact location where his message said he would be. He was the only man to survive the *Napoleon's* disaster who had not been picked up in 1885. Healy's immediate response made it possible for Vincent to return home; it was representative of Healy's humanitarian side.[13]

In the spring of 1888, the *Bear's* crew went to the aid of the disabled whaler *Belvedere,* which had a broken propeller. First, they towed the whaler to Unalaska, then beached her, built a cofferdam around her, pumped out the water, and helped the *Belvedere's* crew to repair the propeller. Only after the whaler was ready to return to sea did Healy leave her and steam a course for the north.[14]

En route to Point Barrow after aiding the *Belvedere,* Healy helped a number of whalers damaged by a severe storm. The same storm had also sunk four whale ships at Point Barrow. When Healy arrived there, he took 150 men from the sunken vessels on board the *Bear* for the return trip to San Francisco. The following spring, the *Bear* departed San Francisco with a load of lumber on her foredeck. The refuge station Healy had been advocating would finally become a reality.[15]

Under Healy, the *Bear* even moved reindeer from Siberia to Alaska. Sealers and whalers had killed much of the game in the north country,

The USRC Bear rescuing whalers trapped in the ice.

which left the native Alaskans with a marginal existence. The inability of the Alaskans to drink in moderation compounded the problem. In 1887, the *Corwin* had found the entire population of St. Lawrence Island dead of starvation.

Two years before that discovery, Lieutenant Cantwell had noticed that the vegetation of the upper Kowak River valley was similar to that of Siberia, where herds of reindeer flourished (see chapter 2). He and Doctor Townsend, the naturalist who accompanied him on his exploration, knew that the Chukchees of Siberia made a good living as herdsmen. Because the Inuits were closely related to the Chukchees, Cantwell and Townsend believed that the Inuits might be able to raise reindeer in Alaska; perhaps domesticated reindeer could be introduced into the territory.[16]

Upon their return to the *Corwin*, the explorers discussed their thoughts with Captain Healy, who followed up their idea by examining the American side of the Bering Sea for food that might support reindeer. Finding an abundance of lichens, moss, and sphagnum, Healy, Cantwell, and Townsend concluded that reindeer could survive in Alaska.[17]

In the summer of 1887, the *Corwin* and the *Bear* sailed into Saint Lawrence Bay. Assisted by a Chukchee herdsman whose son had been saved by the *Bear*'s surgeon, Healy succeeded in acquiring five reindeer. The cuttermen loaded them aboard the *Corwin*, transported them to Port Clarence, and put them out to pasture. When the *Corwin* put in at Port Clarence in 1888, the small herd had grown to eight reindeer. The next year, there were still more deer at Port Clarence.[18]

Reindeer could survive in Alaska. What was needed was a project with public support that could acquire and transport from Siberia enough domestic reindeer to make a difference in the lives of the Inuits. The man at hand who could generate the necessary support was Sheldon Jackson, the commissioner of education for Alaska. Jackson had accompanied the *Corwin* on her 1885 cruise and was also a passenger on the *Bear*'s 1890 cruise to the Arctic. With the experiment of transporting reindeer to Alaska showing every sign of success, he agreed to seek the necessary support.[19]

As soon as the *Bear* arrived at San Francisco in November 1890, Jackson set out for Washington to ask Congress to purchase Siberian reindeer for Alaska. Congress refused Jackson's request, but he raised $2,156 from private donations. After many delays caused by other duties, the *Bear* put in at Siberia on her 1891 cruise. As she sailed up and down the coast, Healy and Jackson bartered for sixteen reindeer. They were among the first of about 1,200 reindeer that the Revenue Cutter Service would transport across the Bering Sea for Jackson by 1902.[20]

The *Bear*'s crew hobbled the reindeer and lifted them onto the cutter's steam launch. When they were alongside the *Bear*, the crew put a sling around each reindeer's belly and hoisted it on board. For the journey across the Bering Sea, the *Bear* became a "cattle" barge, with the deer turned loose in a pen on one of the lower decks. Once the *Bear* reached Unalaska, the process of loading was reversed for the landing.[21] Jackson made another appeal to Congress after he returned to the States in 1891. His effort bore fruit; Congress appropriated $6,000 for the purchase of more reindeer. In 1892, Healy bought 175 reindeer in Siberia.[22]

Jackson chose a location for the reindeer station on the northeast corner of Port Clarence on 29 June 1892. The nature of the harbor, its closeness to Siberia, and the availability of good pasturage and water influenced his decision. He named it Teller Reindeer Station after Henry M. Teller of Colorado. As secretary of the interior in 1885, Teller had authorized establishment of the common school system for Alaska, and he was later influential in passage of the legislation to introduce reindeer into Alaska.

Captain Healy had carpenters and crewmen from the *Bear* go ashore in 1892 to build a frame house at the station. There was not enough lumber to finish the job the first year, so they returned to complete it in 1893. Measuring 20 feet by 60 feet, the house was built with double sides and floors, and tarred paper was installed between the layers. A large lean-to was added to the rear of the house for the herders.

The station had a superintendent and assistant superintendent. Two Americans held the jobs temporarily in 1892. The Reverend W. Thomas Lopp of the American Missionary Association station at Cape Prince of Wales was chosen as the superintendent, but he could not start right away. Captain Healy volunteered 3d Lt. Chester M. White to be acting superintendent until Lopp could take up his duties. The *Bear*'s quartermaster, John Grubin, served temporarily as assistant superintendent. Siberian herders were hired to instruct the Alaskans, and young Inuit men were chosen to study with them. Once they had completed their course of study, they were each given a few reindeer to begin their own herds.

In 1892, 171 reindeer were transported to Port Clarence; 27 of them were lost during the year, 2 wandered away shortly after arriving in

The USRC Bear transporting reindeer from Siberia to Alaska.

Alaska, 12 were injured in transport and either had to be killed or died, and 13 died from various injuries received after their arrival. In the spring of 1893, 79 fawns were born. By 30 June 1893, the herd numbered 222. That summer, 124 reindeer were successfully transported to Port Clarence from Siberia. By September 1893, the herd numbered 346 reindeer.

During the summer of 1894, the station gave 100 reindeer to each of four Christian denominations working with the Inuits and offered deer to others who were interested in caring for them. Native Alaskans began to come from hundreds of miles away to look over the station and its herd. The experiment had worked. Basic problems associated with purchasing, transporting, and distributing the reindeer had been worked out. It was now just a matter of congressional support for the project to succeed, and Congress did support the project. By the spring of 1902, the reindeer in Alaska gave birth to 1,654 fawns that lived to maturity. Herds ranged from Point Barrow in the north to Bethel in the south, and native Alaskans had proven to be good herders and teamsters. They never adapted to the herdsman's life of the Siberians, but they made use of the reindeer in their own way and utilized them as food for many years.[23]

The Revenue Cutter Service continued its involvement in the purchase and transportation of the deer. In the summer of 1894, the *Bear* landed 127 reindeer at the Port Clarence station. Sailing from Puget Sound in June, she made seven trips to the Siberian coast for reindeer between mid-June and mid-August. Doctor Jackson sailed from the States with Captain Healy and accompanied him on four of the Siberian trips. When Jackson went south to inspect the schools between Unalaska and Sitka in July, Healy continued to purchase deer for the station. Whether or not Jackson was along, Lieutenant Jarvis negotiated with the natives for the deer. He was unsuccessful on two trips because the men with whom he was supposed to negotiate were too drunk to carry on the business.

On one of those trips, Jarvis discovered that the captain of the U.S. schooner *Berwick* had purchased reindeer from the natives with five gallons of liquor. This compounded his problems; after the *Berwick*'s visit, the natives refused to trade for anything but liquor. They held to this position until ice threatened to close off the trade for the year and then made their bargains before it was too late. The *Berwick*'s illegal trade prevented the government from acquiring 100 deer that summer. The *Bear*'s cargo ranged between 10 and 26 reindeer on each of the five productive trips. On many of the crossings, the *Bear* had to push through ice to pick up or to land the reindeer; on one trip, she broke ice two feet thick for a distance of seven miles to reach the station at Port Clarence. Between trips for the deer, the *Bear* carried on her regular summer's work, which included her annual cruise to Point Barrow.[24]

In his 1894 report, Jackson thanked the Revenue Cutter Service for its support of his project. "It gives me great pleasure," he wrote, "to again acknowledge the hearty cooperation received from Capt. L. G. Shepard, acting chief of the revenue marine division of the Treasury Department: also the valuable assistance rendered by Capt. M. A. Healy, commanding the U.S.S. *Bear*, Lieuts. Jarvis and White, and also the officers and crew." Knowing that the service assumed this duty "without extra compensation," Jackson appreciated its support, and he felt certain that the men who had so cheerfully cooperated in the movement would "feel well repaid for the same when in after years they see the great results that have been attained."[25]

The Revenue Cutter Service continued to give its wholehearted support to the project, and the results were rewarding indeed. By 1930 the herd had grown to about 600,000 and supported 13,000 native Alaskans.[26]

In 1897–98, some of the offspring of those reindeer brought to Alaska by the *Bear* would play an important role in saving the lives of American whalers trapped in the ice near Point Barrow. Unfortunately, Captain Healy would not be involved in their rescue. Two years before the whalers were stranded, he was court-martialed. His reputation for the tricing-up incidents of 1890 and for heavy drinking probably played a part in his forced retirement.

It was well known in the service that Healy had a drinking problem. He admitted as much and frequently stated his desire to give up alcohol. He even took his wife on one of his Arctic cruises in the hope that her presence would deter him from drinking. Apparently that worked, but, of course, she could not accompany him on a regular basis, and he inevitably returned to the bottle. When he drank heavily, his officers' lives were made miserable.

Dr. James T. White sailed to the Arctic with Healy on board the *Bear* in 1889 and recorded his reaction to a visit he made to the *Rush* on 23 June: "You go on board there," he wrote, "and everything is lively. You are not afraid to laugh and look pleasant, while here you are afraid to do anything for fear of getting a blowing up."[27]

Capt. Michael A. Healy (front row, second from left), with the officers of the Bear.

Between 27 June and 26 July, Healy drank excessively. There were occasions, according to White, when he could not walk straight. On 3 July, he drank three bottles of champagne. White reported at the end of the thirty-day period: "The Captain appears about crazy and is almost blind. He has drunk . . . four gallons of my whisky besides his own and much more from the whaler's beer and wine not counted. This makes four weeks of continuous drunk."[28]

Like so many seamen of the day, Healy's subordinates tolerated their lot until the mid-1890s. By then, professionally trained officers had joined the *Bear's* wardroom, and, knowing their rights, they refused to suffer in silence. In 1895, three officers led by 2d Lt. George M. Daniels charged Healy with drunkenness, abusive treatment of his officers, and endangering the *Bear* while drunk.[29]

Some writers sympathize with Healy. They believe that he was, in part, a victim of ambitious young officers looking for an opportunity to advance in rank. Being of the blunt, old school, Healy offered them plenty of opportunity, and, of course, he did have a drinking problem. The charges led to a court-martial. Following a six-week trial, at which fifty-eight witnesses testified, Healy was found guilty of: "Conduct to the prejudice of good order and discipline. Conduct unbecoming an officer and a gentleman. Tyrannous and abusive conduct to inferiors. Conduct detrimental to discipline. Placing a vessel in perilous condition, thereby endangering the lives and property under his command. Insulting and abusive treatment of officers. Drunkenness to the scandal of the service."[30]

For these offenses, Secretary of the Treasury Carlisle suspended Healy from the service for four years and dropped him to the bottom of the list of officers awaiting assignment. Healy was succeeded in command of the *Bear* by Capt. Francis Tuttle.[31] (In 1902, a new administrator gave Healy command of the *Thetis* for what turned out to be his last Arctic cruise. After returning from the cruise to San Francisco, he retired from the service on 22 September 1903; he died on 30 August 1904.)

On 15 November 1897, Secretary Gage wrote to Captain Tuttle and informed him that eight whale ships were frozen in the Arctic Ocean somewhere near Point Barrow. Gage noted that there were 265 (the actual figure was 275) persons, probably in dire straits, on board the whalers. The conditions called for immediate action. A relief expedition was being organized, and the *Bear* and her captain had been chosen to make the rescue.[32]

Tuttle received Gage's letter right after the *Bear* had returned to Seattle from a six-month Arctic cruise. Yet, he was ready to sail within three weeks, and every man on board the *Bear* volunteered to go. To ensure that the best possible men made the cruise, Gage had instructed Tuttle to choose his officers and crew from volunteers.[33]

Superior officers issued orders granting great latitude to their subordinates, for they could not know the conditions to be faced. Gage, for example, told Tuttle to take food to the trapped whalers and made suggestions about how to do that, but he essentially gave Tuttle a free hand. "Food," he said, "must be gotten to the starving men [and] the best and most feasible method of doing this is to be adopted."[34] Later, when Tuttle put Lieutenant Jarvis on the ice near Cape Vancouver, he granted him full authority to act for the U.S. government.[35]

By 10 December 1897, when the *Bear* reached Unalaska, Tuttle had decided to send Jarvis, 2d Lt. Ellsworth P. Bertholf, Dr. Samuel J. Call, and the reindeer man Koltchoff overland to rescue the whalers. Jarvis, a small, wiry man, was an ideal choice to lead the expedition. He had eight years of experience in the Arctic, spoke fluent Inuit, and knew many of

First Lt. David H. Jarvis

the natives personally.[36] This last qualification was important because Jarvis would have to talk people into supporting his party, even to the extent of giving up their source of a livelihood.

Tuttle had hoped to push the *Bear* farther north than Cape Vancouver before putting the men on the ice, but that proved impossible to do. About 85 miles from Cape Nome, gales, snow, and ice forced the *Bear* to turn to the south. On 16 December 1897, Tuttle hastily landed supplies on Nelson Island, near Cape Vancouver, and turned the *Bear* toward Dutch Harbor, her home base for the winter of 1897–98. Jarvis and his men were on their own.

During the next three months, the rescue party battled the Arctic winter as they attempted to reach the icebound whalers 1,500 miles away at Point Barrow.[37] When they set out from Cape Vancouver, the temperature was around 32°F. By the end of their journey, it would fall as low as −45°F. The men traveled in perpetual darkness. Their sleds were hauled both by dog teams and by reindeer. Dogs were difficult to acquire because the Alaskan gold rush had created tremendous demands for them. The men did not ride on the sleds but hauled, pushed, and drove the sleds over the ice themselves. They preferred to travel along the coast because they could find firewood along the beach, the route was generally smoother than the alternatives, and it tended to head northward. Only weather dangerous enough to threaten lives kept Jarvis from forging ahead. He did not stop even for Christmas day.

Many persons helped to make the expedition a success. Several Alaskan guides provided local knowledge and an understanding of the elements. The Reverend Mr. Lopp and Charlie Artisarlook, a native Alaskan, had provided reindeer to be driven to the whalers. Villagers along the way generously provided rescuers with food, dogs, and clothing from their own pitifully limited resources.

At Tununak, Jarvis hired a Russian-Alaskan trader, Alexis Kalenin, as a guide and bought sleds, dog teams, and supplies to take them across the Yukon delta. He noticed that Kalenin's sleds were lighter and more flexible than those brought from Seattle by the *Bear* and just as tough, so he decided to take three of the Russian sleds and just one of the *Bear*'s. He also learned that there were villages located a day's run from one another between Tununak and Saint Michael on Norton Sound, so he decided to purchase supplies along the way, which would allow him to travel light. On 18 December, his party set out for Ugogamute with four sleds, forty-one dogs, one tent, four sleeping bags, a bale of tobacco, a little food for the men, and 150 pounds of dog food.

The storm that had driven Tuttle and the *Bear* to the south had also blown the ice away from the shores of Nelson Island. This was the usual route to the next village, so the party had to push inland and cross over a mountain to reach Ugogamute. One man went ahead of the party to break a trail through the snow for the dog teams. To stay ahead, he alternately walked and then ran. The sleds followed, pulled and pushed by both men and dogs. In some places, the ascent was so steep that three or four men had to help the dogs pull each sled up the mountain. Progress was slow.

Going downhill presented another problem. The sleds loaded with men and supplies outran the dogs. Jarvis wrapped chains around the sled's runners to slow them down, set the dogs loose, and made the plunge. He wrote of a run down a 2,000-foot mountain: "We flew along at such a rate that in about ten minutes we reached the gentle slope at the base of the mountain and the sleds came to a stop. Here we waited for the dogs, for the little fellows had to come down on foot and were far behind."[38]

During the first few days, Jarvis learned that the best weather for such work was cold, clear, and windless. If it warmed up, the sled's runners stuck to or sank into the snow and ice. If the wind blew too hard, the men had to seek shelter. Given good conditions, the party could cover about twenty to twenty-five miles a day; given perfect conditions, about fifty miles.

When the men stopped at villages, the natives were kind, hospitable, and generous. They almost always invited the party to sleep in their huts, but Jarvis usually chose to pitch his tent. The huts were crowded, filthy, and poorly ventilated. The natives of southern Alaska, he noted, were extremely poor, badly clothed and fed, and none too healthy.[39]

Each night, the men put the sleds up on racks or ice blocks to keep them out of the reach of the dogs, for the ravenous animals would eat almost anything, including leather straps. Feeding the sled dogs was a nightly ordeal. The men chopped up frozen seal meat and gave it to the dogs individually to make sure that some did not starve or get killed by their fellows. They used clubs to keep the bigger, stronger animals from eating all of the meat. After the dogs had eaten, they would curl up and go to sleep, no matter what the weather. In the morning after a blizzard, the men found the dogs buried under the snow with only their noses sticking out.

The men's usual dinner on the trip consisted of beans, hard bread, and tea. Occasionally, they had bacon and "slapjacks" (cakes made of flour and water and fried). Each morning, they rose and traveled all day with just a short break for crackers and tea for lunch.

Three days into the journey, the dogs created a problem for Jarvis. He had started the trip with forty-one animals. Some of them were young and lacked stamina, and Jarvis had planned to replace them, as necessary, along the way. At Ki-yi-lieug, he noticed that some of the teams were exhausted and tried to acquire new ones, but the village dogs were away on a trip to a neighboring village. Believing that he must press on, Jarvis set out for Saint Michael with Doctor Call and the two best teams. Lieutenant Bertholf, Koltchoff, and Kalenin stayed behind to acquire fresh dogs, and they would follow along as soon as possible.[40]

Ten days later, Jarvis arrived at Saint Michael. He had made good time over the snow-free Yukon River, especially after acquiring a fresh dog team from a steamer that was frozen in the river for the winter. His own team had taken a severe beating on the ice, which cut their paws so that they left blood behind with every step they took. At Saint Michael, Jarvis purchased new deerskin clothing and sleeping bags. Their warmth would be needed as he pushed farther north, and the light weight was always an advantage. He also borrowed a fresh team of dogs to carry him as far as Unalaklik. Then he hurried on toward Cape Prince of Wales where he would collect the reindeer herd. Not wanting to be dependent on villagers for supplies as he headed north (they would be fewer and farther between), he left orders for Bertholf to follow him to Unalaklik and then take a short cut from the head of Norton Bay to Cape Blossom on Kotzebue Sound. Bertholf was to transport the necessary cache.[41]

Three days after leaving Saint Michael, Jarvis received news about the stranded whalers. On the trail, he met an Inuit woman whom he knew from Point Hope, a village far to the north. She and her husband were escorting George Fred Tilton to Saint Michael to seek help. Tilton, the third mate on the bark *Belvedere,* had volunteered to walk out of the Arctic from Point Barrow to find help when it appeared that some of the trapped whalers would starve without outside relief. The whalers were eating two small meals a day when Tilton had left Point Barrow. He told Jarvis that the steamers *Belvedere, Orca,* and *Jesse H. Freeman* were caught in the ice west of Point Barrow. The *Orca* had been crushed by the ice, and the *Freeman* had been abandoned. For a while, all of the crews lived on the *Belvedere,* but as her food supply ran low the crews from the other whalers had gone to the refuge station at Point Barrow. Tilton reported the fate of six other whaling ships. The *Rosario* was in the ice west of Point Barrow, the steamers *Fearless* and *Newport* and the four-masted schooner *Jeanie* to the east of Barrow, and much farther east was the bark *Wanderer.* Worst of all, the *Navarch* was a wrecked derelict, and she too was east of Barrow.[42] Tilton's information confirmed what Jarvis knew already; he must forge ahead.

In his book, Tilton writes of his astonishment at meeting Jarvis, heading north, on 3 January. He considered Jarvis's chances of reaching Point Barrow with the deer "a one hundred to one shot." Tilton continues: "Realizing the uncertainty of the safe arrival of the deer at Point Barrow made me all the more anxious to continue my journey to civilization.[43] It is important to recall that Tilton was heading south while Jarvis was heading north. Tilton had left Point Barrow in the fall. Jarvis was going to Barrow in the winter, and he and his men were driving hundreds of reindeer before them.

Jarvis left Unalaklik on 5 January and set out for Port Clarence. Again, the wind had driven the ice to the south, which forced Jarvis, Dr. Call, and their Inuit companion inland where they confronted heavy snow and blizzard conditions. Four men had to break a trail through the deep snow for the dogs, which finally just refused to go on. Ultimately, on 10 January, Jarvis reached the Port Clarence reindeer station. The animals were not there when Jarvis arrived, a Doctor Kettleson, who ran the station, accompanied Jarvis to Golvin Bay, where he replaced his dog teams with reindeer. Jarvis hoped, of course, that reindeer teams would speed his passage to the north.[44]

Neither Jarvis nor the rest of the party was familiar with reindeer, which presented problems. The reindeer started at full speed, so a driver had to be totally ready to go when they set out or he would be left behind. Once the lead deer started, all of the deer followed with a jump, so everyone in the party had to be ready to go at the same time. The deer were timid and, once frightened, according to Jarvis, were hard to control. He learned this in practice on 13 January. While going downhill, his sled bumped the back of a deer's hind legs. The deer bolted and threw Jarvis off the sled. He "held on to the line and was dragged through the snow against an old fish rack at the bottom of the hill." Jarvis turned his head aside, and his shoulder hit the upright and broke it off. When he regained his composure Jarvis was pleased to learn that he had no broken bones, "for such a thing was too serious a matter even for contemplation.[45]

While the party was traveling through a gale that night, with heavy snow falling, Jarvis's deer got tangled up in driftwood. Once again, it spooked, bolted, and ran the sled into a stump. The straps connecting the deer to the sled broke, and the deer ran on. He fell in behind the sleds of Call, Kettleson, and Mikkel, an expert deer handler in Doctor Kettleson's group. Left behind in the sled, Jarvis thought about trying to follow the deer but thought better of it because of the awful conditions. Only when the lead party stopped to consult with Jarvis did the other men learn of his absence. They retraced their route along the trail until they found him. Fortunately, the only thing lost was valuable time.

After several more days of battling blizzards and blinding snowstorms,

Jarvis's party reached Point Rodney, where Charlie Artisarlook and his wife Mary lived. They were Jarvis's friends, but he dreaded his meeting with them. They had a herd of 133 reindeer, built up over time from a few deer loaned to Charlie by the U.S. government. Those reindeer had made Charlie a wealthy man and were the source of living for the entire village. Jarvis had to ask Charlie to give him the herd on the promise that an equal number would be returned, along with 80 fawns to compensate for the herd's natural increase in the spring. Charlie and Mary were persons of great character. They not only gave Jarvis the reindeer, but Charlie signed on as an expert herder to help drive his reindeer the eight hundred miles to Point Barrow. Jarvis bought an additional 5 reindeer at Point Rodney.

On January 20, Jarvis left Point Rodney bound for Cape Prince of Wales. Despite a temperature of −40°F, his party made good time and reached Port Clarence, home of the Teller Reindeer Station, the following day. Jarvis's reindeer team was exhausted, so he replaced it with a dog team and acquired an Inuit assistant. He had left Doctor Call at Point Rodney to prepare the reindeer herd there for the trip to Cape Prince of Wales, where the two herds would be brought together for the final trip to Point Barrow. Jarvis was anxious to leave Port Clarence, but his Inuit assistant refused to travel until the weather moderated. There was a blizzard and the temperature stood at −38°F. On 23 January, with the blizzard still raging and the temperature at −30°F, Jarvis left Port Clarence.

The route north of Port Clarence was the roughest faced by Jarvis on the trip. The ice had been broken in the straits and pushed up against the mountain in a jumble. He had to run over this in the dark. He wrote, "It was a continuous jumble of dogs, sleds, men and ice—particularly ice— and it would be hard to tell which suffered most, men or dogs. Once in helping the sled over a particularly bad place, I was thrown 8 or 9 feet down a slide, landing on the back of my head with the sled on top of me. Though the mercury was −30 degrees, I was wet through with perspiration from the violence of the work."[46]

Later that night, Jarvis reached Lopp's home at Cape Prince of Wales. His sleds were beat up, his dogs played out, and he could hardly move. After a night's sleep, he repeated the appeal that he had made earlier to Artisarlook, with all of the same implications. The reindeer that Jarvis wanted belonged collectively to Lopp, the American Missionary Association, and the Inuits of the village, but Lopp would make the decision for the entire group. He had everybody's respect and the authority to act. On the promise of the government to replace the herd, Lopp gave Jarvis the reindeer and agreed to accompany him to Point Barrow, even though he would have to leave his wife and children, the only white family in the village. Lopp gave Jarvis 292 reindeer, and Jarvis promised to return the same number plus 140 fawns in the summer of 1898. This brought the total number of reindeer that had to be replaced by the government to 645. In addition, Jarvis had bought 9 deer at Cape Prince of Wales, and he had received 9 from other locations. The overland expedition started for Point Barrow with 448 reindeer.

Before the expedition could move on, Doctor Call and Charlie Artisarlook had to bring up the Point Rodney herd. Jarvis hired additional herders to train more reindeer to haul sleds; to build sleds; and to gather tents, harnesses, clothing, and camp gear. Finally, all was in readiness, and the expedition got under way on 3 February 1898.

Because progress was slow the first few days, Jarvis decided to divide the party. He and Call would push ahead along the coast in the hope of finding supplies, guides, and dog teams to speed them along. Lopp and his men, including three native Alaskans, Ootenna, Keok, and Kivyearzruk, would drive the reindeer to Cape Blossom, where Lieutenant Bertholf was expected with a cache of supplies. As things worked out, the native Alaskans along the coast were not much help to the expedition. They were exceedingly poor, their hunting had been disappointing that year, and they had few dogs to spare. The most that Jarvis could convince them to do was to guide him to the next village along the trail. They could not provide food; in fact, they ate far more than their fair share of what Jarvis had. What dogs they did provide usually ate through their harnesses the first night out of their village and returned home. Not believing that food would be waiting at Camp Blossom, the natives left Jarvis after joining his party. Despite his many problems, Jarvis arrived at Cape Blossom on 12 February. Bertholf was there waiting for him; he had arrived the night before.[47]

Jarvis pushed on from Cape Blossom to Point Hope with Call and left Bertholf to wait for the arrival of Lopp and the reindeer.[48] He had sent word to Lopp not to cross the ice of Kotzebue Sound for fear that the entire herd might be lost. Lopp had not received Jarvis's message and was, at that time, successfully crossing the ice, thus saving about 150 miles and two weeks' travel time. Jarvis and Call moved quickly on to Point Hope, making excellent runs in clear, cold weather. Temperatures ranged from −30°F to −42°F. Such low temperatures no longer bothered Jarvis and Call. They changed into dry boots and mittens every night and morning and took good care of their equipment, but weather that would have caused great concern at the start of the journey was now taken as routine.

The natives of the far north were much better off and healthier than their southern brethren and equally generous with supplies. They always offered Jarvis use of their huts and cabins, but he and Call pitched their tents because they slept better in the cold, fresh air. By the time they reached Point Hope, they found that days of 10°F with a strong wind were uncomfortably warm.

At Point Hope, Jarvis met Ned Arey, a whaler who had come down the coast from Point Barrow. Arey told Jarvis that conditions there were bad but not desperate. Although food was scarce, there was enough to last through mid-May. Scurvy was affecting some of the whalers, but an unusual appearance of caribou and native hunters around Barrow had sustained the trapped men through the winter. While this was encouraging news, Jarvis knew that his reindeer would be the only real relief until the *Bear* could arrive at Point Barrow late in the summer.

From Point Hope, Jarvis decided to send Call ahead to Barrow with word that help was on the way. He returned to the south to find Lopp, who had just crossed Kotzebue Sound. Jarvis recalled the doctor and met with Lopp, who was exhausted and suffering from frostbite, to plan the next move.

Jarvis sent Lopp and the reindeer up the Kivalena River. This assured the reindeer of moss for food and avoided the Inuits' dogs on the coast. Jarvis and Call would travel the barren, storm-ridden coast from Point Hope to Point Belcher. Because there were provisions at the Point Hope whaling station, Jarvis left Bertholf there to assist any whalers that Jarvis would send south from Point Barrow in the spring, if this became necessary. He also hired a native named Nekowrah and his wife at Point Hope to help him and Call. The Inuit woman would be especially valuable in caring for the men's clothing.

The last leg of the expedition was the most difficult. Blizzards blew for days, temperatures dropped to −45°F, and ice along the shore was broken and rough. Moss for the deer was scarce, and food for the dogs was in short supply. But each party pushed ahead, crossing paths occasionally and exchanging supplies to keep the herd on its way to the whalers. Finally, on 25 March, Jarvis reached the first of the whalers, the *Belvedere*.

He wrote in his report: "We drew up alongside about 4 P.M. and going aboard announced ourselves and our mission, but it was some time before the first astonishment and incredulousness could wear off and a welcome be extended to us."[49]

The *Belvedere* had taken in the crews from the *Orca*, which had been crushed in the ice, and the *Jessie H. Freeman*, which had been deserted by her crew on 22 September 1897. She then found a "comparatively" safe place behind Point Franklin before she was frozen into the ice. When Jarvis arrived, thirty men were on board the *Belvedere*. The crews of the *Orca* and the *Jessie H. Freeman* had been sent to Point Barrow, along with fifteen men from the *Belvedere*. According to Jarvis, Captain Millard was very sick and looked as if he "would hardly survive the winter." The men were eating just two small meals a day, but there was no real need for Jarvis and his men at the *Belvedere*, so they headed north to Point Barrow.

Two days later, on 29 March, Jarvis reached Point Barrow. He had successfully driven 1,500 miles in the Arctic winter to take relief to the trapped whalers. He reported his reception at Barrow:

> All the population came out to see us go by and wondered what strange outfit it was, and when we greeted Mr. Brower [Charles D. Brower, manager of the Cape Smythe Whaling and Trading Company] and some of the officers of the wrecked vessels, whom we knew, they were stunned, and it was some time before they could realize that we were flesh and blood. Some looked off to the south to see if there was not a ship in sight, and others wanted to know if we had come up in a balloon. Though they had realized their dangerous situation last fall and had sent out Mr. Tilton and Mr. Walker for aid with the first opening of the ice, they had not thought it possible for anyone to reach them in the winter, and had not we and our positions been so well known, I think they would have doubted that we really did come from the outside world.[50]

Jarvis sent word of his mission to the schooner *Rosario* and the steamers *Newport*, *Fearless*, and *Jeanie*. At a meeting with some of the ships' officers and community leaders, he discovered that the men were in no immediate danger of starving, but their supplies were very low. Lopp arrived the next day with his reindeer herd, which relieved concern about the final outcome of the crisis. The relief expedition had set out with 448 reindeer and arrived at Point Barrow with 382. En route, 32 had been killed, either for food or by dogs and wolves, or had died from overwork;

Dr. Samuel J. Call

34 had strayed away in a blizzard. By the end of the overland expedition,
180 reindeer had been killed for food at Point Barrow and 5 at Point Hope
There were still 439 reindeer at Point Barrow and Point Hope because
many fawns had been born in the spring after the expedition's arrival.

The whalers in camp at Point Barrow were in deplorable condition
when Jarvis saw them. On their arrival at the camp, someone had suggested housing them in the old refuge station, which was designed for
about one hundred men. E. A. McIlhenney, who occupied it with three as-

sistants, however, would take only the officers; they were a small percentage of the number needing housing. The only other place available had been the old Kelly house, which Jarvis described as in poor repair. The roof leaked and one end was practically open to the weather, but Bower and some of the men patched it up and built bunks along the walls. The house, which measured 22 by 55 feet, housed seventy-five to eighty men. In that space, and with a stove in the middle of the room, the men could hardly stand up when they left their bunks. The floor was continually wet. Dripping water ran into the berths and soaked the men's bedclothes. Soot from seal oil lamps covered everything, until the men were hardly recognizable. Some of the men stayed in their bunks almost all of the time; all of them were demoralized. Jarvis wrote: "Filth and vermin were everywhere," making it impossible for the men to "keep clean and live decently. . . . [O]nly the cold weather prevented a serious outbreak of sickness."[51]

Doctor Call also wrote of the whalers' condition when he and Jarvis entered the Kelly house:

> Their white, emaciated faces looked like specters as they peered at us from their cold, dark, and frosty berths. They were in all stages of weakness, exhaustion, and despair. Four cases of scurvy had developed, two of which were in a dangerous stage of the disease; others complained of dysentery, loss of appetite, and insomnia.[52]

The masters of the vessels apparently had done nothing for the men. Dr. Richmond Marsh had attended to the sick, and there had been no deaths. In addition to the four men diagnosed with scurvy, however, many more showed signs of it.

Jarvis took command of the situation. He divided the men into small groups and found them decent housing at a schoolhouse and refuge station. Bedding and clothing were cleaned, aired, and, where necessary, replaced, with the generous assistance of the natives. Soap was issued and cleanliness insisted upon. Each man was given 2½ pounds of fresh meat, the only antiscorbutic available, per week. Jarvis noted that before long the general appearance of the men greatly improved. He and Call made daily inspections of the quarters and clothing until the men were taken on board the *Bear*. "They were never allowed to lapse from the conditions of order, discipline, good health, and cleanliness we instituted," he reported.[53] Those who were ill recovered. Later in the spring, signs of scurvy reappeared, and Jarvis increased the fresh meat allotment to 4 pounds per man per week.

After taking care of the health of the whalers at Point Barrow, Jarvis turned his attention to those in the outlying whalers. The schooner *Rosario* was nine miles from Point Barrow; and the *Newport* and *Fearless* forty miles to the east. The steamer *Jeanie* was forty miles to the east of the *Newport* and *Fearless*. The bark *Wanderer*, which had not been heard from, was found at Hershel Island, with her crew wintering on the supplies of the steamer *Mary D. Hume*. Jarvis soon had sleds running to the vessels, and he analyzed their situation. The men on the vessels were in much better shape than those in town. With strict rationing, they had survived on the supplies on board and the birds and game they had hunted. Discipline was better than in town, and Jarvis insisted that the men who were on the whalers stay on them, for the safety of the vessels and for the good order of all. The men suffered from boredom and want of activity; as the weather improved, Jarvis made them play baseball and carry ducks from their shooting camp. Exercise became popular and offered diversion from the monotony of inactivity.

The sea ice began to break up in mid-June. All of the problems were not solved, for the *Rosario* was crushed in the ice on 2 July, but the expedition had provided enough food to last through mid-August, when the *Bear* should arrive at Point Barrow. There was little left to do but wait for the ice to break up and to keep the system of recovery going. By late July, the *Newport*, *Fearless*, and *Jeanie* began to get free of the ice. On 28 July, the *Bear* sailed into view and came as close to Barrow as the ice allowed. Lieutenant Jarvis walked across the ice to the *Bear*, saluted the colors, and stepped on board, where he was greeted by Captain Tuttle and his shipmates.[54]

With the *Bear's* arrival, the whalers' eleven-month ordeal and overland relief expedition came to an end. Jarvis and his rescue party had distributed 12,481 pounds of deer meat, which surely helped to prevent serious illness. The lieutenant had also provided leadership that helped to overcome the suffering caused by inertia at Point Barrow.

Several whalers had died. A middle-aged seaman, Philip Mann of the *Jessie H. Freeman*, suffered a heart attack following the arrival of the relief expedition. Although told not to engage in strenuous exercise, he ate a big meal and then ran along to start a sled. He died on the ice. Two other whalers committed suicide. A man named Kelly from the *Belvedere* drowned himself, and Brower, who had been on the *Navarch*, shot himself.[55]

The crews of the *Orca*, *Freeman*, *Rosario*, and *Navarch* were taken on board the *Bear* and arrived safely in Seattle on 13 September 1898.[56]

At the request of President William McKinley, Congress awarded special gold medals to Jarvis, Bertholf, and Call for their heroic service in the overland expedition.

The gold rush that had made it difficult for the expedition to acquire sled dogs for the trip to Point Barrow had resulted in additional consequences for the Revenue Cutter Service.[57] After gold was discovered on the Yukon River in 1896, it became the easiest route to the gold fields. Captain Tuttle's 1896 cruise report noted that Saint Michael, located adjacent to the mouth of the river, had already taken on considerable importance. Vessels with supplies for the miners put in there, and their cargoes were transferred to steamers going upriver. When Tuttle stopped at Saint Michael that fall, there were nine steamers plying their trade on the Yukon River and its tributaries.

By August 1897, miners had flocked to Saint Michael in great numbers, and more were reported to be on their way. All of the characteristics of an overnight boomtown, including gambling, prostitution, and violence, were in evidence. The *Bear* had provided Saint Michael with law and order before 1896, but she could not cope with the new situation. In addition to the breakdown of the legal system, problems were created by prospectors totally unprepared to survive in the far north. Many had arrived too late to reach the gold fields that fall and had no supplies to take them through the winter or any means of acquiring them. The situation facing those on the river above Fort Yukon was even worse. The river level had dropped so much that vessels could not proceed to Circle City or to Dawson, a frontier town at the junction of the Yukon and Klondike rivers, where provisions were inadequate for the people already there. In response to this crisis, reindeer from the Teller Reindeer Station were sent upriver to feed them. The drivers passed Lieutenant Jarvis, then en route to Point Barrow to rescue the trapped whalers.

The *Bear* remained at Saint Michael a month longer than usual, so that her armed crewmen could patrol the streets. Only after the U.S. Army arrived did Captain Tuttle return the cutter to her normal cruising routine.

While waiting for the ice to melt before pushing into Point Barrow, the *Bear* wintered over at Unalaska. In May 1898, the business community at Unalaska, fearful of the possibility of lawlessness, petitioned Captain Tuttle to delay his departure. The merchants and traders were confident that the *Bear* and her crew could keep law and order by their presence. Tuttle did remain at Unalaska until 14 June. When the *Bear* left for Saint

Michael, many more ships than usual followed her to that thriving port. This probably also helped to ease the fears of the Unalaska businessmen.

That fall, miners discovered gold at Nome. When the *Bear* returned to Alaska in the spring of 1899, under the temporary command of Lieutenant Jarvis, she was called upon to provide that new boomtown with law and order until the army arrived to relieve her, as it had done the year before at Saint Michael. Jarvis then sailed for Point Barrow. On his return south, he found that hundreds of vessels had arrived at Nome with prospectors who would need transportation out of Alaska when cold weather arrived. He delayed his departure until October, when, as he had anticipated, many desperate, sick, and destitute Americans needed his help to return to the States. This scenario was repeated each fall into the early twentieth century.

CHAPTER SEVEN

The Spanish-
American War

W hen Cuba revolted against Spanish rule in 1895, a Cuban underground in the United States prepared to smuggle arms to the island and organized filibustering expeditions. In response, President Grover Cleveland ordered the Revenue Cutter Service to establish a patrol to protect U.S. neutrality. Between 1895 and 1898, the cutters *Boutwell, Colfax, Forward, Hamilton, McLane, Morrill, Windom,* and *Winona* cruised in the Straits of Florida and adjacent waters, seized seven ships for violating U.S. neutrality laws, detained in port another thirteen for suspected smuggling, and broke up two filibustering expeditions.[1]

In 1895, Secretary of the Treasury John G. Carlisle ordered the cutters *Winona, Morrill,* and *Forward* to join the *McLane,* already stationed at Key West, in cruising from Cape Florida on the east coast of Florida to Pensacola on the west coast. In addition to their other duties, the cutters were to enforce the nation's neutrality and quarantine laws.[2]

Frequent attempts to smuggle men and arms to Cuba in 1895 and 1896 caused Carlisle to extend the patrol to Wilmington, North Carolina, and to add to it the *Boutwell, Colfax,* and *Windom.* On 17 September 1895, the *Winona* (Capt. Charles A. Abbey) seized the schooner *Lark* at Bahia Honda, Florida, with thirty-seven men on board. Two days later, the *McLane* (Capt. William H. Hand) seized the steamer *Antinett* off the same port carrying firearms and seven Cubans. The *Winona* and *Forward* (Capt. William H. Roberts), on 5 December, discovered a recently abandoned camp at Middle Cape Sable, Florida, with enough army and medical supplies to indicate that about fifty men had been training there. On 4 March 1896 off Florida's west coast, the *Morrill* (Capt. William J. Herring) seized the schooner *S. R. Mallory*, with a cargo of arms, ammunition, hospital supplies, and army outfits valued at $25,000. In Georgia on the Savannah River, the *Boutwell* (Capt. William F. Kilgore) detained the steamer *Three Friends* with her cargo of munitions, on 23 May. A month later in Biscayne Bay, Florida, the *Winona* (now under the command of Capt. George H. Gooding) seized the steamer *City of Richard,* which was en route to the *Three Friends* with thirty-four Cubans and 449 cases of ammunition on board. All of the vessels and persons seized by the Revenue Cutter Service during 1895 and 1896 were turned over to proper authorities for prosecution.[3]

The following year, Treasury Secretary Lyman J. Gage reported that cutters on neutrality patrol had cruised 75,768 miles, and the *Colfax* and *Boutwell* had served on patrol with the U.S. Navy by order of President McKinley. Gage singled out the *McLane* (Lt. William E. Reynolds) for special mention in his 1897 report. Off Indian Key, Florida on 20 June, the *McLane* had made an impressive seizure of the tug *Dauntless,* with 175 rifles, 300,000 rounds of ammunition, medical supplies, and twenty-seven men on board.[4]

While the Revenue Cutter Service was running the neutrality patrol, unsuccessful and brutal attempts by Spain to quell the Cuban insurrection produced support in the United States for Cuban independence. Destruction of the battleship *Maine* in Havana Harbor on 15 February 1898 raised that support to an emotional enthusiasm, which led to war in spite of McKinley's desire for peace.

U.S. strategic plans called for the navy to destroy enemy naval forces in the Caribbean Sea and the western Pacific Ocean. Once the navy had taken command of the sea, the army would attack and seize Spain's colonial possessions, which strategists believed would cause Spain to accept U.S. peace terms. If it did not, U.S. forces would attack the Iberian peninsula itself.

On 25 April 1898, the United States formally declared war against Spain and made the declaration retroactive to 21 April. Earlier, on 9 April, an executive order had transferred the Revenue Cutter Service to the navy. Subsequently, cutters served in all theaters of the war. Eight cutters served on blockade duty in Cuban waters with Rear Adm. William T.

Sampson's North Atlantic Squadron. One cutter was at Manila Bay with Commodore George Dewey's Asiatic Squadron. Seven cutters, under the U.S. Army, guarded principal U.S. harbors and ports from Boston to the Mississippi Passes, and four patrolled against Spanish raiders on the Pacific Coast. A total of 131 officers and 725 men sailed on twenty cutters, armed with seventy-one guns, that served with the army and navy throughout the war.

Four cutters stationed on the Great Lakes were transferred to the navy, but only one of them reached the East Coast in time to participate in the war. On 20 May, the *Calumet* sailed into Boston, where she served for a few days.[5] The other three cutters, the *Gresham*, *Algonquin*, and *Onondaga*, each measuring more than 200 feet in length, armed with 6-pounders and a torpedo tube, and fast,[6] would have been of value to the navy, but there was a hitch. The locks of the Beauharnois Canal on the Saint Lawrence River in Quebec, Canada, were only 180 feet in length; none of the cutters could fit through the locks. For them to reach the Atlantic, the ships had to be cut in two and reassembled on the other side of the locks.[7] An effort was made to accomplish this task, but the Revenue Cutter Service had trouble with contractors, delays mounted, and only the *Gresham* reached the East Coast before the war ended. She sailed into Boston on 8 August, four days before the protocol of peace was signed with Spain.

Just five days after the United States declared war, the Asiatic Squadron would destroy the Spanish fleet in Manila Bay. The revenue cutter *McCulloch*, under Capt. Daniel B. Hodgsdon, sailed with the squadron. On Sunday, 24 April, McKinley ordered Dewey, whose fleet was then at Hong Kong, to proceed to the Philippine Islands and destroy the Spanish fleet. While Dewey was preparing for his attack at Hong Kong, the Navy Department had sent the *McCulloch* to him. She was in Singapore, on her way from Norfolk to San Francisco via the Suez Canal, when she received her orders, and she arrived at Hong Kong on 17 April.[8]

The *McCulloch*, a new cutter similar to the *Manning*, had been built at Philadelphia by William Cramp and Sons for $196,500 in 1897.[9] A month after her commissioning, she left Hampton Roads, Virginia, for her first duty station at San Francisco. When her ten officers and ninety-five crewmen learned en route that war with Spain was imminent, they were depressed because they believed that they would surely miss taking part in it. In Singapore, when U.S. Consul Gen. E. Spencer Pratt came on board to tell them to join Dewey's squadron, they were delighted.

Capt. Daniel P. Hodgsdon

At Hong Kong, the *McCulloch* went under a naval regime. She took on coal and was painted a leaden gray. From the flagship, according to Captain Hodgsdon, she received "copies of the naval signal books, sets of signal flags and night signals, copies of all existing squadron orders, and instructions regarding the cipher code and its key." To the *McCulloch's* normal battery of four 6-pounders were added two navy 3-inch breech-loading rifles mounted on field carriages. The *McCulloch* never fired these weapons but transferred them to U.S. troops at Manila Bay.[10]

In preparation for action, the Navy Department had purchased the

The USRC McCulloch

British collier *Nanshan* and the supply ship *Zafiro* for Dewey's squadron. Both ships sailed with English crews of merchant seamen. The once dominant U.S. merchant fleet had deteriorated during the late nineteenth century and could not provide the ships needed by Dewey. Although most Americans were content to let foreign-flag vessels carry their commerce, this purchase signaled trouble for the nation's future security.

On 23 April, the governor of Hong Kong had reluctantly notified Dewey that he must leave the harbor by 1600 on 25 April, in order to comply with Britain's neutrality laws. The next day, the *McCulloch* left for Mirs Bay (Dapeng Wan), located thirty miles north of Hong Kong, in company with the *Boston, Concord, Petrel, Nanshan,* and *Zafiro.* The *Olympia, Raleigh,* and *Baltimore* followed on 25 April. Once the squadron reached Mirs Bay, the cruiser *Baltimore*'s cargo of ammunition was distributed. All of Dewey's ships were stripped for action, and the squadron was put on a war footing.[11]

The squadron set sail for the Philippines at 1400 on 27 April, with the fighting ships in one column and auxiliary craft in another. The *McCulloch* sailed in a column with the *Nanshan* and the *Zafiro.* The cruisers and gunboats sailed in a second column led by Dewey's flagship, the *Olympia.*

En route, the vessels were stripped of all ornamental woodwork. Before leaving Mirs Bay, the *McCulloch*'s crew had sent down her square sail yard; dismantled her booms, awnings, stanchions, rails, and gangways; and stored the gear on the *Nanshan.* They covered the boats with splinter shields, barricaded the pilothouse and topgallant forecastle, stored the chronometers and standard compasses below, secured the anchors, filled clips for the rifles, and placed ammunition for the batteries on deck. The carpenter made plugs for shot holes and two stretchers for the surgeon. Barbers cropped the crewmen's hair close to their heads, for comfort in the heat and to make the dressing of wounds easier.[12]

The *Olympia* led Dewey's squadron into Manila Bay in single file around midnight on 30 April. Each ship displayed a single hooded light on her fantail to guide the following ship. The *McCulloch* sailed third from the end, followed by the *Nanshan* and *Zafiro.* When the *McCulloch* passed El Fraile, the flagship was speeding up and the other ships followed suit. As the *McCulloch*'s firemen threw on more coal, gasses in her stack caught fire, which sent up "a pillar of flame like a signal light."[13] From nearby Corregidor, a rocket went up. Shortly thereafter, guns of the El Fraile battery opened fire on the squadron, but they were silenced by gunfire from the *Concord, McCulloch, Boston,* and *Raleigh.*

At dawn on 1 May, the Asiatic Squadron lay seven miles to the west of Manila and an equal distance northwest of Cavite, a small sandy hook south of the city. The Spanish squadron, led by Rear Adm. Don Patricio Montojo, was anchored in a line stretching from behind the hook about a mile toward the city. None of the Spanish ships had steam up.[14]

Dewey left the *McCulloch* in the middle of the bay with orders to guard the *Nanshan* and the *Zafiro*. When fire began, the *McCulloch* advanced as close to the battle as Captain Hodgsdon thought advisable. "In fact," according to Hodgsdon's account, "several shells struck close aboard and others passed overhead" as the *McCulloch* steamed back and forth with a 9-inch hawser at the ready to assist any ship in Dewey's fleet that might be disabled.[15]

The *Olympia*, leading the line of battle and heading directly for Montojo's squadron, was followed in line by the *Baltimore, Raleigh, Petrel, Concord,* and *Boston.* Dewey opened the battle at 0540 with the famous words, "You may fire when you are ready, Gridley." At 5,000 yards (2½ miles), the *Olympia* opened fire with her 8-inch guns. The squadron made five runs past the Spanish front, three from the east and two from the west, with the ships turning each time with a port helm and the range varying from 2,000 to 3,000 yards.[16]

At 0745, Dewey ordered a withdrawal into the bay. Through a communications error, he was led to believe that the *Olympia* was running out of 5-inch shells. During the lull, he took the opportunity to serve breakfast to his crew and to meet with his commanding officers. At 1045, he renewed the fighting but broke it off again at 1230 after the Spanish raised a white flag.[17] Just before the renewal of the battle, the *McCulloch* had intercepted the British mail steamer *Esmeralda* on orders from Dewey. She then took up her position near the fleet and stood by again to render assistance as needed.[18]

Montojo's casualties were heavy: 318 men killed or wounded, three ships sunk, eight burned, and two captured.[19] In contrast, Dewey could report that only seven of his men were slightly wounded, the damage to his ships was light, and they were all in fighting shape. No Americans were killed in battle, but Frank B. Randall, chief engineer on board the *McCulloch,* died after the cutter's smokestack had caught fire. Randall had collapsed of heat prostration in an engine room that reached a temperature of 170°F. The death of the portly engineer cast a pall over the *McCulloch*'s officers and crew for some time, for he was a popular man. At 1600 on 2 May, the *McCulloch* took the *Olympia*'s chaplain on board and steamed down the bay. Twenty minutes later, Randall's body was committed to the deep.[20]

After the battle of Manila Bay, Dewey moved to establish American supremacy in the Philippines. This included cutting the cable that con-

*Chief Engineer Frank B. Randall. Courtesy
of Naval Historical Foundation.*

nected Manila and Hong Kong, which broke the defenders' communications with Madrid. It also severed communications with Washington, and Dewey needed a dispatch boat to carry news of his victory to a waiting world. On 5 May, the *McCulloch* was dispatched to Hong Kong. She arrived two days later and wired news of Dewey's victory to Washington, which set off a national victory celebration and established Dewey as an American hero. On her return trip to Manila the next day, the *McCulloch* carried supplies, mail, and word of Dewey's promotion to rear admiral.[21]

Emilio Aguinaldo, a leading Filipino insurgent, had petitioned for a ride to Manila on the *McCulloch* when she was in Hong Kong to send news of Dewey's victory, but Dewey's aide, Lt. Thomas M. Brumby, refused the request. He did, however, carry Aguinaldo's message to Dewey, who authorized passage on the *McCulloch*'s second trip to Hong Kong. Aguinaldo and thirteen of his followers sailed on the *McCulloch* on 16 May and arrived at Cavite three days later. During the crossing, Aguinaldo kept to himself.[22]

Dewey hoped that Aguinaldo would help the American cause by rebelling against Spain, but he gave little thought to the long-range consequences of encouraging Aguinaldo to attack the Spanish. When the United States established sovereignty over the Philippines, Aguinaldo decided to resist U.S. control.

Meanwhile, halfway round the world, the revenue cutter *Hudson* was winning great acclaim at Cárdenas Bay, Cuba.

On 22 April 1898, President McKinley had signed a congressional proclamation ordering a blockade of the ports between Cárdenas and Bahia Honda on Cuba's northern coast and the port of Cienfuegos on the southern coast. That same day, Admiral Sampson had led the North Atlantic Squadron to the coast of Cuba. Lacking adequate resources to carry out the blockade, Sampson did the best he could with the forces at hand. He employed battleships, monitors, and even torpedo boats on the blockade, but the latter could not carry enough coal or supplies for blockade work.[23] For about a month, while his bigger naval vessels were planning to attack the Spanish fleet, revenue cutters alone maintained the blockade of the north coast of Cuba.[24]

On the forenoon of 11 May, three vessels set out to break Spanish communications with the outside world by cutting the cables between Cienfuegos and Santiago de Cuba. The USS *Marblehead* (Comdr. Bowman H. McCalla), which had been on the blockade for several weeks, was joined in the effort by the USS *Nashville* (Capt. Washburn Maynard) and the revenue cutter *Windom* (Capt. Samuel E. Maguire).[25]

The cable landing was located on the beach. The water being shoal, it was necessary to send in several rowboats and two steam launches to do the work. The naval vessels opened the engagement by shelling the bushes on the beach and driving the defenders away. Then, men in rowboats moved in to cut the cables. The defenders, perhaps one thousand strong, moved back into position after about an hour and opened fire with small arms, one-pounders, and machine guns. One man in a rowboat was wounded and bled to death before anyone knew he had been hit. Another, a marine, had his jaw badly disfigured but stayed at his work. Finally, after two of three cables had been cut, the men retreated to the bigger vessels. No supporting gunfire had been possible during the ordeal because the men in the small boats were within thirty yards of the beach. After they returned to their vessels, the *Windom* avenged U.S. losses by forcing the defenders to seek cover in a lighthouse that had been fortified.

She toppled the lighthouse with a 4-inch shell and sent the Spaniards racing inland to escape her fury.[26]

The *Windom*'s crew received a richly deserved "well done" from Captain Maguire for their accurate shelling of the lighthouse. He reported that the *Windom*'s battery fired eighty-five shells during the action and that almost every shot struck the lighthouse or fort from which the enemy was firing.[27] Following the fight, the first in which Americans were killed in the war, the *Windom* carried the wounded to Key West and arrived there on 14 May.

Also on 11 May, an even bloodier engagement took place at Cárdenas Bay. While using the mouth of the bay as a rendezvous, four U.S. vessels on blockade duty between Matanzas and Cárdenas were challenged by three small Spanish gunboats. Two or three times a day, one or more of the gunboats approached the blockaders, circled around, and retreated to the safety of the shallow water of the bay. At night, they posed a threat to the blockading ships. Quickly, the blockaders turned their energies to engaging the gunboats in battle.[28]

Cárdenas Bay is a shoal-water lagoon measuring about ten miles in diameter, with islands obstructing the entrance. The mined ship channel had just 10½ feet of water at one place.

Navy Comdr. John F. Merry, the senior officer, had four vessels under his command: the USS *Machias*, his own gunboat; the USS *Wilmington*, (Comdr. Chapman C. Todd), a gunboat built for service on the rivers in China; the torpedo boat USS *Winslow* (Lt. John B. Bernadou); and the revenue cutter *Hudson* (Lt. Frank H. Newcomb). During the morning of 11 May, the *Hudson* and the *Winslow* scouted out the entrance to the bay. Just before noon, Merry sent three of the vessels into the bay; his ship drew too much water and could not participate in the engagement. The *Winslow* and the *Hudson*, drawing the least water, led the way through Blanco Channel. Once in the bay, the *Wilmington* took the lead, with the *Hudson* on her starboard side and the *Winslow* on her port.[29]

Commander Todd ordered the *Winslow* to locate the gunboats. To do this, she had to run directly into the sun for 1½ miles and take on three boats, plus Spanish guns ashore. After she had gone ½ mile, the *Winslow* came upon buoys that Bernadou thought were channel markers. He learned his mistake—they were range markers—when a gunboat to the east opened fire with deadly accuracy. The first shell just missed the *Winslow*; the second destroyed her steering gear. A round crashed into

The USRC Hudson *rescuing the* Winslow *at Cardenas Bay.*

the deck and wounded Bernadou in the groin. Another wrecked the hand-steering gear, which left the *Winslow* helpless.[30]

The *Wilmington*'s 4-inch rifles hammered the batteries, and the *Winslow*'s three 1-pounders joined in, but the batteries kept up their fire.[31] The Spanish gunners used smokeless powder, which made them difficult to locate, and the Americans' black powder prevented the *Hudson*'s crew from seeing the fight clearly. Lieutenant Newcomb maneuvered the cutter to the west to escape the smoke and kept firing his two 6-pounders. Each shot "shook the *Hudson* from stem to stern, while to those serving them it was like a box on the ears," according to Lt. Ernest E. Mead, the *Hudson*'s navigation officer.[32]

As the totally disabled *Winslow* drifted toward shore, Newcomb maneuvered the *Hudson* close enough for his crew to throw a line to the crippled boat, while enemy rounds hit the water all around them. The first line fell short, and the water was so shallow that the cutter's propeller stirred up the bottom. As Newcomb approached the *Winslow* for a second attempt to get a line to her, Ens. Worth Bagley and four crewmen gathered along her rail. "The next instant," Lieutenant Mead reports, "they were gone."[33]

Finally, with the line made secure, the *Hudson* towed the *Winslow* out of the bay. It had taken at least a half hour under constant fire to accomplish this feat, and Newcomb found it hard to believe that the *Hudson* had escaped without serious damage. En route, the *Winslow* took a heavy sheer and parted the line, but, by then, the vessels were in deeper water and the *Hudson* easily got into position, put another line on the *Winslow*, and towed her to safety.[34]

Ensign Bagley was the only naval officer killed in the war with Spain. The other men killed on board the *Winslow* were an oiler, two firemen, and a cook, and five men were wounded. Nearly one third of the sixteen men killed afloat during the war lost their lives on board this ship at Cárdenas Bay. Following the engagement, the *Hudson* returned to Key West.

The attack on Cárdenas, which destroyed two Spanish gunboats, was the first raid to hurt Spanish gunboat operations in Cuban waters. According to Commander Todd, it reduced the likelihood of attacks by night. The battle also gave clear evidence of the value of smokeless powder.[35]

In response to the heroism of the officers and crew of the *Hudson*, President McKinley recommended that Congress present a gold medal to Captain Newcomb, a silver medal to each of his officers, and a bronze medal to each of his crewmen. A joint resolution of Congress carried out the president's wishes and properly recognized each man on board the *Hudson* for bravery under fire.[36] Newcomb received the only gold medal awarded by Congress for participation in the war.[37]

Not all revenue cutter jobs were as exciting as those of the *McCulloch* and *Hudson*. The forty-year-old paddle wheeler *McLane*, commanded by Lieutenant Reynolds, guarded Sampson's main communication line, a 130-mile telegraph cable linking Key West and Sanibel Island off the Florida coast. For four months, the *McLane* ran back and forth along the cable, and some of her crew stood a daily twenty-four-hour watch on the cable where it came ashore on Sanibel Island. After the war, Lieutenant Reynolds described the duty in a report to the secretary of the navy. "The report, though covering a long period," he wrote, "will necessarily be brief, for while our work was exacting, trying, and, owing to the excessive heat and the great number of mosquitoes, wearing on officers and crew alike, it was monotonous in the extreme and entirely devoid of exciting incidents."[38]

Panic spread along the East Coast of the United States during the early phase of the war. This led to demands from many coastal cities for protection and to the division of the North Atlantic Squadron. A portion of the squadron, a so-called Flying Squadron under the command of Com-

Lt. Frank H. Newcomb

modore Winfield Scott Schley, was organized at Norfolk to protect the coast. Fortunately for the United States, the Spanish fleet under Adm. Pascual Cervera posed no threat to either the coast or the North Atlantic Squadron. Otherwise, the division of forces could have proved fatal.

Also in response to the panic, the army was assigned the duty of protecting harbors along the coast. It provided this protection with forts, guns, and mines. Because the army required boats to protect U.S. shipping in the mine fields and to patrol these areas, it sought the navy's assistance. The navy had no vessels to spare and ordered the revenue cutters to operate with the army. Between 15 April and 9 May, seven cutters, mounting ten guns and manned by thirty-three officers and 163 enlisted men, were assigned the task: the *Smith* and *Galveston* at New Orleans, Louisiana; the

Winona at Mobile, Alabama; the *Dallas* at Boston; the *Dexter* in Narragansett Bay, Rhode Island; the *Penrose* at Pensacola; and the *Guthrie* at Baltimore. The latter was serving with the navy when she was assigned to army duty.[39]

Other cutters spent long months on blockade duty, escorted troop transports, performed scouting missions, carried army dispatches, transported Cuban insurgents, provided gunfire support for landing operations, and removed men trapped under enemy fire from dangerous beaches.

The *Manning* (Capt. Frederick M. Munger) participated in a great variety of operations in Cuban waters. Her main battery of two 4-inch rapid-fire rifles and secondary battery of one 4-inch gun and four 6-pounders fired about 600 rounds during the war. She blockaded communities on both the northern and southern coasts. Prior to the arrival of Cervera's ships, the *Manning* was stationed at Bahia Honda to watch for the enemy fleet. She confirmed the international legitimacy of the blockade when the German warship *Geier* tried to run out of Havana without communicating with the blockading fleet. The *Geier* was intercepted after a chase of a few miles, during which the *Manning* turned up to about 17 knots. The *Manning* also convoyed transports carrying the Fifth Army Corps to Santiago de Cuba, carried dispatches between the U.S. Army's Cuban headquarters at Daiquiri and more advanced positions, guarded army supplies at Daiquiri, and engaged Cuban shore fortifications at Santa Cruz del Sur in company with a navy squadron. At the war's end, she was praised for outstanding service and especially fine gunnery. Navy Commander Todd, who was the senior officer present on the *Manning*'s blockading stations on both coasts, wrote that Captain Munger was always alert and his ship ever ready for the duties assigned.[40]

The cutters on blockade duty off Cuba headed for home on 14 August. The *Manning* stayed behind to carry word of the war's end to Cienfuegos. She arrived there on 15 August and then sailed for the United States. When they returned home, the *Manning* and *Woodbury* were singled out for having patrolled crucial areas of the blockade and for having done outstanding jobs.

After Dewey's victory over Montojo's fleet in the Philippines, the *McCulloch* cruised on blockade duty and served as the boarding vessel for the Asiatic Squadron. On 25 May, she moved to an anchorage berth next to the *Olympia*. Thereafter, she kept up steam and was prepared to get under way on short notice, especially in response to orders from Dewey's flagship. According to the official record, she kept the scope of her anchor chain as short as weather conditions permitted. Under these conditions, she occasionally got under way in two minutes and her average time was about five minutes. To enforce the blockade, the *McCulloch* intercepted all vessels sailing into Manila Bay.[41]

Captain Hodgsdon was detached from the cutter on 17 June, and First Lt. Daniel P. Foley replaced him in command.[42] Five days earlier Admiral Dewey had written to Secretary of the Navy John D. Long to commend "the zeal and efficiency" of Captain Hodgsdon while serving under his command:

> The *McCulloch* steamed from Hong Kong to Manila Bay in the squadron formation and ran the batteries at the entrance with the squadron, and while not placed in the line of battle at the battle of Manila Bay, was kept near by and in readiness to assist any vessel that might be disabled. Since joining my command, Captain Hodgsdon has kept the *McCulloch* in a high state of efficiency and ready to move at a moment's notice and made her a valuable auxiliary to the squadron.[43]

Dewey concluded by requesting that the department communicate his report to the secretary of the treasury.

Germany was the only neutral nation that did not respect the U.S. blockade of the Philippines. The German fleet of five vessels anchored where it chose to, the ships sailed into the blockading squadron at night, and the fleet commander, Vice Adm. Otto von Diederichs, did as he pleased. Because his fleet was bigger than the U.S. squadron, his assertiveness was most objectionable. Finally, fed up with Diederichs's behavior, Dewey made a personal reconnaissance of the German position. According to Sargent, Dewey hoisted "his flag on McCulloch, . . . steamed down to Marweles Bay, passed around the German ships anchored there, and left again without communicating with them, allowing them to draw their own conclusions from his visit."[44]

It is perhaps significant that Dewey chose to make this reconnaissance run in the *McCulloch*. The Revenue Cutter Service had a long history of combining naval power with its reputation for peaceful humanitarian service. Thus, the government often chose to use a cutter to make a diplomatic point when use of a naval vessel might convey too much hostility.

The *McCulloch* participated in amphibious operations when the U.S. Army seized the city of Manila. On 12 August, she stood in close to the transport *Kwonchoi* and sent four boats to convoy soldiers from the transport to the city. Her crew also restored the lighthouse on Corregidor, which Spanish authorities had extinguished when hostilities began.[45]

During the Spanish insurrection, Dewey planned to use the *McCulloch* to attack the new enemy's towns, vessels, and strongholds, if such attacks proved necessary. The only significant operation of this variety took place late in September, when the *McCulloch* was ordered to capture the insurgents' gunrunning steamer *Pasig.* Despite Dewey's fear that a sharp battle was inevitable, the *McCulloch* accomplished her objective without a fight.[46]

An executive order, dated 29 October 1898, returned the *McCulloch* to the Treasury Department. On 6 November, she sailed from Manila on her long-delayed trip to San Francisco and arrived there on 4 January, just eight days short of a year after leaving Hampton Roads. She was the last of the cutters to leave naval service at the end of the Spanish-American War.

Her duties had been most confining to her officers and crew. From 24 April to 30 September, no liberty was granted. Between 1 May and 13 August, all lights except standing lights were extinguished after 1900. No visits for pleasure were allowed between ships. The men endured intense heat in May and June and torrential rains until August. Gun crews often slept near their guns, searchlights shone constantly, and officers and crew lived under considerable strain.[47]

On board the *Manning,* in Cuban waters, the general health of the officers and crew was excellent, but there were several cases of malaria.

Such hardships were richly rewarded. Participation in the war alongside the navy led to greater recognition of the Revenue Cutter Service by the nation and to acceptance of the service's value in time of war. In large part because of the service's role in the Spanish-American War, Congress voted in 1902 to give revenue cutter officers retirement rights comparable to those enjoyed by army and navy officers.

In spite of passage of H.R. 6723, on 2 March 1895, that allowed for retirement of aged and infirm revenue cutter officers who were on active duty on that date (see chapter 5), the service had a shortage of qualified officers for duty on board ship within a few years. As a result, in 1901, the service was forced to give the responsibility of command to first lieutenants. Secretary of the Treasury Gage had pleaded with Congress to amend the 1895 law in every annual report from 1899 through 1901. In each report, he recounted the shortage of officers and stressed that their duties were arduous to the extreme, more dangerous in peacetime than a naval officer's duties, and most important to the nation. None of his arguments seemed to work.[48]

Then, in 1902, the Senate Committee on Commerce published its report on S. 1025, a bill to promote the efficiency of the Revenue Cutter Service, which emphasized the role played by the Revenue Cutter Service in the war with Spain. The report pointed out discrepancies in the treatment of its officers versus officers in the other services:

> Officers of the Navy rank with officers of the Army. Officers of the Cutter Service should by right and fairness rank with both. They have earned, by faithful service, devotion to duty, and heroic effort in peace and in war, this right and not to confer it would be an unjust discrimination against a valiant and devoted body of men who bear the commissions of the President, by and with the advice and consent of the Senate, upon the same terms as do officers of the kindred services.[49]

The Senate report also recounted the role played by the cutter service in earlier wars. It noted that the Revenue Cutter Service had been an active participant in the war with Spain and extensively cited official correspondence relating to participation in that war by revenue cutters.[50]

On 12 April 1902, Congress addressed the desperate situation facing the officer corps of the Revenue Cutter Service by passing a law to promote the efficiency of the service. The law recognized the military character of the Revenue Cutter Service, placed its officers on "an equal footing with those of the Army and Navy," conferred "upon its commissioned personnel rank, pay, and allowances of officers of the Army up to and including the grade of major, U.S. Army," and provided "for retirement from active service because of age or physical infirmities, on the same lines with provisions of law in force for the other military services."[51]

The impact of the law was immediate. By 30 June 1902, the service had retired, under the law, nine captains and five chief engineers because of age and one chief engineer, one third lieutenant, and two assistant engineers because of physical disability.[52] The effect of the law was also long lasting. In 1915, when the U.S. Coast Guard was created by uniting the Revenue Cutter Service and the Life-Saving Service, Congress formally recognized the new service as part of the Armed Forces of the United States.

CHAPTER EIGHT

Operational Highlights, 1898–1914

Betweeen the Spanish-American War and World War I, the Revenue Cutter Service answered the nation's call on the high seas in a variety of situations requiring responses from the U.S. government. The following are illustrative of the service's actions during this period:

- the *Nunivak*'s operations on the Yukon River in Alaska at the turn of the century
- the *Winona*'s assistance in preventing the spread of yellow fever in the Gulf of Mexico in 1905
- the response of six cutters to the needs of San Francisco following the earthquake of 1906
- the *Gresham*'s rescue of the *Republic*'s crew off the coast of Massachusetts in 1909
- the *Androscoggin*'s rescue of thirty American fishing vessels locked in the ice off the coast of Newfoundland in 1912
- the *Seneca*'s removal of derelicts from the nation's shipping lanes after 1908
- the *Seneca*'s and *Miami*'s operation of the ice patrol after 1912

Revenue cutters also performed a myriad of other duties that served the national interest; these ranged from medical care for deep-sea fishermen to preparations for assisting the U.S. Navy in time of war.

In 1897, the cutter service started construction of the *Nunivak* at San Francisco for service on the Yukon River. She was a wooden stern wheeler, 209 feet long, 35 feet in the beam, and a draft of

6 feet, with two tandem steam engines that could generate 600 horsepower. First Lt. John C. Cantwell, who had explored the Kowak River, successfully sought command of the new vessel in a personal letter to the commandant, Capt. Charles F. Shoemaker. Cantwell took command on 6 April 1899 and recruited veterans of the Bering Sea Fleet as his executive and junior officers.[1]

Cantwell's cruise orders, dated 24 April, were much like those issued to other officers bound for Alaska in the nineteenth century. He was to enforce the nation's trade laws, uphold law and order, make hydrographic notes, chart the Yukon River and its tributaries, collect flora and fauna samples, study the natives of the Yukon River valley, and transport destitute Americans out of Alaska.[2]

The *Nunivak* left San Francisco on 2 May under tow of the *Rush*.[3] Almost immediately, the 4,000-mile trip turned into a nightmare. Hog chains supporting the hull broke loose, beams broke, seams opened up, the hull flooded, and steam pumps quit working. An exhausted crew was forced to run the cutter into Eureka, California, for emergency repairs, but the town had no marine railway capable of handling the cutter. The crew patched her up on the beach, and the *Rush* towed her to Seattle for more permanent repairs. There, the yard recalked her seams, sheathed her bottom with half-inch spruce planks, strengthened her kingpost, and added heavy keelsons amidships. With her hull strengthened, the *Nunivak* set out again, still under tow, for Saint Michael, where she arrived on 14 July, a month and a half after leaving San Francisco.

Cantwell started up the Yukon River on 9 August with a pilot on board. During his first year on the Yukon, he would prepare a chart of the river; take a census of river traffic; visit every important settlement and mine within a thousand miles of the river's mouth; enforce U.S. customs and navigation laws; protect the interests and health of natives, miners, and missionaries alike; and successfully winter over on the river.

On 4 September, Cantwell chose the Dall River, which flows into the Yukon, as the site for the *Nunivak*'s winter quarters. He left Rampart for the Dall on 18 September and stopped en route to take on board all the coal available from a nearby supplier, who had just forty-five tons (not enough for the winter). The wind picked up to a howling gale and heavy snow began to fall, so Cantwell headed for the Dall on 21 September and reached it two days later at 0800. He selected a site about a mile from the river's mouth for his winter quarters and hauled the cutter onto the riverbed. She rested there on an even keel for the winter.

Although Cantwell planned to have his men live on the cutter, he had them spend the first week to ten days in preparing a log house on shore as an emergency dwelling. They stored all superfluous and flammable materials, including paint and oil, ashore and then settled in for eight months on the river.

Cantwell's greatest immediate concern was to cut and haul enough wood to supplement the cutter's inadequate coal supply. This caused trouble. The crew, insisting on being discharged, claimed that they had signed on as sailors, not woodsmen. Some of the crew had planned to leave the cutter for the gold fields, but Cantwell laid down the law. He ordered the crew to cut wood and said that no requests for discharge would be entertained. After that, except for minor cases of moodiness, there was little trouble.

The river began to freeze over on 3 October. A week later, it could hold a man. On 6 November, the first mail delivery arrived by dog sled.

With hunters and miners traveling through the area constantly, the trails were kept open, and they afforded the opportunity for plenty of exercise. Some of the crew hunted during their off-duty hours; others preferred to read, smoke, and sleep. Cantwell allowed them to do as they pleased because, even when temperatures dropped as low as −20°F to −40°F, the crew got plenty of outdoor exercise.

The routine of duty and recreation was soon well established, and only one personnel case required severe discipline to maintain order. The exception occurred on Thanksgiving eve. Somehow, the crew had acquired a supply of liquor and they all got drunk. When the officers tried to quiet them, one of the crew became so defiant and disrespectful that Cantwell court-martialed the man, gave him a dishonorable discharge, and sent him on his way to the closest town. That seems to have quieted the crew, for no other case during the rest of the winter resulted in more than a short confinement to quarters.

In November, the weather had turned clear and cold with periods of snow. Cantwell marveled at the beauty of the aurora borealis, which, he noted, brought both officers and crew outside to watch for as long as they could stand the cold. During the days, they cut and hauled wood in preparation for the colder, darker month of December. By the end of November, they had hauled about 160 cords to the cutter.

With this new supply of fuel, Cantwell turned on the dynamo each day from 1400 to 2400, thus providing the ship with electric lights. The light improved the men's spirits, and no new trouble developed. Between 8 December and 5 January, there was some natural light for four hours a day, even when the sun failed to rise above the nearby mountain, and moonlit nights were nearly as light as day.

For three days during the first week in January, temperatures ranged from a high of −56°F to a low of −62°F. Although it was impossible to keep the ship comfortable, the crew did not suffer severely from the cold. During this bitter season, however, half a dozen traveling parties sought refuge on the cutter. They brought their dog teams with them, and the dogs numbered up to fifty at a time. The dogs fought bloody battles and bayed at the moon, sometimes all night long.

In the late winter and early spring, a steady flow of native Alaskans passed by on their way to the nearby hills to hunt moose and caribou. One old Alaskan shocked Cantwell by telling him that he had left his mother behind. When Cantwell asked how she would survive, the son responded that she would probably starve.

Melting snow in March made hauling wood to the cutter difficult but also made it possible to cut the ship out of the ice. By 3 April, she was clear and free to float, once the ice on the river broke up. On 28 April, the thawing river picked up the cutter from her muddy perch and floated her free, but ice continued to flow in the river until 14 May. On 17 and 18 May, Cantwell took the *Nunivak* three miles up the Dall to avoid ice flooding into the river from the Yukon, but the *Nunivak* had successfully wintered over in the Arctic and was soon free to renew her Yukon operations.

Traffic on the Yukon was booming by 1900. That year, the continuing rush to the gold fields at Nome added still more traffic on the river and increased the workload of the *Nunivak*, which had extended Alaskan operations to the mighty rivers.

Far to the south in New Orleans, authorities first announced the 1905 yellow fever epidemic on 21 July (the same day of the year as a similar announcement in 1878), but the disaster was well advanced at that time. By the end of the month, there had been more than 20 new cases and 3 or 4 deaths each day. The situation grew steadily worse until the end of August, when a comparison of figures for the 1905 and 1878 epidemics indicated that progress was being made in the fight to combat the disease. Finally, on 27 October, the *New Orleans Times-Democrat*, which had been covering the epidemic on its first and third pages every day for months, stated that the few cases and deaths were no longer worth reporting. Four deaths from the disease had occurred in the city during the previous week. Since July, totals of 3,369 cases, 437 deaths, and 2,873 persons treated and discharged had been reported. On 25 October, 59 persons were still under treatment.[4]

Dr. J. H. White of the Marine Hospital Service and the Public Health Service deserves much of the credit for controlling the disease in New Orleans. The U.S. surgeon general put White in charge on August 6. White knew what caused yellow fever, and he took immediate action to eliminate it. He ran several notices in the *Times-Democrat* that began with the declaration (in capital letters), "KILL ALL MOSQUITOES"; held public meetings to educate the citizens; and brought experts from Havana to give lectures on the disease. He fumigated homes, boats, and trains; put up screens to contain mosquitoes; and enforced a quarantine. None of this was easy. Some citizens refused to let officials into their homes. Italian Americans in Iberville parish attacked and nearly killed a quarantine officer because they thought he had infected a person who subsequently died of the disease. Town fathers tried to play down the scope of the disaster for economic reasons. Of greatest importance, however, was the fact that only about 10 percent of the population believed the "mosquito theory," as it was called, yet the city of 125,000 persons was asked to accept the theory and to act upon it. As a result of White's efforts, by the end of the disaster, 90 percent of the people of New Orleans understood the cause of yellow fever.[5]

The *Journal of the American Medical Association* wrote that New Orleans was making world history by its effort to control the disease. The city, it said, had followed the best medical advice, and the people, the business community, and the government had all banned together to fight the disease.[6]

The revenue cutter service played a role by helping to contain the epidemic in the Gulf of Mexico. The fever disrupted business and caused great economic losses, which caused cities and states on the Gulf to impose a quarantine on ships and persons from Louisiana. Detention centers were established and fumigation stations set up. Tensions soared, and conflict broke out. In response, the federal government ordered revenue cutters to establish and preserve the peace and to enforce a quarantine between Louisiana and Florida.

On 28 July, Dr. Eugene Wasdin of the Public Health Service and the Marine Hospital Service had been put in charge of a quarantine of the Gulf Coast outside of New Orleans. That same day, he took control of a patrol made up of revenue cutters and small state-owned boats. Secretary of the Treasury Leslie M. Shaw placed the revenue cutter *Winona* (Capt. Edmond C. Claytor) at Wasdin's disposal and ordered Claytor to prevent ships from New Orleans from landing in Mississippi. Captain Claytor detained ships sailing from New Orleans and escorted them to Ship Island, where they were fumigated. Ultimately, Wasdin ordered all ports in the Gulf to detain vessels for quarantine and inspection; by the end of the crisis, six cutters were patrolling the Gulf to prevent the spread of yellow fever by water. They were assisted by seven chartered vessels that were also under the command of revenue cutter officers. In cooperation with the Public Health Service and the Marine Hospital Service, two hundred officers and men of the Revenue Cutter Service stopped and/or examined 1,923 merchant vessels and held more than 250 of them for fumigation. Most important, according to Secretary Shaw, "Not a case of yellow fever entered any locality by water within the limits of the patrol."[7]

In early August, the *Winona* became entangled in a serious conflict between Louisiana and Mississippi. An armed Mississippi quarantine patrol, consisting of the oyster commission boat *Grace* and the *Tipsey*, prevented Louisiana fishermen and merchants from entering Lake Borgne or the Lake Borgne Canal on 1 and 2 August. The fishermen returned to port and informed Louisiana officials of the incident. Louisiana's governor, Newton Crain Blanchard, responded by sending the Louisiana Naval Militia to sweep Mississippi boats from the lake. On 5 August, the militia accomplished its mission by seizing both Mississippi vessels and imprisoning their crews at St. Bernard parish. Louisiana then manned the *Grace* with a prize crew and ordered her to seize the revenue cutter *Winona*. At this point, communications between Secretary Shaw and Governor Blanchard ended the confrontation. The governor returned the *Grace* to Mississippi authorities, gave orders that the *Winona* was to come and go as she pleased, and issued a statement that he was not fighting the federal government. The Louisiana Naval Militia remained on guard, but revenue cutters continued to detain Louisiana vessels on quarantine at the Ship Island station. Shaw then ordered Capt. Worth G. Ross, commandant of the Revenue Cutter Service (since 1 April 1905), to New Orleans to take personal charge of the cutters in the Gulf under the direction of the Public Health Service and the Marine Hospital Service. The *Winona* and five other cutters served directly under Ross until 23 October, when the crisis passed.[8]

The USRC Winona

Ross played an active role in the yellow fever crisis. He established temporary headquarters at Gulfport, Mississippi, on 8 August 1905. Almost immediately, he set up systematic patrols by the six cutters and seven chartered vessels under his control and maintained the patrols night and day during the epidemic. Not content to stay on shore at Gulfport, he sailed on inspection tours with Captain Claytor on board the *Winona*. With his men, he endured the oppressive heat, rain, storms, and mosquitoes of the Gulf. Two of the men on the *Winona* became ill during the epidemic, seaman H. Meihner with typhoid fever and fireman Harold Berg with yellow fever. In spite of such trials, Ross and his men were totally satisfied with the job they had performed in the Gulf.[9]

On 23 October 1905, Doctor Wasdin expressed personally his satisfaction with their fine work: "In all the history of our quarantine patrols, there is no record of service equal to that which you have rendered to the Public Health and Marine Hospital Service, to the Nation and to the State."[10]

Capt. Worth G. Ross. Courtesy of U.S. Coast Guard Academy Museum.

When an earthquake and subsequent fires wracked San Francisco on 18 April 1906, six cutters and their crews responded with professional competence to the disaster. The quick response of the crews of the *Bear, Thetis, McCulloch, Hartley, Golden Gate,* and *Perry* helped to contain the fire and relieve the suffering of the people who lived around San Francisco Bay. The cutters cooperated with the U.S. Navy and local officials, and their crews earned the praise of those with whom they worked and those to whom they gave aid.[11]

From the perspective of the Revenue Cutter Service headquarters in Washington, anarchy seemed to prevail and there were questions about the U.S. Navy's control of cutters. On the scene, however, cooperation and understanding existed. The city was placed under martial law early in the crisis, with Rear Adm. C. F. Goodrich, commander-in-chief of the Pacific Squadron, in charge. Capt. Oscar C. Hamlet, who commanded the cutters on the scene, cooperated willingly with the admiral, as did U.S. Army personnel.[12]

The officers and crews from several cutters distinguished themselves during the earthquake and the conflagration that followed. In reporting the disaster, many officials singled out the response of Lt. C. C. McMillan, assistant engineer on the *Bear;* also praised was the work of First Lt. John C. Berry of the *Thetis* and the crew of the *Golden Gate.*

McMillan rescued the family and friends of a lieutenant on the *Bear;* carried refugees and injured persons from the Presidio to Oakland; provided the *Golden Gate* to the navy for use in fighting the fires in San Francisco; detailed William Criep, chief oiler of the *Thetis,* to act as engineer in the Appraiser's Building; carried blankets to Fort Baker for the army; transported stores to Sausalito for the Red Cross; and distributed stores to refugees. Superintendent Frank A. Leach and 141 brave men saved the U.S. Mint at San Francisco in the face of heat, smoke, and flames that threatened to destroy the building. John T. Bell, a citizen of Oakland, noted in a letter to Secretary Shaw that Leach and McMillan were two of the most heroic saviors of the mint.[13]

Berry set up a curbside relief office to assist persons looking for friends and relatives after the disaster. He assisted Capt. E. O. C. Ord, a retired army officer, in establishing order in the relief work, furnishing needed transportation, and providing food for the needy.[14]

The *Golden Gate*'s crew fought fires along the waterfront; saved about sixty people; helped the homeless and the helpless; patrolled along the wharves day and night to prevent pillaging; guarded the custom house and Appraiser's Building in San Francisco; took $23,000,000 in notes and securities from the Crocker Woolworth Bank onto the cutter for safekeeping; saved papers belonging to the Pacific Mail Company; transported refugees to Sausalito; and distributed food throughout the bay area.[15]

The crews of the *Thetis, Bear,* and *McCulloch* also deserve mention. They performed guard duty and opened their cutters to refugees. Also, they assisted in saving the Appraiser's Building, controlled crowds and prisoners, fought fires, saved paintings at the Art Institute, transported sick persons to the hospital; removed patients from Waldeck Sanitarium, saved books and valuable papers of the Main Street Iron Works, and assisted injured and dazed victims of the earthquake.[16]

Immediately upon receiving news of the earthquake on 18 April, Capt. John Cantwell of the *McCulloch* set sail from San Diego and arrived at San Francisco at 0600 on 20 April. He reported to an army officer in charge, who asked him to go to Sausalito to protect that city from rioting and pillaging. Cantwell proceeded to Sausalito, where, for a while, he was put in charge by the county supervisors. Thirty men from the *McCulloch* patrolled the city. Others distributed food and clothing to the homeless and destitute and kept order.[17]

These services were not rendered without cost. A wardroom mess attendant on the *Bear* tried to commit suicide and was admitted to the U.S. Naval Hospital at Mare Island on 20 April. The hands and faces of the *Golden Gate* crewmen were blistered by the fires they fought, and the cutter's paint was also blistered. The *Thetis* and *Bear* lost their chronometers to the fires.[18] There were rewards, as well. Many citizens and officials praised the work of the Revenue Cutter Service. These included the boards of trustees of the towns of Sausalito and Mill Valley and Rear Admiral Goodrich.[19] Most important, President Theodore Roosevelt offered his hearty appreciation to the officers and men of the Revenue Cutter Service for their "prompt, gallant, and efficient work" during the earthquake.[20]

The revenue cutters continued to assist helpless ships and seamen at sea throughout the era. One dramatic rescue involved the cutter *Gresham*, when she made her way through 150 miles of dense fog to reach the sinking steamer *Republic* on 23 January 1909. The *Gresham*, a *Manning*-class cutter built in 1895 by the Globe Ironworks Company of Cleveland, Ohio, was accepted by the government on 10 February 1897 and placed in commission on 30 May of that year. She was one of fewer than a score of cutters equipped with wireless sets before 1910. Her rescue of the *Republic*'s crew was facilitated by the wireless; along with other such rescues, it proved the value of wireless in saving lives at sea. By 1915, the entire fleet of cruising cutters was similarly equipped, which significantly expanded the cutters' effectiveness.

The *Gresham*'s district stretched from Portsmouth, New Hampshire, southward to Vineyard Haven, Massachusetts. While she was anchored in Provincetown harbor, Massachusetts, at 0810 on 23 January, her skipper, Capt. Kirtland W. Perry, received a message from the Wellfleet Marconi station that the White Star liner *Republic* was sinking twenty-six miles southeast of Nantucket, Massachusetts. Perry ordered steam and got under way in thick fog at 0820. After rounding Cape Cod, the *Gresham* turned up to full speed, even though Captain Perry could not see the length of his ship. She reached the Nantucket lightship in the evening and spent that night and the next morning searching for the *Republic*, while constantly changing course in response to wireless messages intercepted by her operator, Charles Blankinship. At 1110, the *Gresham* sighted the *Republic* nine miles southeast of the lightship.[21]

On 22 January, the *Republic* had sailed from New York on a cruise to Gibraltar and Genoa with 422 passengers and a crew of 300 under the command of Captain William Inman Sealby. The next morning at 0530, the Lloyds Italian liner *Florida*, bound from Naples, Italy, to New York with 800 immigrants on board, rammed the *Republic* in dense fog. The collision killed three of the *Republic*'s passengers, injured several more, and cut the *Republic* to the waterline. As soon as he learned the extent of the damage to his ship, Captain Sealby ordered abandon ship and told Jack Binns to send a wireless message appealing for assistance. Holding a broken key together by hand and using emergency power in a dark cabin, Binns managed to send out the "CQD" message, which was then the distress call. Binn's message brought assistance and surely avoided a tremendous loss of life. He became the hero of the hour.[22]

The wireless station at Siasconset on Nantucket received Binn's message and relayed it. Several ships at sea, including the *Florida* and the White Star Liner *Baltic*, also received the wireless message. One particularly dramatic aspect of the rescue was the transfer of the *Republic*'s passengers by small boats, once to the *Florida* and a second time to the *Baltic*, which also took on board the *Florida*'s passengers. The transfer of passengers to the *Baltic* was made in the fog. Fortunately, the sea was calm. The *Baltic* arrived in New York on 25 January with more than 1,650 rescued persons. Although the *Florida*'s first two compartments were flooded and she was down at the bow, she steamed into port on her own power. Captain Sealby and a volunteer crew of fifty had remained on board the *Republic* in an effort to save her.[23]

Four revenue cutters received the *Republic*'s call for help and set out for the scene of the accident, but the *Gresham* was the first to arrive. The *Seneca* (Capt. William E. Reynolds) arrived later the same day. She steamed to the accident from 105 miles off Sandy Hook, New Jersey, after receiving orders sent from the Fire Island wireless station by Assistant

Secretary of the Treasury Beekman Winthrop. The other two cutters never arrived at the scene. The *Mohawk* ran aground on Palmers Island in New Bedford harbor while en route, and the *Acushnet*, stationed at Woods Hole, Massachusetts, was diverted to Vineyard Sound to rescue another vessel.[24]

After reaching the *Republic*, Captain Perry agreed to try to tow the damaged steamer to shallow water south of Nantucket. The *Republic* was a heavy tow. She had taken on water in her boiler room, engine room, and several additional compartments until she drew forty feet aft. According to the cutter's report, her steering gear was disabled, so the British steamship *Furnessia*, which had arrived on the scene shortly before the *Gresham*, dropped astern of the *Republic* and took a line from each quarter to assist in steering.[25]

During the afternoon, the wind and sea picked up and the Republic's captain, fearing his vessel would sink, sent his crew over to the *Gresham*. Sealby stayed with his ship, and the second mate, R. J. Williams, refused to leave his captain. The liner's officers worked out a signal with a blue light to inform the cutter if the *Republic* should be about to sink during the night. The *Gresham*'s crew bent the cutter's 9-inch hawser onto the eye of the wire cable so that the tow could be cut away, and Captain Perry stationed the ship's carpenter at the hawser with an ax for that purpose.[26]

When the *Republic*'s executive officer boarded the *Gresham*, he asked if he could take charge of the rescue boat in case the *Republic* sank, and he requested the help of some men from the *Gresham*'s crew.[27] This was arranged, with four men from each vessel assigned to the rescue boat.

During the night, when all hope of the *Republic*'s staying afloat ended, Captain Sealby and Second Mate Williams burned a blue light and fired a pistol to signal that they were abandoning ship. Williams went over the side into the water. Sealby left the ship only when she sank beneath him.[28]

When the *Gresham*'s crew saw the blue light flash at 2010, they noted that the liner was sinking rapidly. Because the *Republic*'s executive officer could not be found immediately, gunner Carl Johansson of the *Gresham* jumped into the rescue boat and took charge, while the carpenter performed his duty with the ax. Thirty-five minutes later, the gunner returned with both men. He had rescued Sealby from a floating hatch cover and Williams from some of the ship's gratings. "Both men were exhausted and they were immediately taken below, rubbed down, provided with hot stimulants, and put to bed."[29]

Captain Sealby later wrote: "I cannot express my appreciation of what was done by the officers and crews of the *Gresham*, under Capt. Perry, and the *Seneca*, under Capt. Reynolds."[30] This was the *Gresham*'s eighth rescue that winter.[31]

That night, the *Gresham* and *Seneca* headed toward Gay Head, Massachusetts. At 0630 the next day, the cutters stopped at Vineyard Haven lightship, where their captains consulted. Afterward, they transferred the *Republic*'s officers and crew by boat to the *Seneca*, which took them to New York, while the *Gresham* proceeded to Woods Hole for fresh water.

The cutter's report stated:

> During all of the above operations, the wireless apparatus of the *Gresham* was in constant use, the operator rendering most exceptional, efficient, and arduous service. While interferences were encountered, dispatches of the most important character were sent and received, and after the rescue three messages were sent out for Captain Sealby, which not only assured those personally interested in himself and crew but gave information to the country at large in this important affair.[32]

The Boston Daily Globe reported that all persons on board the *Republic* probably would have been lost but for the wireless; no vessels had come within hailing distance of the *Republic* except those responding to her wireless message.[33] The chief clerk of the Steamboat Inspection Service, William F. Gatchell, reported that wireless was indispensable to safe navigation, and used the rescue of the *Republic*'s passengers to support his case. Marconi himself said that the rescue of the passengers was an overwhelming reward for his work on wireless telegraphy.[34]

On 27 January, the produce exchange adopted a resolution favoring international legislation to mandate wireless telegraphy on oceangoing passenger ships. Motivated by a letter from a constituent who was sure he would have perished on board the *Republic* except for the wireless, Representative Francis Burke of Pennsylvania introduced legislation in the U.S. House of Representatives that would require any ship carrying fifty or more passengers to be equipped with wireless before it could clear from the United States for an ocean crossing.[35] This proposal made good sense, but it would take the devastating loss of the *Titanic* in 1912 to stimulate legislative action.

Several months before the sinking of the *Titanic*, the collector of customs at Gloucester, Massachusetts, reported on 15 January that thirty American fishing vessels, with $500,000 worth of frozen herring on board, were stuck in ice floes off the coast of Newfoundland and threatened with destruction. Assistant Secretary of the Treasury Bailey ordered the revenue cutters *Androscoggin* and *Gresham* to go to the fishermen's assistance. The former, stationed at Portland, Maine, which was 850 miles from the scene of the potential disaster, was the closest cutter. Built of wood, the 210-foot *Androscoggin* had limited ice-breaking abilities and a top speed of 12 knots. She got under way during the same afternoon that she received the message. The *Gresham*, which had to take on supplies at Boston before departing for Newfoundland, sailed after the *Androscoggin*.[36]

Initial reports indicated that two U.S. schooners, the *William F. Morrissey* and *Helen G. Wells*, had been driven ashore. In fact, a blizzard that raged for a week had destroyed the two schooners, in addition to two Newfoundland schooners and several big power-driven fishing boats. Hurricane-force winds, accompanied by zero-degree temperatures and a blinding snowstorm, drove the *Morrissey* onto the ice along Newfoundland's western shore. Newfoundland natives reported that the schooner's officers and crew just escaped death. The *Wells* went ashore at St. Georges Bay, where she was destroyed, but her crew saved the schooner's 2,400-pound cargo of codfish. The two schooners, valued at $16,000, were owned by the Gordon Pew Fisheries Company of Gloucester.[37]

Twenty-five schooners were frozen in the ice on Newfoundland's western shore, eighteen at the Bay of Islands and seven at Bonne Bay. A northeast gale made their predicament treacherous and necessitated the rescue mission.[38]

In spite of the treacherous weather, the *Androscoggin* made good time and reported sighting the vanguard of the schooner fleet at the Bay of Islands on 18 January. The *Gresham* was a few hours behind the *Androscoggin*. The next day, a fortuitous change of wind drove the pack ice offshore, and the cutters convoyed the eighteen schooners at the Bay of Islands to the safety of the Gulf of St. Lawrence. The seven schooners at Bonne Bay took advantage of the opening on the following day and also sailed for home, but they were caught in the ice again later that day. On 21 January, they freed themselves once again, and all of the schooners made for Gloucester.[39]

Capt. George Metcalf Daniels of the *Androscoggin* had sent a wireless message to a customs collector on 20 January, in which he reported that the Gloucester fishing schooners were free and bound for home. There was a moderate gale, Daniels reported, and a snow squall from the north-northwest, but the barometer was rising. On 25 January, the *Portland Evening Express* reported that the *Androscoggin* was expected to enter Gloucester harbor at 1800 that evening. She was returning a number of schooner owners who had accompanied her to Newfoundland. When the mission was accomplished, the cutter would return to her home port.[40]

Two weeks later, in a public address, Secretary of the Treasury Franklin MacVeagh praised the officers and crew of the *Androscoggin* for their successful rescue of the trapped schooners.[41]

Some years before the sinking of the *Titanic*, Congress had assigned a new duty to the Revenue Cutter Service, one that would later prove important in relation to the international response to the *Titanic* disaster. On 12 May 1906, partly as a result of the lobbying efforts of the Maritime Association of the Port of New York, which wanted a cutter "equipped to cruise for and destroy derelicts and obstructions to navigation," Congress had authorized the service to build a derelict destroyer.[42] The vessel, which would be steam powered and equipped for service in bad weather, was to cost no more than $250,000.[43]

In his 1978 Newcomen lecture at the U.S. Coast Guard Academy, schooner expert Charles S. Morgan stated that "the floating derelict, her decks awash and her masts gone" posed a danger to all shipping. He added: "Only heaven knows how many vessels, both sail and steam, disappeared without trace after tearing out their bows on an unsighted derelict. Wooden vessels, laden with lumber, may survive like a half-tide rock for months after being abandoned."[44] He went on to tell the story of the *Carrie A. Buckman,* a 287-ton, three-masted schooner that was dismasted en route to Cuba with a cargo of lumber in 1882. An Italian bark picked up the schooner's crew, but the schooner drifted for two years before she was picked up and towed to a U.S. port. During that time, she was sighted near the coast of Ireland.

The Revenue Cutter Service contracted with the Newport News [Virginia] Shipbuilding and Drydock Company to build the derelict destroyer. The *Seneca*, a 204-foot-long cutter with a speed of 12 knots, was commissioned in November 1908. She cost $244,500.[45]

Between November 1908 and 30 June 1914, revenue cutters recovered or destroyed 177 derelicts. The *Seneca*, which dedicated almost all of her efforts to that purpose, destroyed or removed more derelicts than any other single cutter, but the service called on other cutters to perform this duty when feasible. The *Seneca* normally cruised between the ports of Portland, Maine; Sable Island, Nova Scotia; Bermuda; and Charleston, South Carolina. If circumstances warranted, she had the authority to cruise outside of those limits. A review of 68 derelicts and other obstructions to navigation removed during fiscal years 1910–12 reveals that the service destroyed 49 of the obstructions, delivered 5 to their owners, and towed another 14 into a port or a beach. The *Seneca* removed 31 of these.[46]

All branches of the government and the entire maritime community cooperated heartily in the effort to locate derelicts. Steamship lines, individual shipowners, and coastal and international shipping interests provided information to the Revenue Cutter Service and the Hydrographic Office in Washington and to major U.S. ports. This information was distributed to the public in bulletins and monthly charts released by the Hydrographic Office and in articles on shipping published in the nation's leading newspapers.[47]

Removal of sunken derelicts within the nation's three-mile limit was the obligation of the Chief of Engineers, War Department, who called on either revenue cutters or private contractors to do the work. Outside the three-mile limit, both sunken and floating derelicts were the Revenue Cutter Service's obligation. The vesting of jurisdiction over sunken obstructions in the War Department caused delays because it was necessary for the department to correspond with the cutter service before a derelict could be removed. This problem was solved on 2 April 1913, when the War Department promulgated regulations that authorized any cutter to remove sunken obstructions without prior correspondence.[48]

Capt. Ellsworth P. Bertholf, who had succeeded Ross as commandant of the Revenue Cutter Service on 19 June 1911, published a booklet, *Methods of Searching for Derelicts at Sea,* in 1913. Probably meant for skippers of cutters performing this difficult work, it includes "Two Methods for Searching for Derelicts at Sea," by First Lt. William H. Munter, and "Method of Searching for Derelicts at Sea," by 2d Lt. Stanley V. Parker. All of the recommended methods are based on mathematical probability and seem complicated to the layman. Courses to be steered include parallelograms, sectors of circles, and others. More practical and simpler advice is also included. Commanding officers are told to try to cover the greatest possible area while consuming the least possible amount of coal. The booklet states that it is important to know the appearance of a derelict, for

The USRC Seneca

thc bottom of a capsized vessel probably would be visible with difficulty at a distance of one mile on a clear day, whereas a derelict with masts still standing probably would be seen at eight or ten miles on a similar day. In planning his search, a cutter captain has to consider the extent of the derelict vessel exposed to the wind, the direction and force of the wind blowing on the derelict, the direction and speed of the current, and the status of all of the above from the time of the wreck until he arrives at the site of the derelict. The commandant expects his officers to get such information from the closest lightship or any other available source.[49]

The stories of two abandoned schooners that cutters towed to their owners in 1910 are worth mentioning. Between 11 and 16 February, the *Seneca* delivered the three-masted schooner *Sadie C. Symner* to her owners at Norfolk after a tow that took six days.

On 6 March, the *Onondaga* and *Mohawk* delivered the four-masted schooner *Asbury Fountain* to her owners, also at Norfolk. Early in the morning of 3 March, the steamer *Jamestown* of the Old Dominion Steamship Company had rammed the *Asbury Fountain* about eighteen miles southwest of Winter Quarter Shoal Light on Virginia's Eastern Shore. The *Fountain* was en route from Mobile to New York with a cargo of lumber. Her skipper and his eight-man crew tried to save the schooner, but she was a waterlogged floating derelict by 0530 and the captain gave the order to abandon ship. He and his crew were taken on board the *Jamestown*, which headed into Norfolk and left the schooner floating in the coastal shipping lane. Information of the wreck first reached Norfolk by wireless from Atlantic City, New Jersey. That same day, the cutter *Onondaga* set out from Norfolk in search of the *Fountain* and was joined by the *Mohawk* from New York. Three days later, the two cutters towed the derelict, valued at $40,000, into Norfolk.[50]

Steamers were also rescued by the cutter service. On 22 October 1913, the *Androscoggin* towed the derelict steamer *Templemore* into Boston harbor and turned her over to the underwriters. The 6,200-ton steamer had caught fire on 11 October, and her crew abandoned ship. The *Templemore* continued to float and drifted into a trans-Atlantic shipping lane while still ablaze. Two steamships that tried to tow the burning ship gave up the task before the cutter arrived on the scene. The *Androscoggin* sighted the vessel, which was still burning, on 13 October, but rough seas forced her crew to wait until the next morning before boarding her. After throwing grappling hooks over the rail and climbing on board, they tied lines to her quarter bitts because the bow was too hot to approach. With her awkward tow, the *Androscoggin* steamed slowly toward Boston. At times, she made only two knots and, during a gale on 17 October, steamed just five miles in twelve hours. After enduring fogs and more gales, the *Androscoggin* finally reached Boston with her tow.[51]

Some of the derelicts could not be towed into port or beached. The cutters destroyed them where they lay, sometimes ramming them but more often using gunfire or explosives, which cuttermen called mines. Because no cutter carried a weapon bigger than a 6-pounder in peacetime and some derelicts had cargoes of wood products that made them almost impossible to sink, they had to be blown apart. This work was most dangerous. In such cases, the cutter's gunner boarded the hulk and placed a mine on board. As he was rowed away from the derelict, he trailed a wire for detonating the mine. If a hulk was floating bottom side up, the gunner had to stand on an often slippery bottom while he cut a hole in the hull for the mine. This was not work for a novice, for mistakes would be costly indeed.[52]

Cutters continued to pursue the job of removing derelicts and other menaces to navigation, and this was done vigorously during 1914. "Probably no task accomplished by the Revenue Cutter Service," according to the secretary of the treasury, afforded "greater security to the marine interests of the country, as well as to all travelers by sea, than the work performed in this important field."[53] The service destroyed or removed thirty derelicts that year and towed others, valued at $145,000, into port. By then, derelict destruction had served as a precedence that provided the Revenue Cutter Service with the authority needed to operate an international ice patrol.

On the night of 14 April 1912, the supposedly unsinkable White Star liner *Titanic* ran into an iceberg off the coast of Newfoundland and sank. Of the more than 2,200 persons on board, 1,503 perished. Tragically, lifeboats were available for only about half of those on board, six warnings of icebergs in the area had been ignored, and the radio operator of a nearby ship had stopped monitoring his radio a half hour before the accident occurred.[54]

The largest ship afloat in 1912, the *Titanic* measured 46,329 gross tons, 852 feet in length, 92 feet in the beam, and 175 feet from the keel to the top of her funnels. Powered by engines that could generate 50,000 horsepower, the *Titanic* could turn up to 24–25 knots. In size and appointments, she was the pinnacle of passenger liners of her day.

She sailed from Southampton on her maiden voyage under the command of Capt. Edward J. Smith, the line's senior officer with thirty-eight years of experience. Her passengers included the rich and famous, along with immigrants on their way to start a new life in the United States. Among those on board were Thomas Andrews, the managing director of the Harland and Wolff yard in Northern Ireland, where the *Titanic* was built, and J. Bruce Ismay, the managing director of the White Star Line.

Forty minutes before midnight on 14 April, the lookout spotted an iceberg and gave a warning, but it came too late for the ship's officers to avoid the iceberg. Persons onboard were conscious of a slight grinding noise. Snow fell on deck, and an inspection of the ship's hull revealed that the collision had ripped a hole in the hull that stretched the length of the first five bulkheads. When told of this, Andrews knew that they faced a most serious problem. The ship could survive the flooding of four compartments, but those from the fifth one aft had low bulkheads—water would spill over them from compartment to compartment until the *Titanic* sank.

At 1205, Captain Smith ordered the radio operator to send out a distress call. The closest ship to the *Titanic*, the *California*, had a radio on board, but her operator had stopped listening a half hour earlier. Flares fired from the *Titanic* were observed by persons on board the *California*, but Capt. Stanley Lord assumed that the *Titanic* was celebrating and made no response. In contrast, when the radio operator of the *Carpathia* heard the *Titanic*'s call for help and informed his skipper, Capt. Arthur H. Rostron sprang into action and steamed toward the scene of the disaster. The *Carpathia*, however, was fifty-eight miles and four hours from the *Titanic*, which had about two hours to live.

The issue of who got into the *Titanic*'s lifeboats was a matter of life or death, for the ship had boats enough for only 1,178 persons of the 2,200 on board. Unfortunately, even the available lifeboats were about half full when they put to sea. Passengers in first class had a much better chance of boarding the boats than those in second or third class. Only 4 women in first class died, 3 by choice—they refused to leave their loved ones. Of the 93 women in second class, 15 died, as did 81 of the 179 women in third class. All children in first and second class survived; 23 of 76 children in third class perished. Some officers in charge would let no men into the boats, but others were not so particular. The most flagrant case was that of Ismay. Although not in the formal chain of command, he had interfered with the operation of the ship and might have been responsible for her steaming at 18 knots in the ice field. Ismay sneaked on board one of the lifeboats and lived out the rest of his life as a guilt-ridden recluse in Ireland.

After the collision, the ship's orchestra played ragtime until the final minutes approached, when it switched to the English hymn "Autumn." Many passengers were praying.

At 0220, when the *Titanic* sank, 1,500 persons waiting on deck were plunged into the sea. About 60 of them were rescued by the lifeboats. The *Carpathia* later picked up those who had succeeded in boarding the boats. The rest perished. Captain Rostron was the hero of the tragedy. Captain Lord of the *California* was the only person punished for his part in the affair. He lost command of his ship, but he later received another command.

The British government conducted two investigations into the loss of the *Titanic;* the American government conducted one. The White Star Line was held responsible for not having enough lifeboats for all passengers on board and for failing to slow down in the ice field. Significant results of the investigations included requirements that passenger liners must have enough lifeboats for every person on board and that they must maintain a twenty-four-hour radio watch. Of great importance, especially to the Revenue Cutter Service, investigators recommended the establishment of an international ice patrol.

Following the *Titanic* disaster, during May and June 1912, two scout cruisers of the U.S. Navy maintained an efficient ice patrol, but the navy announced in the spring of 1913 that it had no vessels available for the patrol that year. As soon as they learned of the navy's decision, Willard U. Taylor, president of the Maritime Association of the Port of New York, and J. S. Holton, president of the Philadelphia Maritime Exchange, wrote letters to Secretary of the Treasury William G. McAdoo. Each informed McAdoo of the unanimous vote by his organization's board of directors that the previous year's ice patrol had been very important to the safety of North Atlantic shipping and that it should be maintained in 1913. Because the navy had found it impossible to run the patrol, both organizations asked McAdoo to require revenue cutters to patrol the danger zone and send out wireless messages to ships transiting the area. On 29 March 1913, after convincing a reluctant McAdoo to give his permission, Bertholf ordered the cutters *Seneca* and *Miami* to proceed to the Grand Banks to establish a patrol.[55]

In part, the Revenue Cutter Service acquired the obligation to run the ice patrol because Captain Bertholf sought the duty as a means of increasing both the importance and the public awareness of the service when it was under attack by the Cleveland Commission, a federal body looking for ways to save tax money (see chapter 11). One of the commission's recommendations was complete elimination of the cutter service. Bertholf had started his campaign to save the service by convincing a reluctant MacVeagh, the previous treasury secretary, that cutters should do the job. Then Bertholf further convinced him that the service had all the authorization it needed to run an ice patrol, which came from its authority to destroy derelicts and remove obstructions to navigation.[56]

Between April and June 1913, the *Miami* and *Seneca* alternated on patrol, with each cutter staying on station for fifteen days at a time (not counting transit time). When relieved on station, each cutter went into Halifax, Nova Scotia, for coal and supplies in preparation for relieving her sister at the end of the patrol. During their patrols, each cutter determined the southern, eastern, and western edges of the ice fields or icebergs and broadcast that information at specified times to ships at sea, to the U.S. Hydrographic Office at New York City, and to Boston or Newport radio stations. Each cutter kept a record of ice conditions and, at the end of the patrol, wrote a report for the season, which was sent to headquarters in duplicate.[57]

The *Seneca* (Capt. Charles E. Johnston) sailed from Tompkinsville, New York, on 3 April 1913 and arrived on her patrol grounds five days later. On 13 April, she sighted her first iceberg at latitude 44–36 N and longitude 48–09 W. Johnston sent daily reports to the Hydrographic Office in New York. He had to relay his messages via steamers at sea because he could not communicate directly with the East Coast of the United States from east of longitude 55. Just before noon on 20 April, the *Miami* (Capt. Aaron L. Gamble) relieved the *Seneca*, which thus completed the first ice patrol conducted by a revenue cutter.[58]

During her first patrol, the *Miami* helped to repair the trawling gear of the French barkentine *St. Christopher.* She fired a 6-pound shot at an iceberg, but it had no appreciable effect. At no time between 20 April and 1 May did she report any ice within 200 miles of steamer lanes between the United States and Fastnet, England, or within 90 miles of the westbound lane from Glasgow, Scotland.[59]

On 1 May, Captain Johnston relieved Captain Gamble without personal contact because the fog was so thick that they could not see each other's ships. The relief was carried out by radio message after the *Seneca* arrived on her cruising grounds. Between 16 May and 4 June, the *Miami* lay in a trough with her staysail and mainsail set to conserve coal. On 25 May, the *Seneca* picked up two French fishermen (from their dory) who had lost their ship in the fog. The next day, Johnston returned them to their mother vessel, the barkentine *Arabia*.[60]

Captain Johnston recommended discontinuing the patrol for the season on 8 June because it was no longer necessary. From 25 to 28 June, Captain Gamble and the *Miami* made a final search of a rectangle between meridians 41 and 42 and parallels 42 and 43–30 but did not see any large icebergs. At 1600 on 28 June, Captain Gamble set the *Miami*'s course for the banks and ended the Revenue Cutter Service's first season on ice patrol.[61]

With his *Reports of Vessels on Ice Patrol in the North Atlantic Ocean* in 1913, Bertholf published Johnston's observations for the season.[62] Johnston reported that ice on the Grand Banks had been in the form of bergs from Greenland. In April, about 100 bergs had drifted south of latitude 50 N; in May, 114 bergs; and up to 16 June, 35 bergs. The largest berg he had seen "was about 400 feet long by 300 feet wide, by 70 feet high out of water; the smallest was about 225 feet long, 100 feet wide and 35 feet high." No two were shaped alike, according to Johnston. The highest berg he had seen was about 150 feet high and looked like the Matterhorn. "One berg," he wrote, "had a protuberance on its side that bore such a striking resemblance to the profile of the late Queen Victoria that several officers exclaimed in unison, 'Victoria!'"

On an unusually clear day, Johnston had observed ice at 18 miles, but the average distance of sightings on a clear day had been 12–15 miles. Clouds reduced these distances by about 2 miles. Fog obviously reduced the range at which bergs were seen: from 2 miles in light fog to 200 yards in dense fog. In drizzle, Johnston reported seeing bergs at 2½ miles. This was the same distance at which he could see a berg in bright moonlight. In starlight alone, the distance was 1 mile.

Bergs might or might not give an echo. Although an echo indicated an obstruction, its absence indicated nothing. Johnston reported that a berg had little impact on air temperature. Some bergs, he wrote, were covered with birds, some had none. The birds' presence generally indicated nothing about the presence of bergs, except that he considered murre an indication of bergs. He had seen mallard ducks, puffins, hogdon gulls, petrels, jaegers, plovers, Arctic terns, red phalaropes, lesser auks, and murre on bergs, but no harbor, herring, or kittiwake gulls.

Bergs were observed to drift with surface currents. "Where two currents meet," Johnston noted, "the dominant one eventually takes charge." The greatest distance he had observed a berg drift in a day was 32 miles. On the Grand Banks, winds occasionally "overcame the strength of the tidal current." But usually bergs drifted with the flood tide to the north and the ebb tide to the south.

The weather in 1913 was mild and foggy. Johnston reported fog on about 50 percent of the days in April, 60 percent in May, and 30 percent in June. The wind blew over force 8 on two days in April, three days in May, and one day through 16 June.

In Johnston's opinion, skippers in areas where there were icebergs should stop in heavy fog on dark nights and then run slowly. He did not consider icebergs dangerous in clear weather. At night and in fog, he advised posting a lookout as low down as possible, for he calculated that an observer high on a big ship could look right over a berg in such weather. "In addition to this," he observed, "the vigilance of the officer of the watch should be unremitting."

In July, the New York Maritime Exchange and the international maritime community thanked McAdoo and Bertholf for the valuable service just completed. They wrote that the ice patrol had made both the passengers and professionals on the trans-Atlantic runs more comfortable. The success of the patrol in improving the safety of all shipping on the North Atlantic led the maritime community to ask that it be continued annually and resulted in the government making it a permanent duty of the Revenue Cutter Service.[63]

McAdoo had continued his opposition to the service running the ice patrol until the maritime community made it an international obligation in 1914. In 1912 and 1913, the United States ran the ice patrol as a national program and paid the bills, which seemed unfair to McAdoo. He thought that ships could avoid the ice by simply taking a longer, more southerly route. The British steam-whaler *Scotia* had done scientific work on ice conditions in the crucial area, which, he thought, might constitute a duplication of efforts. But, clearly, running a longer route across the Atlantic Ocean cost more than a shorter route, and the *Scotia*'s methods of operation failed to warn ships of ice dangers on the North Atlantic, in contrast to the success of the cutter's methods. Finally, in 1914, an acceptable solution to the problem was found. On 12 November 1913, fourteen nations had met in London at an international convention for the safety of life at sea. Captain Bertholf was one of a dozen delegates representing the United States at the convention, which decided that nations interested in an ice patrol would participate in it and would pay for the service according to the volume of their shipping. Because the agreement would not go into effect until 1 July 1915, Great Britain asked the United States to run the patrols in 1914. On 7 February 1914, President Woodrow Wilson ordered the Revenue Cutter Service to undertake the task. The *Seneca* sailed from New York on a preliminary investigation of the ice area on 19 February. After 1 April, when ice began to advance into the shipping lanes of the North Atlantic, the *Seneca* and *Miami* resumed their routine of the previous season and operated the patrol through June.[64] Subsequently, the Coast Guard ran the patrol for the international community, and the maritime community of the world paid for the service.

In addition to responding to calls for assistance, cutters performed a myriad of other duties for the nation, including, but not limited to, enforcing navigation, immigration, quarantine, and neutrality laws; preventing smuggling; patrolling regattas and marine parades; suppressing mutinies; saving lives and property in disasters on shore; protecting marine species; cooperating with the Life-Saving Service; providing medical aid to fishermen; and maintaining the military skills necessary for cooperation with the navy in time of war.

On 5 September 1890, the *Seattle Post-Intelligencer* had reported an interview with Capt. Russell Glover, then stationed at Port Townsend, Washington. Five days earlier, the *Wolcott*, under Glover's command, had seized the steamer *George E. Starr* in Juan de Fuca Straits bound for the United States with a cargo of opium. Glover, who was described by the reporter as "a gentleman of stout build, a profusion of black side-whiskers with the hearty manners of a thorough-bred seaman," was asked if there was much smuggling in Puget Sound. He had responded, "A great deal of it, . . . the rascals are extremely hard to catch, too. We give them a futile chase, but unless the breeze fails them or some accident befalls them they generally elude us." The Revenue Cutter Service, he had said, needed a fast cutter on the order of a torpedo boat to catch the smugglers—they

Capt. Russell Glover

could identify a cutter at a distance and usually escaped. Opium, with a duty of $10 a pound on it, was the most important article smuggled, he said and added that "the temptation to avoid custom dues is great." Almost as an afterthought, Glover added that the service also had to contend with the illegal immigration of Chinese nationals, who tried to migrate from British Columbia in violation of the law.[65]

The service continued to enforce laws prohibiting the entry of opium and Chinese migrants, but as a secondary rather than a primary obligation. In his 1912 annual report, Commandant Bertholf wrote that cutters, especially on the Pacific Coast, had assisted immigration authorities when requested but only as the availability of equipment allowed. He added that on 2 March 1912, the *Hartley* had seized the *Morning Star* in Oakland Creek and arrested both her crew and twenty-one contraband Chinese.[66]

Judging from the 1912 annual report of the secretary of the treasury, signed for the secretary by W. E. Curtis, such seizures were rare. The report states that the "Congress should give its full attention to the opium situation," which he evaluated as "horrible." Smuggling was rampant, and the United States had failed to do its full share of the work to stop it.[67]

The Revenue Cutter Service participated in efforts to protect a variety of marine species from encroachment by Japanese vessels during that era. On 9 July 1909, cutters seized the Japanese schooner *Tenyse Maru* for illegal sealing. The following June, they seized the *Tokai Maru* for fishing in U.S. waters, in violation of legislation dated 14 June 1906, and arrested the skipper of the *Korei Maru* for sealing illegally. In January 1910, the *Thetis* sailed from its home port at Honolulu to islands in the Hawaiian chain to enforce federal laws against alien plumage hunters. On the Laysan and Lisianski islands, the *Thetis* arrested twenty-three Japanese subjects for killing birds illegally and seized $112,470 worth of plumage in their possession.[68]

On occasion, prior to 1914, cutters had sailed with a medical doctor on board—usually on cutters bound for the Arctic Ocean—but all requests for the regular assignment of doctors had been turned down. Then, on 24 June 1914, in response to a request from Captain Bertholf, Congress authorized the secretary of the treasury to assign Public Health Service doctors to cutters as necessary to provide medical care to deep-sea fishermen. By 1915, ten cutters had been assigned a doctor, which greatly enhanced their ability to serve America's seagoing community. The doctors treated anybody in need, not just deep-sea fishermen. A cutter without an assigned surgeon carried a medical handbook prepared for the use of officers and enlisted men.[69] It was understood that written directions were a poor substitute for a physician or surgeon; in cases of serious sickness or injury, the man in charge was expected to obtain medical assistance as soon as practicable. The handbook described the symptoms of a few of the more common diseases and gave basic treatments for various types of disease and injury.

The service continued to maintain its military readiness. In 1910, it participated in naval drills and took target practice with rapid-fire guns and small arms.[70] Two years later, the report of the secretary of the treasury acknowledged that appropriations for the service had been inadequate to purchase modern ordnance. The report added that first- and second-class cutters, armed with 6-pounder rapid-fire guns, were being fitted out with new guns of similar caliber, thanks to the generosity of the Navy Department. Most of the cutters had been so equipped, and the remainder would be similarly equipped before the end of the year. The service had modernized its small arms and was instituting the navy's system of gun drills and target practice.[71]

During this period, the Revenue Cutter Service lost two cutters. Both were lost in Alaskan waters. The old 161-foot iron-hulled steamer *Perry* went aground on Saint Paul Island in the Pribiloffs in dense fog in July 1910, and the steamer *Tahoma* (191 feet, 8 inches in length) grounded on an uncharted reef near Buldir Island in the western Aleutians on 20 September 1914. No lives were lost in either accident, and Commandant Bertholf, who had sailed on many cruises in Alaskan waters, was understanding in his response to the sinkings. He considered the grounding unavoidable and wrote that "not a single island west of Unimak Pass is correctly charted; the positions of the islands themselves are incorrectly shown, the coast lines are incorrect, and the soundings and outlying dangers are, for the most part, left to the conjecture of the navigator. These facts, together with the ever-present fog, make navigation in those waters a precarious undertaking, but it must be done. In performing the duty of enforcing the law, and the treaty for the protection of the fur seal and sea otter, Coast Guard cutters are obligated to take many risks, and it is not surprising that the *Tahoma* struck an uncharted reef; indeed, the surprising thing is that the cutters have navigated these waters these many years with so few mishaps."[72]

One could rationally say similar things about the loss of just fourteen cutters in the 124-year history of the Revenue Cutter Service.

CHAPTER NINE

The Revenue Cutter
School of Instruction

fter Sumner Kimball reformed the officer corps of the Revenue Cutter Service by eliminating officers who were unfit to serve (see chapter 1), he granted rank commensurate with their abilities to those who were retained. He then persuaded Congress to establish a training school to ensure a steady supply of competent, well-trained officers. Congress authorized the school on 31 July 1876.

Capt. Hopley Yeaton, the first seagoing officer commissioned under the U.S. Constitution, had appreciated the need for a formal training program for young revenue cutter officers. In 1808, he asked the Treasury Department for permission to add four boys to the crew of his cutter, the *New Hampshire,* so that he could train them as seamen, navigators, and pilots. His request shows that he was ahead of his time on the subject of training officers, but like the ideas of many forward-thinking people, it was turned down.[1]

Alexander V. Fraser, the first military commandant of the Revenue Cutter Service, was also the first officer actually to run his cutter, the *Lawrence,* as a training ship. On a year-long cruise from Washington, D.C., to San Francisco in 1848–49, Fraser confronted heavy storms, breakdowns, and delays. His problems were exacerbated by a wardroom of incompetent junior officers, but there was a positive side to these unhappy events. Burdened by inexperienced officers, Fraser ran the *Lawrence* like a schoolship. He established a small shipboard library and required his officers to study and take examinations in surveying, law, seamanship, and navigation.[2] Without headquarters' support, the program died when Fraser retired.

Building on Fraser's foundation, Kimball used the topsail schooner *Dobbin* as a schoolship. Constructed in 1853 by J. M. Hood at Somerset, Massachusetts, the *Dobbin* sailed out of Wilmington, Delaware, and Savannah, Georgia. In December 1860, she was stationed at Savannah when Capt. Napoleon L. Coste turned over the revenue cutter *William Aiken* to Charleston, South Carolina, authorities. Capt. John A. Webster, Jr., the *Dobbin's* skipper, tried to escape to sea in the cutter, but foul weather and adverse winds kept him from sailing downriver and the customs collector of the port refused to give him a tow. On 3 January 1861, a mob seized the Dobbin in Savannah, put her crew in irons, and held her officers as prisoners on parole. At daylight, a tug towed the *Dobbin* downriver with the Palmetto flag at her peak. The mob ran her ashore under the guns of Fort Pulaski at high tide, took all of her boats, and went to the fort. At three o'clock that afternoon, the mob returned, accompanied by an officer from the fort, who assumed command of the *Dobbin* in the name of Georgia. That same day, collector John Boston learned what had happened and appealed to Georgia's governor, Joseph E. Brown, to allow the cutter to proceed to sea, in keeping with the orders of Secretary of the Treasury Salmon P. Chase. With regrets for the illegal action, Governor Brown ordered the cutter and officers released and the cutter towed to sea. Captain Webster lost no time getting under way and headed north in the only southern-based cutter to escape to the north before the Civil War.[3]

Following the war, the *Dobbin* served along the East Coast of the United States. In May 1877, headquarters ordered her to proceed on a practice cruise with the first class of cadets of the Revenue Cutter School of Instruction. She served as the school training ship until the summer of 1878, when she was replaced by the *Salmon P. Chase*. The *Dobbin* sailed thereafter as a cutter until 6 April 1881, when the service sold her to Henry Brothers of Baltimore, Maryland.

The *Chase*, a graceful little bark with a clipper bow and rounded stern, was designed by Capt. James H. Merryman and built by Joseph Allen of New York. She measured 106 feet between perpendiculars, 25 feet in the beam, and 154 tons burden, and she carried four broadside guns. She was fitted out to accommodate cadets, who lived in steerage in one of six staterooms. Each room was furnished with two berths, a washstand, and lockers for clothes. Training was not to interfere with the cutter's performance of her legitimate duties. In addition to serving as the schoolship, she discharged the regular work of a cutter from her home base at New Bedford. Capt. John A. Henriques, commander of the *Chase*, was in charge of all cadet instruction.[4]

Congress authorized the appointment of cadets in July 1876 to fill vacancies in the officer corps at the rank of third lieutenant. Cadet candidates had to be between eighteen and twenty-five years of age. A cadet ranked below third lieutenants, and the total number of cadets and third lieutenants could not exceed the number of third lieutenants authorized for the service. Cadets were promoted to third lieutenant after completing a two-year training program and passing the necessary examinations. Their pay was three quarters of a third lieutenant's pay. When a cadet was promoted to third lieutenant, another cadet could be appointed.[5]

Candidates of good moral standing who passed a required physical examination could take the written examination given annually at the Treasury Department. Appointments were awarded on the basis of merit, in strict accordance with scores on the examination. Candidates were given a number to write on the examinations, and officers graded the examinations without knowing the identity of the candidates until all grading had been completed. Political influence was prohibited in the rank ordering of candidates, which set a precedent still in effect today. The admissions examination covered reading, writing, spelling, grammar, arithmetic, algebra, geography, and U.S. history. Candidates had to score 75 out of a possible score of 100 to qualify for an appointment. Different values were assigned to the subjects on the examination: arithmetic was given a value of four, grammar three, and geography one. The general average was "obtained by first multiplying the average of a candidate's marks in each subject by the relative value of the subject, adding the results obtained for the respective branches, and dividing the aggregate by the sum of the values." Ezra Clark, chief of the Revenue Marine Bureau in 1881, explained how appointments were made after the examination had been graded: "When the final averages have been affixed, the names of the candidates are placed upon a list in the order of the proficiency exhibited by them in the examination, and from this list appointments are made to fill vacancies, beginning at the head of the list and taking the names in regular order."[6]

The USRC Salmon P. Chase *on a cadet training cruise.*

Ten of nineteen young men who took the first entrance examination passed it. Eight of the successful candidates received instructions to report on board the *Dobbin* at Baltimore, whence they sailed on a summer training cruise on 24 May 1877. The cadets sailed into New Bedford to start their academic program on 15 October. Six cadets completed the two years of study and graduated in 1879. One of them, Worth G. Ross, would overcome adversity to become the first school graduate to receive an appointment as commandant of the Revenue Cutter Service. On 13 July 1877, less than two months after sailing on his first cadet cruise, Ross was detached from the *Dobbin* and placed in a waiting orders status. A week later, Captain Henriques reprimanded him for "licentious and scandalous conduct." Although the correspondence on his case does not specify Ross's specific offense, it is clear that the service came close to expelling him from the academy during his first summer there.[7]

During the first five years of the school's history, 176 candidates reported for medical examinations, and 31 failed at that stage of the admissions process. Of the 145 who took the academic test, 38 passed and 29 received appointments to the cadet corps: 8 in 1876 (for the first class on the *Dobbin* in 1877), 5 in 1878, 4 in 1879, 8 in 1880, and 4 in 1881.[8]

The *Chase* tied up just above the bridge at the north end of Fish Island, where it provided a home for cadets during the winter. The government leased buildings on the north end of the island and used the Mitchell Boat Company buildings for classes, drills, and storage. Most classes were held on board the *Chase*.[9]

Ross (class of 1879) later described the early school of instruction in an article for *Harper's New Monthly Magazine*. The cadet routine in port included daily recitation in academic courses, physical exercise, professional studies, and time for recreation. Cadets engaged in "simple athletics, rowing, and going aloft." They studied navigation, seamanship, gunnery, and signaling. The administration granted liberty on Wednesday and Saturday afternoons and after an inspection on Sunday. Cadets ate alone in a mess catered by a person of their own choosing. They could neither drink alcoholic beverages nor smoke. They wore a uniform, which they purchased, and were given demerits for infractions of academy rules.[10]

Each year was divided into two terms, the first from June to January and the second, January to June. During the first term, classes ran for fourteen weeks, there was a three months' cruise on the *Chase*, and cadets received a one-week vacation at Christmas. During the second term, classes ran for twenty weeks. Each term ended with an examination given in December and May, respectively.[11]

Edwin Emery, who had been appointed by Kimball, taught most of the

TABLE 9-1 CURRICULUM: REVENUE CUTTER SCHOOL OF INSTRUCTION	
FIRST TERM	SECOND TERM
Junior (first) year:	
Algebra (14 weeks)	Geometry (20 weeks)
English (14 weeks)	Composition and rhetoric (20 weeks)
Arithmetic (10 weeks)	History (20 weeks)
History (4 weeks)	
Senior (second) year:	
Law (14 weeks)	Composition (20 weeks)
Composition (14 weeks)	International law (16 weeks)
Geometry (10 weeks)	Astronomy (16 weeks)
Trigonometry (4 weeks)	Revenue law (12 weeks)
Philosophy (10 weeks)	Trigonometry (8 weeks)
Steam engineering (4 weeks)	Algebra (4 weeks)
	Steam engineering (4 weeks)

academic program. Like Kimball, he had graduated from Bowdoin College in Brunswick, Maine. Emery had taught school and served as principal in public schools. In the Union Army during the Civil War, he fought at Spotsylvania and in the Battle of the Wilderness. He was "wounded twice, decorated for bravery, and commissioned on the battlefield." He served on the faculty from the school's beginning to its temporary closing in 1890. Charles F. Emery, Ph.D., from New York, who also served as a consulting engineer for the Revenue Cutter Service, supplemented Edwin Emery's course on steam engineering.[12]

In accordance with the admissions requirements, the curriculum emphasized the study of mathematics and English, with some attention given to history and philosophy (physics). To prepare cadets for their profession, courses were also offered in steam engineering and law. All cadets studied the curriculum shown in Table 9-1.

Ross describes the course of instruction, as he remembered it several years later:

> It takes up arithmetic, algebra, geometry, astronomy, and trigonometry (plain and spherical); the history of the origin and growth of the English language; composition, rhetoric, and correspondence, in which the cadets are required to write upon abstract, imaginary, descriptive, and professional subjects, and to construct official letters, reports, and

forms; philosophy and steam-engineering, the latter being treated both practically and theoretically, and supplemented by lectures of Consulting Engineer Charles E. Emery, Ph.D., of New York; history of the world in general, and of the United States in particular; that part of international law which deals with the rights of nations in peace and war, rights of jurisdiction over the sea, and of commerce; embargoes, law of contraband, blockade, right of search, offenses against the law of nations, piracy, etc. In constitutional law the history of the Constitution is taught, and the legislative, executive, and judicial departments, and powers of Congress, are discussed, while the revenue law comprehends all that relates to the duties of an officer of the customs, such as the regulations of commerce and navigation, collection districts, and ships papers.[13]

Comments by Ezra W. Clark, chief of the Revenue Marine Bureau, in his 1881 annual report indicate that the school emphasized training, that those in charge of the service were aware of the program's limitations (they asked for an additional year of study), and that they were proud of what they were able to accomplish in the two years available to them. Clark states that a considerable amount of time was allotted to teaching seamanship. Additional time was allotted to instruction in small arms, great guns, and signaling, and, in the study of physics, particular attention was given to the study of steam engines. Clark conceded: "This course of study seems meager when compared with that of a university, or of the Government military and naval academies." Yet, he added, because of the competitive nature of the admissions process, good students were recruited and better results were "accomplished with the course of study . . . than might casually appear to be the case."[14]

Cadets received a considerable amount of their professional training during the summer. About 1 June, the *Chase* put to sea for a three-month cruise under the command of Captain Henriques. Walter Wyman, a U.S. Public Health Service and Marine Hospital Service surgeon who accompanied Henriques on the 1881 summer cruise, describes him as "a fine-looking man of about fifty years of age, more than six feet in height and broad in proportion," with blue eyes and a fair complexion. He wore "an iron-gray beard neatly trimmed."[15]

According to both Ross and Clark, the system owed much of its success to Henriques. The cutter sailed from New Bedford in the summer of

1881 with three lieutenants, Doctor Wyman, two classes of cadets (a total of thirteen cadets), a crew of thirty, and one cook. At sea, the seniors assumed some of the duties of an officer, and the juniors assumed some of a petty officer.[16]

According to Ross, a cadet's "endurance, pluck, and energy" were tested on the summer cruise, for he was "subjected to many of the inconveniences and discomforts incident to a sea voyage, at the same time having to perform all the duties belonging to the vocation of a sailor." Also, according to Ross, if one was "actually unfit for the sea, physically or otherwise," it was "brought to the surface" and provided early in the program an opportunity to turn away from "a career in which he would not be likely to succeed."[17]

The objective of the cruise was to impress upon cadets the duties of a deck officer, and they were divided into watches. They kept a rough log and studied the evolutions of the vessel. When placed in charge of the deck, they worked the ship in tacking and wearing operations. They learned marlinspike seamanship and the names and uses of everything on board. When the weather was calm they reset the rigging and rattled it down. They were drilled constantly "in raising shears, stepping masts, reefing, furling, and shifting sails, and in sending up and down yards." Each cadet took his turn at the wheel, learned how the compass and steering gear worked, and was introduced to slush and tarpots.[18]

The cadets practiced using the sextant in navigation. Each day, they determined the latitude, longitude, and position of the cutter. They learned signal codes and the use of small arms, broadswords, and gunnery. Fire drills were conducted.

On practice cruises, according to Ross, the *Chase* usually put in "at some foreign port for supplies and mail, having been on different occasions to England, France, Spain, Portugal, Gibraltar, the Azores and Bermuda Islands."[19] In 1881, for example, she called at the city of Coruna, Spain. The weather was good, and the cutter had the honor of being visited by the provincial captain general. The American consul took the officers and cadets on a tour of the city. After a week of sightseeing by the ship's company, the *Chase* sailed for Fayal in the Azores. The 1,000-mile trip took more than two weeks, as the *Chase* was buffeted by gale force head winds that forced her to heave to.[20]

By mid-July, the cadets had composed a "catechism" that revealed something about their training and poked fun at themselves and all third lieutenants. One cadet asked the questions while the others responded in unison:

Q. Who made the earth?
A. Captain Henriques.

Q. What is the most godlike being that walks the earth?
A. A captain in the revenue marine.

Q. What is the most contemptible thing that crawls?
A. A cadet.

Q. Who brings head winds?
A. Cadets.

Q. How do you know that cadets bring head winds?
A. Because the captain always lays for them when there are head winds.

Q. What is the rank of cadet?
A. Next below that of mess boy.

Q. What is a third lieutenant?
A. That is what the third lieutenant would like to know.[21]

The *Chase* usually returned to the United States in August and the last part of the cruise was devoted to nautical exercises in the bays and harbors. After leaving the Azores on 6 August, the *Chase* made a stormy but fast passage (twenty days) to Gardiner's Bay, Long Island. Until 3 September, the cadets practiced commanding and sailing the bark in the bay. Then she sailed into New Bedford on 4 September, and the cadets left the cutter for thirty days of leave.

During Leonard Shepard's tenure as the school's superintendent from 15 June 1883 to 9 April 1887, the *Chase* made three cadet cruises to European waters.[22]

On the 1884 summer cruise under Shepard's command, the *Chase* proved herself a good training ship. The *Gallatin* towed her to sea from New Bedford early in June in thick fog. From the first Friday at sea to the following Monday noon, winds blew a full gale, and the *Chase* drove through heavy seas under reefed topsails, reefed spanker, spencers, fore-topmast staysails, and reefed foresail. All of the cadets except one and half of the bluejackets (crew) on board got sick, but the watch officers praised the *Chase* as a very good sea boat. She arrived safely at Brest, France, sometime before 3 July. From there, she sailed to the Azores, then on to Greenport, Long Island, where she arrived in mid-August.[23]

While sailing as a cadet on the 1887 summer cruise, John Cantwell served as a correspondent for the *New Bedford Chronicle*. His letters to the newspaper reveal that Shepard kept cadets busy with full days of training and education. Cantwell emphasized that cadets studied law, particularly as it related to the Treasury Department and international law. Under way, the cadets rose at 0600, reported on deck at 0630, and began their day furling and loosing sails if the weather was good. They ate breakfast at 0730, and reported to the first lieutenant at 0830 for work assignments. Three hours later, they reported to the navigator for instruction in the use of the sextant and to work up the ship's position. At 1200, they took observations and worked them up between 1300 and 1400. Seamanship training filled the rest of the afternoon. From 1630 to 2000, the cadets were free to enjoy themselves. Cantwell reported that music, reading, and playing checkers and shuffleboard were common forms of recreation.[24]

The *Chase* put in at a European port for water, and Shepard granted liberty, which thrilled the cadets. On the return trip, the *Chase* visited the western islands en route to Gardiner's Bay, where cadets handled the cutter without the officers' assistance for two weeks. They practiced clawing off of a lee shore, sent down spars and masts, handled small boats, and took pride in working from sunup to sundown. The *Chase* then sailed for home, where Shepard granted ten days' leave. During the cadets' absence, Shepard had the *Chase* overhauled and painted in preparation for the new academic year, which started on 15 September.[25]

Classes at the school were small during the first decade. Only thirty-one cadets had graduated by 1885. The largest graduating class had numbered eleven, the smallest three. As noted above, the school varied in size to fill the needs of the service for thirty-six cadets and third lieutenants. Graduation took place in Washington, D.C. Each cadet's position in the class was determined by his academic performance, deportment, and examination averages.[26] The relative position of the graduates when they entered the

The class of 1904 was a small class.

officer corps was based on their averages for the two years at the school and their results in the examination for third lieutenant.[27]

Clark had nothing but praise for the officers produced by this new system. In 1881, he wrote: "Without ostentation, I think the claim may now justly be asserted, that not elsewhere in the public service will be found a corps of officers better qualified in their profession, more zealous in their devotion to duty, more intelligent in their methods of work, more faithful, more self-respecting than those now comprising the roll of the

Revenue Marine."[28] It says something about Clark's character that he attributed these results to efficient management and acknowledged that "the reorganization of the Service was principally effected during the incumbency of the former Chief, Mr. Sumner I. Kimball."[29]

In spite of the obvious success of the school, it was closed by the government in 1890 (see chapter 3). Shepard deserves credit for reopening the school in 1894.

As a result of the rapid expansion of the U.S. Navy in the 1890s, that service needed all of the Naval Academy's graduates, with none left for revenue cutter duty. Shepard, who had been the second commanding officer of the *Chase*, must have been delighted with the opportunity to renew cadet training, and he seized the opportunity. In May 1894, he ordered the *Chase* refitted, so that the practice of having cadets live on board in port eight or nine months a year for academic and professional instruction could be resumed. The *Chase* would cruise during the other three or four months for practical instruction in seamanship. This regimen lasted just one year.[30]

In April 1894, Shepard ordered Capt. Joseph W. Congdon to take command of the *Chase* and to fit her out for a cruise with a new class of cadets. Congdon was an experienced *Chase* sailor, having served on her as both a first lieutenant and an executive officer. Prior to taking command of the training ship, he had commanded the *Colfax* on the North Carolina station and served as president of the board that examined the cadets trained on the reactivated *Chase*.[31]

Before Congdon arrived in New Bedford, the Revenue Cutter Service had begun the work of completely overhauling the *Chase* under the supervision of Captain Henriques. The service replaced her decks and spars, fitted her out with new boats, and overhauled her running and standing rigging, with wire generally replacing the old rope rigging. Three-inch breech-loading rifles replaced the *Chase*'s antiquated brass cannons, and a coat of jet black paint, on which her gold work stood out strikingly, covered her hull.

The ship's complement consisted of 2d Lt. Daniel P. Foley, who served Congdon as executive officer; 2d Lt. David H. Jarvis, navigation officer; 3d Lt. Henry L. Peckham; surgeon Edgar Strager; and twenty-seven petty officers and seamen. The department assigned no special teachers to the faculty in 1894; the cutter's officers taught all courses.

The curriculum was broad based. In port, cadets studied seamanship,

In 1895, the service cut the Salmon P. Chase *in two and added forty feet amidships.*

gunnery, signaling, law (revenue, international, and constitutional), navigation, and steam engineering and learned to use the cutlass. At sea, seamanship, navigation, and drill dominated their lives.

In May 1894, twelve cadets entered the class of 1896 after passing the competitive examination administered in Washington. Eleven of them were from the East Coast, and the twelfth came from Michigan. (Two of these young men, Frederick C. Billard from Maryland and Harry G. Hamlet from Massachusetts, later became commandants of the Coast Guard.) Members of the cadet corps received $500 a year and one ration a day.[32]

In 1895, when old and infirm officers were placed on the waiting orders list, the school enlarged the *Chase* by cutting her in two and adding forty feet amidships. The longer *Chase* could accommodate twenty-five cadets. Commandant Charles F. Shoemaker appointed Oscar C. Hamlet as the *Chase*'s new skipper and assigned Ellsworth P. Bertholf as his executive officer. Only cadets who had already completed most of their education were admitted to the school. For two years, they would concentrate almost exclusively on what Shoemaker described as "instruction in the technical branches of the profession," that is, on practical seamanship. In 1897, the *Chase* cruised for seven months; worked in port for four months, with occasional practice under way; and one month was set aside for cadet leave and to overhaul, clean, and paint the *Chase*.[33]

The *Chase* had no permanent home port under Hamlet. Instead, she put into various ports, usually in the South, including Wilmington, Charleston, Key West, Tampa, Pensacola, and Mobile. The school sponsored a limited athletic program during winter layovers and fielded football and baseball teams against local talent. William J. Wheeler, who was a cadet at the time, wrote that the school's teams were fairly successful and recalled that "celebrations following victories were not soon forgotten." Social life, he wrote, centered around receptions on the cutter for local dignitaries, who occasionally reciprocated with an invitation to a formal dance ashore.[34]

Officers who trained at the school of instruction in the 1890s were defensive about their education, as evidenced by a letter that Wheeler wrote to Albert A. Lawrence in 1938. Lawrence, who was working on a history of the Coast Guard with Stephen Hadley Evans, wrote to Wheeler, then the commander of the New Orleans Division of the Coast Guard, to inquire about his early years at the school of instruction. Wheeler generously sent back a cover letter and a typed nine-page response. In the cover letter, Wheeler, who had entered the school of instruction on 26 May 1896 and graduated on 21 April 1898, wrote at length about the entrance examination and course of instruction. A few years before Wheeler wrote this letter to Lawrence, an ensign had written that "in the early days the entrance examinations were most rudimentary and instruction entirely practical." Wheeler was concerned about the ensign's work: "This is liable to be very misleading and give the younger officers a very poor opinion of the older ones," he wrote. Wheeler distinctly recalled "that the first graduate of the *Chase*, late Captain Myrik, whom I knew in his later years, was a Harvard graduate. Others of the early classes on the *Chase*," he wrote, "were educated men." Then Wheeler revealed the essence of the school during its seagoing-only phase: "The course of instruction when I was a cadet was very thorough," he added, "along professional lines."[35]

The foregoing is not meant to dispute Wheeler's recollections. In fact, the entrance examination probably was demanding in 1896. About forty candidates for the ten vacancies that year took the examination at either Washington or San Francisco, and only nine passed with the required grade of 75. As Wheeler recalled, 86 was the highest grade and 75 was the lowest. Many of those who took the examination, perhaps a majority, he recalled, "were college men, and a considerable percentage were college graduates."[36]

The class reported to the *Chase* at Baltimore, where the cadets had to wait for about a week until the schoolship was ready to receive them. While he waited, Wheeler boarded with four other cadets at 25 South Broadway. In the meantime, Oehm and Company of Baltimore made the new cadets' uniforms. Finally, on 17 June 1896, Wheeler and his classmates reported onboard the *Chase*, where they were berthed in the *Chase's* steerage with fourteen members of the class of 1897. They quickly learned that the class ahead of them "had rather strict ideas of class distinction."[37]

Captain Hamlet called them to his cabin, where he gave them a "sensible" talk. Essentially, he told them that class distinction was part of their training. "Bear in mind," he added, according to Wheeler, "that it is always best to exercise a large degree of self-restraint, as the fewer complaints, the better." During his tour of duty at the school of instruction, Hamlet influenced the careers of many young men who went on to become senior officers in the Revenue Cutter service. Wheeler described Bertholf as "afterwards a brilliant Commandant of the Service," and also noted that 2d Lt. S. P. Edmonds, the navigation officer, and 2d Lt. E. V. D. Johnson, an instructor, had graduated from the Naval Academy and Edmonds had earned a master's degree in mechanical engineering from Cornell University.[38]

Wheeler's first summer cruise on the *Chase* was a success, which revealed Hamlet's skill as a sailor. On the first leg of the cruise from Baltimore to Boston, according to Wheeler, "the vessel anchored to await daybreak and it was then found that a head wind was blowing. Without hesitation, Captain Hamlet got under way and tacked up the channel through the Narrows to anchorage off the New England docks, Boston. This excited a great deal of favorable comment, both from newspapers and from seagoing men, as it had been many years since a square rigger had stood up to the Boston wharves against a head wind."[39]

From Boston, the *Chase* sailed to Gibraltar. The Atlantic crossing took thirty days, during which cadets "were allowed two quarts of fresh water per day, one quart being supposedly for washing, but there is much doubt as to this subdivision." While the *Chase* lay at Gibraltar, cadets visited Granada, Algiers, Funchal, and Madeira, learning at Funchal of Presi-

Capt. Oscar C. Hamlet

dent William McKinley's victory over William Jennings Bryan. From Gibraltar, the *Chase* sailed for Tampa Bay, via the Cape Verde Island and St. Thomas. She sailed the last leg of the summer's cruise in a hurricane of moderate intensity that drove the bark along at eleven knots under reduced sail. The *Chase* arrived at Tampa Bay about 20 December, just short of six months after leaving Baltimore.[40]

Wheeler wrote that for one week on the return trip the ship's company had been reduced to eating hard tack, rice, and tea without sugar. The cadets had spent almost all of their money on sightseeing, so the ship had been provisioned only for a normal crossing. Then they ran into a storm that delayed their passage. To add to their troubles, the steward spilled a kerosene lantern into the rice. Wheeler thought it interesting that they could still do the strenuous work of sailing the cutter in spite of their diet. And he wrote that he would never forget their second meal ashore after the crossing. They had hurriedly eaten bread and jelly on the wharf, then headed for the Tampa Bay Hotel, where they pooled their funds. "The head waiter carefully selected a large table in the center of the immense dining room and he assigned the two best waiters." The cadets consumed one order of everything on the menu, to their own great satisfaction and, Wheeler wrote, apparently to the delight of the other guests.[41]

From Tampa, the *Chase* sailed to St. Petersburg, Florida, where she stayed for three months, and then to Charleston, South Carolina. Tragedy struck on 6 May 1897. While cruising east of Charleston, close-hauled on a starboard tack, the *Chase* was rammed by the schooner *Richard F. C. Hartley.* The *Hartley* smashed into the Chase's bow during the mid-watch, so most of the men on board were asleep when the collision occurred. The carpenter, after inspecting the Chase's hull, assured Captain Hamlet "that all damage was above the main deck," according to James F. Hottel, a retired rear admiral. "Daylight," he added, "disclosed a terrible mess which was cleaned up and an improvised rig set up."[42]

After the *Chase* limped into Charleston, the service towed her to Baltimore for repairs, which took two months to complete. During that time, the school gave the cadets leave. Subsequently, the *Hartley* was found responsible for the accident.[43]

During the Spanish-American War, the service graduated the class of 1898 early, without ceremony, on 21 April. The class had requested an early commencement in hopes of participating in the war, but Paul C. Prince was the only member of the class who received an assignment to a cutter that went into action; he was on the *Manning.* The school's superintendent from 1887 to 1890, Capt. Daniel B. Hodgsdon, commanded the *McCulloch* at the Battle of Manila Bay and served with distinction under Commodore Dewey.[44] By then, Shoemaker was in charge of the service.

Following the Spanish-American War, Capt. David A. Hall commanded the schoolship *Chase.* A native of Warren, Rhode Island, Hall had compiled a distinguished record in the U.S. Navy during the Civil War; he entered the Revenue Cutter Service on 8 March 1871. He was a good choice to lead young men, for he had a good disposition and was known for the "keen interest he took in the welfare of his many friends in the service."[45] In the summer of 1899, on his first cruise as skipper of the *Chase*, Hall took the cutter into New London, Connecticut, and New Bedford, then returned to Charleston for the winter. Toward the end of the following summer's cruise, he received orders to sail the *Chase* to Arundel Cove, Maryland, which was to become her new home port.[46]

Hall's orders marked the successful culmination of an idea developed by Lt. John C. Moore, a young engineer who wanted the Revenue Cutter Service to move into its own yard, where, he believed, repairs and maintenance could be done more reasonably than at commercial yards. Realizing that Congress might balk at funding a yard for the service, Moore convinced Captain Shoemaker that having the yard serve double duty as a site for a new school of instruction might help to sell the idea. Once convinced, Shoemaker provided $500 to take out a lease on a parcel of land at Arundel Cove. In 1900, the *Colfax* steamed into the cove, where her crew began to build a bulkhead and several small buildings. The *Chase* joined her there in November, and her crew immediately joined in the effort. A two-story shingled school building and a 400-foot, L-shaped pier were soon in place on the shores of the cove.[47]

At the end of 1900, Congress authorized $30,000 to purchase sixty-five acres of land at Curtis Bay, Maryland—the effort to create a yard and a site for a school had paid off. Unfortunately, Congress also removed from the service's budget $65,000 that had been designated for construction of a new cutter for the West Coast. The yard would be a permanent facility, however, so Moore and Shoemaker could be more than satisfied with their accomplishment.[48]

Facilities at Arundel Cove were spartan indeed. Johnson and Earle describe them as consisting "of a small carpenter shop, a boat shed, a store house, a dwelling, the Academy classroom building and a dock for the *Chase*."[49] Until 1906, when the school acquired the *Oriole*, built in 1838 as a sloop-of-war, to serve as living quarters, drill hall, and dance hall, cadets lived on board the *Chase*. The *Oriole* offered better accommodations, with four cadets to a cabin.

The classroom building had a drill hall on the first floor, three classrooms on the second floor, and storage space for the *Chase*'s sails and gear on the third floor. According to Capt. John P. Gray,[50]who had attended the school at Arundel Cove from 1906 to 1909, however, the school was the *Chase:* "Cadets, you see, spent most of their school lives aboard the sailing ship, the barkentine (it was a bark) U.S.S. Salmon P. Chase, sleeping and eating at their mess in cadet steerage. And during three summer months the ship was at sea, we cadets handled old-time deepwater chores from standing watches to slus[h]ing down the topmast. . . . It was a good life and a tough one."

Gray remembered living in two-man cabins in steerage that opened to the cadet mess. They had their own mess steward and treasurer and ate very well because, Gray wrote, they bought their own food out of their $500 annual pay. "The deck was a sanctuary for us," he wrote, "where we smoked—pipe and cigars only, and no chewing tobacco—and listened to salty yarns by the ship's sailors, most of them seamen with years before the mast."

Because there were so few cadets—there were thirty when Gray arrived at the school—there was no hazing. He remembered discipline as strict. For misdemeanors, cadets were deprived of liberty, which they normally received on Saturday evenings and Sunday afternoons. "All of us went up to Baltimore," Gray wrote, "taking the yard launch to Jack Flood's pier, then walking to the streetcar that went to town via the old Light street bridge. . . . Social activities included an occasional meal at the Rennert, visits to Ford's, the Auditorium and the Academy of Music and, of course, dates with young ladies." Dances were held at Arundel Cove; the cadets' dates came in from the city by streetcar. Many cadets met their future wives at those dances, according to Gray; he was one of them.

Cadets were kept busy from reveille to lights out, both on board the ship and on shore, but they found time for some recreation, such as baseball, the school's only organized sport, in the yard, where, according to Gray, they occasionally played against "St. John's, Maryland Agriculture, City College, and Gettysburg." They "also played Virginia Theological at Alexandria." (Johnson and Earle note that some cadets enjoyed informal tennis matches and sailing in local waters.[51])

By the time Gray arrived at Arundel Cove, the school had adopted a three year curriculum with emphasis on practical seamanship.[52] It also had a new superintendent. On 6 November 1902, William E. Reynolds relieved Hall as commander of the *Chase* and as superintendent of the

The cadet baseball team at Curtis Bay in 1903.

school. Reynolds, who would lead the school for five years, had an impressive background and a promising future. As a member of the sled party from the *Corwin* he had searched for the *Jeannette* on the Siberian coast (see chapter 2), and he had served on all U.S. coasts. He earned a law degree from Georgetown University, attended the Naval War College, commanded the Bering Sea Patrol, and fought in the Spanish-American War on board the *McLane*. After serving as the school superintendent, he went on to command the derelict destroyer *Seneca* and, ultimately, to lead the Coast Guard as its commandant.[53] While at the school, Reynolds made many significant changes.

When the school first went ashore at Arundel Cove, the administration restored some of the classes that had been eliminated during the seagoing-only phase of development. Changes in naval technology had

Capt. William Edward Reynolds

created a need for more knowledge of mathematics and science; in 1903, the school responded by adding a third year of instruction. In information provided to prospective cadets by MacVeagh in 1909, he listed the courses to be studied by cadets: "seamanship, navigation, gunnery, mathematics, naval architecture, marine engineering, English, history, international law, navigation law, physics, chemistry, electricity, wireless telegraphy, surveying, and French, and infantry and artillery drills, boat drills under oars and sails, etc."[54]

Significant changes were made at the school in 1906. In an act dated 23 June to promote the efficiency of the service, Congress provided for the appointment of cadet engineers for six months of training and authorized the school to hire two civilian instructors, one at a salary of $2,000 per year and another at $1,800. Newly commissioned third lieutenants were paid $1,700 a year at that time. Candidates for appointments as cadet engineers were required to have six months of practical experience in marine engineering, to be between twenty-one and twenty-six years of age, and to pass a competitive examination. While at the school, they received a salary of $75 a month plus one ration per day. Upon completion of their training, they filled positions as second assistant engineers.[55] The training period for engineering candidates was extended to one year in 1914, and, in 1926, all distinctions in the training of engineering cadets and cadets of the line ended. In 1906, the school used the two civilian openings to hire Professor Chester E. Dimmick to teach mathematics and Professor B. A. Carman to teach English and Spanish.[56]

In 1907, the U.S. Navy agreed to transfer the former gunboat *Bancroft*, an old Annapolis training ship, to the Revenue Cutter Service for use at the school. Secretary of the Treasury Leslie M. Shaw had begun campaigning to replace the *Chase* in 1904 when he told Congress that the wooden practice cutter was in desperate condition and not worth repairing. He wanted to replace the *Chase* with a new vessel and asked Congress to appropriate $70,000 for that purpose. The following year, Shaw specified "a seagoing sailing ship, with auxiliary steam power" to replace the *Chase*, but his efforts were only partially successful when Congress ordered transfer of the *Bancroft*.[57]

A two-masted auxiliary sailing vessel, the *Bancroft* was equipped with twin screws and triple-expansion reciprocating steam engines; she could be used for training under both steam and sail. Measuring 190 feet in length and 32 feet in the beam, she accommodated fifty cadets. The navy had built her in 1894 to replace the venerable *Constellation* as a training ship for the Naval Academy, but she proved to be too small for that purpose and Annapolis kept her for just two years. Essentially a miniature cruiser, the *Bancroft* was armed with fourteen 5- and 6-pounders, a torpedo tube, and a Gatling gun and carried armor plating. In 1907, she went into a Baltimore shipyard, where she was refitted with new water tube boilers, rerigged as a brigantine, and divided into separate, watertight compartments. The Revenue Cutter Service named the restored ship the *Itasca*.[58] In the words of former cadet John Gray, the *Itasca* "never held the place in our hearts occupied by the *Chase*."[59]

Shortly before her decommissioning, the *Chase* passed in review before
140 ships of the world's navies as part of the Virginia tercentennial celebration in 1907. According to Johnson and Earle, she "went out in a blaze
of glory. . . . A witness remembered it this way:

> The entire Atlantic fleet, with many foreign vessels, lay at anchor in
> stately array in Hampton Roads. Flying on before a fair breeze, with
> every sail drawing and gleaming white in the sunlight, spars beau-
> tifully clean and glistening with varnish, rigging taut as a bow string
> and all sheets home alike to the veriest inch. *Chase* stood gallantly
> down the line of warships, an incarnation of the spirit of romance
> and beauty of the sea, rounded to and dropped anchor in the exact po-
> sition assigned her in the formation."[60]

The service decommissioned the *Chase* that spring and reduced her to
service as a quarantine station at Baltimore.

The *Itasca*, commanded by Captain Reynolds, cruised to Europe and
the Mediterranean during the summer of 1907. The cadets had to swing
hammocks and store their gear in lockers and seabags, but visits to Mar-
seilles, France; Naples, Italy; and Algiers, North Africa, and their training on modern equipment must have made up for their former staterooms on the *Chase.* The *Itasca* returned to Baltimore via Saint Thomas
in the Virgin Islands and San Juan, Puerto Rico. She arrived home on
8 October.[61]

Capt. John E. Reinburg, who succeeded Reynolds as superintendent of
the school in January 1908, continued Captain Reynolds's policy of taking summer cruises to Europe and the Mediterranean. On the 1909
cruise, Gustavus U. Stewart, a new cadet from Kansas, kept a diary. Unfortunately, he filled the last page of his book just before reaching Venice,
Italy, the ultimate destination of the cruise, and no manuscript has been
found for the remainder of the trip. Stewart's diary is interesting, informative, and well written. The school placed considerable emphasis on
neatness and the correct use of English in written work. First Lt. Harold
D. Hinckley, executive officer on the 1909 summer cruise, demanded that
cadets submit neat papers when defending their conduct. It must be "free
from erasures . . . with close attention paid to the English used, to spelling,
and to punctuation," according to Cadet Fourth Class John B. Barrett,
who quoted Hinckley in his "Seamanship Notebook." The weekly hull-
board reports of the cadets are neat and well written.[62]

On 26 May 1909, a revenue cutter tug towed the *Itasca* out of Arundel Cove and beyond the drawbridge, where it anchored for the night. Cadet Stewart recorded feelings that night that most cadets have probably experienced: "I'm dreading the top a little but I wouldn't back out if I could as everybody at home wishes me to stay and it would look cowardly. I'll stay a year or two at any rate, if I can keep up in studies."[63] Stewart stayed for three years, graduated from the school in 1912, and retired from the Coast Guard as a captain in 1946.

Stewart quickly overcame his fear of climbing the rigging. On 27 May, he went aloft four times, twice before breakfast, but going aloft was dangerous. His concerns were reasonable and perhaps prudent. On 5 July, while the *Itasca* was sailing up the coast of Spain, a third classman, who subsequently left the school without graduating, fell from just eight feet below the top of the mainmast. Fortunately, he caught hold of the ratlines and escaped injury.[64]

Unforeseen by Stewart, but soon to be part of his life, was seasickness, which he never completely overcame during the first half of his fourth-class cruise. After the *Itasca* left Norfolk on 6 June, some of Stewart's shipmates were soon sick, which seems to have amused him. About 1700, he was sick himself and "let her go pretty good." Although the next day was another fine day, Stewart didn't feel well. He climbed the mainmast and recorded that he didn't care whether he fell off or not. "Almost everybody was more or less sick," he added. That night, he kept down his dinner and felt slightly better the following day, but he was "not at all well." On 9 June, he felt OK. As the *Itasca* was sailing at her maximum speed, about nine knots, Stewart was aloft. The ship was rocking, but he did not mind: "It's a case of simply holding on or fall for good, and it comes easy to hold on." The next day, he wrote that he felt very good and almost had his old appetite back. He had eaten his first "salt horse" (corned beef) and proclaimed it "not bad." But, on 11 June, he wrote that he could have been sick again, and the next day the ship pitched and rocked, and he felt bad.[65]

Another form of sickness common to young persons away from home for the first time gripped Stewart and held on. By 3 June, he wished he was at home. His high school's graduation was approaching, and he thought he might never see some of his school friends again. Ten days later, he wrote: "I read some old letters from home and elsewhere but stopped as it soon made me homesick (I'm bad enough already)." On 16 June, when Plymouth High School was having its graduation ceremonies, Stewart lamented his fate: "Oh! If I only could be there." He hoped that his parents would attend the ceremonies, even though he could not. Thereafter, his thoughts turned to other matters, but homesickness occasionally returned and Stewart was unable to explain why.[66]

The thought of visiting Europe excited Stewart. Just three days out of Arundel Cove, he expressed delight at the prospect of getting there. And what a trip the school had planned for the summer of 1909. The *Itasca* made a short stop at Ponta Delgada in the Azores, then visited Lisbon, Portugal; Gibraltar; Valencia, Spain; Villefranche-sur-Mer, France; and Genoa, Naples, Messina, Catania, Bari (to take on coal), and Venice, Italy. Despite his anticipation of seeing new lands and peoples, Stewart grew tired of the cruise about halfway across the Atlantic. On 11 June, he wrote of reaching the midway mark: "I'm glad for I am beginning to get tired of this life same as the rest. It's so dreary." The next day, he exclaimed, "How this blamed trip lags."[67]

On 24 June 1909, thirty days after leaving Arundel Cove, the *Itasca* moored at Lisbon to take a pilot on board, then proceeded to custom's house square and tied up. "The city is beautiful," Stewart wrote. The next day, he had shore leave from 1300 to 2200. He toured a church where the royal family was buried, went to an arsenal that held a collection of naval guns used by the Portuguese navy since 1500, and enjoyed a good meal in a restaurant. Again on 27 June, he had a great time in Lisbon.[68]

On 29 June, the *Itasca* sailed from Lisbon, bound for Gibraltar. Two days later, before the ship moored at Gibraltar, Stewart had his first look at Africa.[69] He went to a Spanish bullfight there on 4 July, but he did not mention the pageantry of the event, its nearly mystical religious nature, or its importance to Spain's heritage. His reaction was thoroughly American: "I have [had] enough of Spanish bull fights. . . . We sat beside the band on stone seats in the blazing sun. We only saw 3 of the 6 bulls killed but it's fierce. They have old decrepit horses which they blindfold + urge forward for the bull to gore which he does in good shape. Several of the horses had the entrails hanging out + if they didn't die they were sewed up + sent back until the bull buried his horn in a vital spot." Stewart described the rest of the bullfight, down to the matador killing the bull, and concluded: "How the people enjoy such things is more than I know."[70]

Stewart's attitude changed through the remainder of the journey; his diary reveals mood changes, frustration, boredom, and a desire to leave

Europe. On 8 July, he was homesick again. Four days later, he declared Villefranche "a beautiful place." Then at Naples, on 21 July, he got a cold, became hoarse, and could hardly speak. Before reaching Naples, the cadets had to box a compass correctly before they could go ashore. Stewart met the challenge and received shore leave on 24 and 28 July. He spent his first day at Pompeii, the last at Naples, which he found fairly dull; he added, "I'm getting sick of this dirty hole of Naples." Having reached the midpoint of the summer's cruise, he wrote that he hoped the last half would go faster than the first half. Three hours and forty-five minutes of leave gave him all he wanted of Messina. "Well," he wrote, "I've seen all I want to of wrecked Messina in that short time." He ended his diary, on the inside back cover, on 6 August, two days before the *Itasca* reached Venice, her final destination for the summer cruise.[71]

Stewart, along with the other cadets, trained throughout the cruise. He rowed a great deal, helped to sew a canvas cover for a medicine chest, participated in several ceremonial functions, stood his share of watches, tended sails, performed abandon ship and collision drills, and learned to navigate.[72]

Captain Reinburg led the school from 1908 to 1910. During his first year in charge, he began a campaign to find a new site for it. Arundel Cove had become overcrowded with the additions of a third year to the curriculum and new engineering cadets. The shipyard at the depot was noisy, and new facilities were needed so that the school could further expand its curriculum. Both Commandant Ross and Secretary of the Treasury George B. Cortelyou supported Reinburg's efforts to find a suitable location for the school. In 1908, Cortelyou told Congress that Curtis Bay was difficult to get to, had undesirable surroundings, and was "not suitable for the proper development and progress of the school." After considering various alternatives, Cortelyou concluded that Fort Trumbull, located on the Thames River in New London, Connecticut, was a proper site. He informed Congress that the War Department, which had jurisdiction over the fort, was willing to turn it over to the Treasury Department if Congress approved.[73]

In 1910, Cortelyou's efforts bore fruit. The War Department vacated the fort that summer, and the *Itasca*, with fifty cadets on board, sailed into her new home port at New London. The Treasury Department was most grateful. Praising the Revenue Cutter Service and its leaders, the new secretary, Franklin McVeagh, said:

This has enabled the department to gratify a cherished ambition of the service to enlarge and improve its facilities for instruction and extend its curriculum, and thus tone up its personnel. . . . The long and credible record of this well-disciplined service is secure in the hands of men of the right spirit, who are justly proud of the worthy traditions of the service.[74]

There is some disagreement about the basic character of the Arundel Cove site that the school left behind. In contrast to the official view of it as an unsatisfactory industrial area, Gray remembered it as "a lovely spot." While acknowledging that noise from the service's yard played a role in the decision to move, he remembered that "the only industry was farming. In early summer, we'd see all manner of small sailing boats heading up Curtis Creek, laden down with bedding belonging to the Baltimorians headed for Anne Arundel farms to pick fruit and berries." In another passage, he wrote: "We said good-by to the clear, crab filled waters of Arundel Cove."[75] Perhaps Gray's memories were just the nostalgic recollections of an older man looking back on his youth.

William V. E. Jacobs, ninth superintendent of the Revenue Cutter School of Instruction, oversaw the institution's move from Arundel Cove to New London. Jacobs had entered the school as a cadet on 14 September 1885, when it was located in New Bedford. Following his graduation in 1887, he served on board several cutters on the Atlantic and Pacific coasts and at Shields Cove, Minnesota. His service career included a tour of duty with the Life-Saving Service and a tour on board the *Hamilton* during the Spanish-American War. He then returned to the training ship *Chase* as a junior officer after she had moved to Arundel Cove. On 15 October 1902, Jacobs went back to sea on the *Tuscarora* at Milwaukee, Wisconsin. He later served on the *Manning,* commanded the Bering Sea Patrol as captain of the *Thetis,* and returned again to the school in March 1910, this time as superintendent and skipper of the *Itasca.*[76]

Jacobs loaded up the *Itasca* with cadets and as much of the Arundel Cove school as he could get on board. In New London, the reception for the *Itasca* and the cadets was anything but hospitable. When, on liberty, the cadets went to the Casino at Ocean Beach, the management refused to admit them in uniform. This brought a strong protest from Jacobs and a resulting apology from the Casino's management. Equally unpleasant was the fact that Fort Trumbull had no showers. Some cadets were even

Capt. William V. E. Jacobs

allowed to go home for a few weeks until the place could be made more habitable. Most of them lived on the *Itasca* until December.[77]

The new twenty-acre site did offer easy access to Long Island Sound and the open ocean. Captain Jacobs and his officers went to work to make it an acceptable school. They converted a low wooden building into a barracks and classrooms. A two-story stone structure became their administration building, and they made a small parade ground by cutting the weeds. On 15 September 1910, the army formally transferred the fort to the Revenue Cutter Service, which raised its colors over the venerable military site.[78]

The cadets were discouraged by the place. Rear Adm. Earl G. Rose recalls that the fort was "tall in weeds, a stony and forlorn looking place, devoid of creature comforts." Vice Adm. J. E. Stika remembers having to go to the Crocker House each week for a bath, until plumbing was installed in the basement of the barracks.[79]

The first class of sixteen cadets graduated from Fort Trumbull on 10 December 1910. The following year, President William Howard Taft formed the Cleveland Commission, which recommended complete elimination of the Revenue Cutter Service (see chapter 11). This had a profound impact on the school.

Between 1911 and 1914, the future of the school looked bleak indeed. In 1911, the secretary of the treasury recommended changing the law governing the filling of third lieutenant billets in the Revenue Cutter Service to permit graduates of the Naval Academy to fill those billets. His annual report for the year notes: "The duty of recruiting the commissioned personnel of any service is a most serious one, and is second in importance only to the duty of performing the work for which the service is maintained, for the future efficiency of a military service depends most upon the quality and training of the young men selected to fill the vacancies in the lowest grade."[80]

As Curtis, who signed the report for the secretary, had calculated the service's needs in 1911, there would be twenty-nine vacancies in the officer corps over the following fourteen years, or an average of two vacancies per year. There were twenty-eight cadets of the line at the school in 1911; when the last of them had graduated in 1913, the known vacancies in the line would be filled. For fourteen years after 1913, he believed, the service would need only two new officers per year, and such a small number would not justify the expense of keeping the school open. Thus, he recommended modifying the law to allow Naval Academy graduates to fill revenue cutter billets.[81]

The following year, Curtis changed his mind, but by then Congress had passed the sundry bill for 1913, which declared: "No additional appointments as cadets or cadet engineers shall be made in the Revenue Cutter Service, unless hereafter authorized by Congress." Curtis found himself in the awkward position of being unable to fill ten vacancies in the officer corps because of that bill. Between 30 June 1911 and 1 July 1912, 14 officers had died, resigned, or retired, and 1 would retire in 1912. Thirteen of the eighteen cadets at the school would fill vacancies existing prior to 1 July 1911; five cadets remained to fill the fifteen vacancies that had occurred since that date. The service would fall 10 officers below its authorized number of 242 officers, which resulted in a large percentage indeed in such a small officer corps. Reversing his evaluation of 1911, Curtis recommended changing the cadet authorization. Captain Bertholf, in his annual report for 1912, also recommended relief from the previous year's congressional measure.[82]

Bertholf's support of Curtis might have been motivated in part by concern about the use of the *Itasca* as a relief vessel when she was not actively employed on cadet cruises. This practice made good sense—it allowed the service to repair cutters on the Atlantic Coast without leaving a station defenseless—but it might have indicated to Bertholf the truly precarious state of the school.[83]

The appeals of the secretary and the commandant bore fruit. In its sundry bill for 1914, Congress authorized the appointment of seven cadets in 1915. The school was saved, and the service now asked for the authority to appoint seven cadets each year to fill the average number of officer vacancies in the service.[84] Granting this request would guarantee a cadet corps of twenty-one young men.

In 1914, Captain Billard relieved Jacobs as superintendent. Jacobs went on to serve another twelve years in the Revenue Cutter Service and the Coast Guard. He retired at the mandatory retirement age of sixty-four, after more than forty years of service. Before his retirement, Jacobs would serve a tour as superintendent of the U.S. Coast Guard Academy from October 1919 to March 1923. This was the second change of name for the school in as many years. Billard changed it to the U.S. Revenue Cutter Academy shortly after he took charge; a year later, it became the Coast Guard Academy.[85]

Cadets at the school in its final years under the Revenue Cutter Service were required to be U.S. citizens of good moral character, between the ages of eighteen and twenty-five, and at least 5 feet 4 inches tall. Applicants took an entrance examination, administered by the Treasury Department in Washington at their own expense. (This marked a change from the procedure in 1908, when officers administered examinations for cadet and cadet-engineer candidates at nineteen locations on the Atlantic, Pacific, and Gulf coasts and on the Great Lakes.) Cadet candidates first had to pass a physical examination given by a board of officers from the Public Health Service and Marine Hospital Service. Then, they became eligible to

take a competitive academic examination administered by the officers of
the Revenue Cutter Service. Each officer on a board of examiners read
each candidate's examination, and the mean marks given by all of the
board members was taken as a candidate's mark for each question. The
candidate had to earn a grade of 70 to pass the examination.[86]

The competitive examination took about four days to finish. It consisted of the following subjects and assigned weights:

spelling	10	physics	7
algebra	10	grammar	5
geometry	10	composition	10
geography	7	English literature	8
world history and		modern language (French,	
constitution of		German, or Spanish)	5
the United States	8	general information	5

The board also considered a candidate's suitability for the service, which
was worth 5 points, and took into account letters of recommendation
and a candidate's bearing and general appearance, as rated by members
of a subboard who had met the candidate.[87]

The way the service administered the examination, its content, and
the weights assigned to the various subjects reveals important information about the service and the society it served. Because each candidate
had to travel to Washington to take a four-day examination, one can
safely conclude that almost all of the candidates came from the upper and
upper-middle socioeconomic classes. Successful candidates had to know
a considerable amount of world history, English literature, and a European language, which indicated the western orientation of the society
they represented. Mastery of the liberal arts determined more than two
thirds of the examination grade, and more than one fourth came from
knowledge of the English language alone, about the same weight assigned to science and mathematics combined. By comparison, today's
academy counts a candidate's score on the mathematics section of the
standardized Scholastic Aptitude Test twice, whereas his or her score on
the verbal section of the test is counted only once. Also, candidates today
can take the examination at almost any high school in the nation.

Secretary MacVeagh's 1909 booklet of information for prospective
cadets (mentioned earlier) included nine pages of sample questions that
had been given in a previous examination. The successful candidate

clearly needed a good educational background. He was expected to spell correctly such words as transient, scythe, sovereign, nuisance, tendency, miscellaneous, and convalescent. His first task on the grammar section was to analyze a complicated sentence without using a diagram. He had to write an essay of at least three hundred words on a designated subject; it was marked for errors in form, spelling, capitalization, punctuation, syntax, style, and adherence to subject.

In English literature, the candidate had to name the authors of ten works, including *The Prisoner of Chillon, The Compleat Angler,* and *Utopia;* name the books in which ten (listed) characters appeared and the authors of those works; write about such persons as Cotton Mather, James Boswell, and Samuel Pepys; and give a brief account of Jonathan Swift, Alexander Pope, or Thomas Macaulay. He had to translate a substantive historical passage from English into French, German, or Spanish (his choice of language) and another paragraph from the chosen foreign language into English. The vocabulary of the passages to be translated was difficult, and the verb structures were complicated, according to Professor Attilio DeFilippis, who taught French and Spanish at the Coast Guard Academy from 1967 to 1993 (personal conversation).

The section on world history and the U.S. Constitution ranged from questions about the preamble of the Constitution to when it is necessary for the chief justice to preside over the Senate; from giving a brief account of the Spanish Armada to giving accounts of Charlemagne, Talleyrand, Scipio Africanus, Danton, and the Duke of Alva; and from explaining the Missouri Compromise to writing about George Mason and John Slidell. The examination sought general information about the identity of the speaker of the House of Representatives, the U.S. ambassador to England, and the president of Harvard University. A successful candidate was expected to know the ranking officer in the navy; how often the nation took a census; the names of five continental railroads in North America; and something about J. P. Morgan, William P. Frye, and Alexander Graham Bell. In geography, a prospective cadet had to name all of the seaboard states in the United States and give their capitals; name the three rivers that rise in the mountains of Colorado; describe the general course of the Gulf Stream; fix the positions of the Balkans and of the Pyrenees, Himalayas, Altai Mountains, and Hindu Kush Mountains; and name five large islands in the Mediterranean Sea.

The mathematics, geometry, and physics sections of the examination were time-consuming and quite difficult. A candidate was expected to be able to use the cube root in problem solving. Peter Seaman, a recent Coast Guard Academy graduate who was first in his class, indicates that today's cadets would need about one semester of physics at the academy to answer the questions posed in that field (personal conversation).

The successful candidate had to deposit $150 with the school superintendent to defray the cost of uniforms. While at the school, each cadet received a salary of $500 per year plus one ration per day. The school took $10 from his pay each month to pay for officer uniforms, which would be needed when he successfully completed the three-year course of study. Upon graduation as a newly commissioned third lieutenant, he would receive a salary of $1,700 per year.[88] It should be noted that a cadet's pay was not a salary given for services rendered. It was provided so that cadets could pay for their uniforms, books, and other incidental expenses, including travel to and from their homes.[89]

The newly named U.S. Revenue Cutter Academy that a successful candidate entered in 1914 emphasized practical professional knowledge for the full three years of study and drew a sharp distinction between line and engineering cadets.[90] Billard ran the academy under the control of the secretary of the treasury and the commandant of the Revenue Cutter Service. As a line officer of captain's rank, Billard controlled all property at the academy, presided over the board of instruction, and commanded the practice cutter *Itaska.* He was the only officer assigned to the academy who had no teaching assignment.

Billard's executive officer was responsible for security, discipline, the government of the academy, and maintenance of all buildings and grounds. On cruises, the executive officer took responsibility for all practical and theoretical work related to seamanship; he also taught seamanship on shore. He inspected cadet uniforms and quarters daily, assigned sleeping quarters and seats at the mess, and kept a daily conduct report on each cadet.

The senior engineering officer took charge of the *Itasca*'s machinery afloat and of cadet education in all work related to steam engineering.

Of the four junior officers, the officer of the line below the executive officer navigated the *Itasca* at sea and was in charge of navigation instruction. A commissary officer ran the mess. Any officer or civilian faculty member could be assigned by the superintendent to supervise cadet athletic exercises, and all officers, except the superintendent, executive officer, and senior engineering officer, rotated as duty officer. A medical officer from the Public Health Service cared for sick and injured cadets, assured proper hygienic conditions at the academy, gave each cadet a physical examination at the end of each term, prescribed physical exercise for cadets, and supplied the superintendent with daily sick call information.

A board of instruction considered matters related to the course of instruction, the general system of training, and cadet discipline. All officers and civilian instructors assigned to the academy made up the board, but civilians and the medical officer did not vote on matters of discipline or on the fitness of cadets for service, except that the medical officer voted on a cadet's physical fitness to serve. A majority of the members present for duty constituted a quorum, a majority of which was required for a decision. Each member had one vote and had to cast it. In case of a tie vote, the superintendent, who was president of the board, had one additional vote. Minority reports could be filed. Meetings were called by the president or by a written request from any three members. The action of the board was confidential.

In general, the board considered the course of instruction at the academy and any cadet's deficiency in academic performance, conduct, or suitability for the service. Within five days of the end of each term, the board met to decide upon each cadet's suitability for service. It could recommend that a cadet resign or that he be dismissed. All board members were obliged to report any cadet whom they thought unfit for duty. The board then considered the case and took action. If it decided that the cadet was fit to serve, it kept no report. If it decided the cadet was unfit, it wrote a report and sent it to the Treasury Department, with a recommendation for action. The board sought the opinion of the medical officer and each civilian faculty member in each case, although these individuals did not vote, except the medical officer, as noted above, on issues of medical fitness.

The cadet corps consisted of three classes of cadets of the line and one class of cadet engineers. Senior cadets were first classmen, second-year cadets were second classmen, and new cadets were third classmen. Cadet engineers took precedence after first classmen in positions at formations, assignment of quarters, and seats at table.

The school year, consisting of two academic terms and one sea term, began on 1 June and ended on 31 May. The sea term ran from 1 June to 14 October, the first term from 15 October to 31 January, and the second term from 1 February to 31 May. The sea term included a practice cruise and practical instruction at the academy. The superintendent could grant leave to cadets meriting it, except for the new cadets, from the end of the cruise to 14 October. He could grant liberty on all federal holidays, any days between December 24 and January 1, and when in port during the sea term. When a cadet went on liberty, he personally had to sign out and back in at the academy and note the time of his departure and return.

A cadet's life was dominated by "thou-shall-nots." He could not smoke tobacco, consume alcoholic beverages, or gamble. He had to get permission from the executive officer before he could discuss his grades with an instructor. Except at night, he could not lie on his bed. He could not contract a debt, go swimming, or go onto ice without permission from the superintendent.

Cadets earned liberty by good conduct and avoidance of demerits for violating regulations. Cadets who stood at the top of their class in this regard were granted liberty every Saturday from 1300 to 2330, every Sunday from after church to 2155, and every Thursday from 1615 to 1800. In addition, first classmen were given liberty every Tuesday from 1615 to 1800. Cadets who just barely merited liberty, but who were not restricted, were free from 1300 to 1800 on the first and third Saturdays of the month and on the fifth Sunday, when there was one.

A cadet's daily routine, except for Saturday and Sunday, began with reveille at 0630 and ended with taps and lights out at 2205. He formed up for morning roll call at 0700, followed by breakfast. Immediately after breakfast, he returned to his room and prepared for inspection. At 0800, he formed up to go to his first recitation period, which lasted until 0845. Between 0845 and 0930, he studied in his room. (Sick call, for those who needed it, was at 0900.) A second recitation period ran from 0930 to 1015 and a third from 1015 to 1100.

The executive officer, at his own discretion, inspected cadet rooms between 1100 and 1110, when a forenoon drill or exercise was scheduled, followed at 1215 by lunch formation. After lunch, a fourth recitation period ran from 1300 to 1400 or, at the discretion of the instructor, until 1500. After a cadet was released from recitation, he studied in his room until 1500. Dinner formation was at 1800. Call to rooms for study at 1930 followed dinner, and the study period lasted until 2130. Warning call sounded at 2155, followed by tattoo at 2200 prior to taps and lights out.

The routine on Saturday and Sunday was somewhat relaxed. The academy held classes in drawing and signaling on Saturday morning, which were followed by an inspection of quarters by the executive officer at his discretion. The school gave deserving cadets liberty at 1300. Dinner was scheduled for 1800, as usual, but nothing else was scheduled for the rest of the day until warning call. Sunday's reveille was not until 0700. At 0900, cadets mustered, then went to their rooms, where they remained until recall from inspection. They formed up for church at 1000. Nothing else was scheduled for the rest of the day except meals and the formal ending of the day.

All cadets had to attend church in New London on Sunday. If there was no church of their denomination and if it would offend their beliefs to attend any of the churches there, they could be excused, but they had to present written confirmation of the facts from their parents.

In 1914, the academy emphasized practical training for the professional officer. The board of instruction had developed a curriculum heavily weighted in professional subjects, and it selected all textbooks, which were approved by the Treasury Department.

Cadets of the line took six terms of seamanship, navigation, French, signals, hygiene, and drawing, with seamanship and navigation rated most important. Navigation included some astronomy during the third-class year and some surveying during the second term of the first-class year. Service regulations were studied every semester except the first, and cadets studied mathematics and drill every semester except the first two. They studied five additional courses in each of the last four terms at the academy (gunnery, navigation law, naval architecture, steam engineering, and radiotelegraphy). They took English, history, and electricity in both terms of the third-class year; international law in both terms of the first-class year; one term of civil government in the first term at the academy; and one term of military law in the last term.

Cadet engineers took two terms each of seamanship, drill regulations, naval architecture, English, steam engineering, service regulations, French, signals, hygiene, and drawing, and one term each of navigation, gunnery, navigation law, international law, electricity, and radiotelegraphy.

The *Regulations for the Academy* stressed that, in addition to the theoretical instruction in the subjects studied, "practical work and instructions to the fullest extent possible shall be given in each subject where the nature of the subject and the equipment available permit." The faculty had to make every effort "to develop in the cadets the qualities of zeal, energy, judgment, thoroughness, and promptness of action essential to the proper performance of their future duties as commissioned officers. All drills and practical exercises" were to "be so conducted and the performance of all duties so supervised as to instill in the cadets the habit of obedience and to train them to the best advantage in the discharge of responsibilities and in the exercise of command." Finally, the academy imparted "practical instruction in the duties of an officer by detailing cadets of the first class as officer of the day, and during the practice cruise as officer of the deck. Practice in the handling of men [was] given by placing cadets in charge of boats and of working parties and by detailing them to conduct drills."[91]

There was a tremendous dissonance between the demanding academic admissions examination required of all cadets and a curriculum that was heavily weighted in professional subjects taught in a most practical manner. The emphasis of the academy in 1914 was clearly on training, rather than education. Perhaps the years of accepting only cadets who had completed their education and then providing them with two years of seagoing training continued to have a residual impact on the academy in 1914.

In addition to their academic classes, cadets participated in drills and exercises. They drilled with pistols, rifles, artillery pieces, bayonets, and cutlasses; took target practice with small arms and rapid-fire guns; and learned to handle boats under sails and oars and to run a power launch. They practiced making rescues with the breeches buoy apparatus used by the Life-Saving Service, and they fenced, danced, and exercised regularly.

During sea terms, cadets of the line studied seamanship, navigation, and engineering in each of their three years at the academy. To that base, they added signals during their third- and second-class years and radiotelegraphy during their first-class year. Cadet engineers studied seamanship, navigation, engineering, and signals during their sea terms. In addition, every officer on the *Itasca*, except the medical officer, marked every cadet, on a weekly basis, for adaptability for service during all but the cadet's last sea term, when he was marked for professional fitness.

The academy gave examinations in each subject at the end of each term. The instructor made out his examination and submitted it to the board of instruction for approval before administering it. Any examination marked unsatisfactory by an instructor was marked independently by a second instructor designated by the superintendent. If the two marks were within 5 points (out of 100 points) of each other, the first mark stood. If the two independent marks varied by more than 5 points, the two instructors graded the paper together and the mark they decided upon was final. At the end of each month and at the end of each term, the superintendent sent a report of marks to each cadet's parents. The reports for January and May included the cadet's marks for the first and second terms, respectively.

A board of officers from the Public Health Service gave a final physical examination to each cadet who successfully completed the academic and sea terms at the academy and met the requirements for conduct. If he passed his physical examination, the board of instruction recommended a cadet of the line for a third lieutenant's commission and an engineering cadet for a third lieutenant of engineer's commission.

CHAPTER TEN

The U.S.
Life-Saving Service

T he federal government established the U.S. Life-Saving Service (LSS), a shore-based service, in 1848 to save the lives and property of shipwrecked mariners. The first such effort had been made by the Massachusetts Humane Society, incorporated in 1791, which built small, unmanned huts on the outer beaches of Massachusetts. These were crude one-story buildings that housed a stove and food for use by shipwrecked mariners. In 1807, the society built the first lifeboat station at Cohasset. After that lifeboats became increasingly common. In the winter of 1836–37, two shipwrecks on Long Island increased interest in the construction of lifeboats for use from shore as well as on board ship. New York boatbuilder Joseph Francis designed and built a lifeboat with watertight compartments around 1837. Volunteers at Rockaway, New York, had one by the end of that year, and newspapers began to urge their use all along the New York and New Jersey shores. By 1845, the Massachusetts Humane Society operated eighteen lifeboat stations and many huts of refuge on the coast of Massachusetts.[1]

In 1839, a New Orleans packet advertised its intention to sail with a Joseph Francis lifeboat, which it claimed could sustain all passengers. The next day, an editorial remarked that life-saving devices were of much greater importance "than damask tablecloths, silver forks, or anything which is merely intended to please the eye." Nonetheless, many lives were lost over years of sailing before adequate lifeboats were provided for passengers.

The same was true of life preservers. Following the loss of the Black Ball liner *Albion* on the coast of Ireland in 1822, which resulted in a great loss of life, two men demonstrated a life-preserving dress in waters around Governors Island, New York. Apparently, life preservers were subsequently sold to any passengers who cared to buy them, but they were not widely used until after a wreck off Hatteras, North Carolina, in 1837, when some passengers wearing them survived. They seem to have been provided thereafter only to coastal steamers, and a very long time passed before the government required operators to provide them for all passengers.[2]

A national rescue organization had to await the shocking loss of life that attended the flood of immigrants following the Irish potato famine of 1846 and the unsuccessful revolution of German states in 1848. Most of the merchant ships carrying immigrants to America arrived at New York, the busiest port in the nation. As the ships piled up along the New Jersey and Long Island beaches, many were tragically lost. Between 1818 and 1848, an average of ninety ships were destroyed each year. Several of the wrecks each resulted in the loss of more than a hundred lives off the coast of New York.

Congress responded by appropriating $5,000 for the rescue of shipwreck victims in 1847. Because marine disasters often occurred near lighthouses, whose keepers had traditionally offered assistance to mariners, the Treasury Department initially assigned the job of lifesaving to them. That same year, the voters of New Jersey elected William A. Newall to Congress. A physician by training and profession, he had witnessed the wreck of the Austrian brig *Terasto* with the loss of thirteen lives. He added an amendment to a lighthouse appropriations bill, dated 14 August 1848, that created the Life-Saving Service. The bill appropriated $10,000 to purchase surfboats, rockets, carronades, and other rescue equipment to be used at stations between Sandy Hook and Little Egg Harbor, New Jersey. Supervision of the effort was to be assigned to a Revenue Cutter Service officer designated by the secretary of the treasury.[3]

Secretary Robert J. Walker appointed Capt. Douglass Ottinger to the job. Ottinger built eight stations along the prescribed stretch of beach, the first one at Spermacetti Cove near Sandy Hook. The first stations, according to York, were "little more than crude one-and-a-half-story frame boathouses, 16 feet wide by 28 feet long. The single room on the first floor housed the surf-boat and other rescue equipment while a small loft above was used for storage. On the outside, each was covered with two or three layers of shingles on the walls and roof and painted or whitewashed."[4]

Shoemaker notes that Ottinger placed in each station the equipment that existed for making rescues: "hawsers, hauling lines, shot-lines, rocket frames, rockets and lines, blocks and tackles, mortars and balls."[5]

Ottinger also claimed to have invented the iron lifecar, but Francis, who built the first lifecar, challenged Ottinger's claim of invention. This led to a long controversy that has left most historians accepting Francis as the inventor. More important, Sumner Kimball believed that Francis had invented the lifecar.[6] He, of course, knew both men well and was familiar with all aspects of the LSS and its history.

The lifecar was essentially a covered metal boat that could be hauled back and forth from ship to shore on the surface of the water. It was shaped like a football with a hatch on top, for entry and exit, and a big ring at each end, for securing lines. The only unique piece of equipment purchased by Ottinger, it was especially useful in very heavy surf, when a wreck occurred at a great distance from shore, or when injured persons had to be rescued. Six or seven persons could fit into the lifecar.[7]

Untrained volunteers could haul the simple device through the surf to and from a wreck. On the occasion of its first use, the lifecar saved 248 of the 249 persons on the wrecked British immigrant ship *Ayrshire*, which was driven ashore at Squam Beach, New Jersey, on 12 January 1850. John Maxen of the lifesaving station there fired a line to the ship with a mortar and used a Francis lifecar as a rescue vehicle. The weather was so severe that no boat could have survived in the surf. In sixty trips, the lifecar carried 47 crewmen and 201 passengers to safety. A passenger named Bell, who insisted upon clinging to the outside of the car while the lifesavers hauled his family to the beach, was washed away and drowned.[8]

After Newall's initiative, Congress passed additional legislation to expand the Life-Saving Service. In 1849, Lt. John McGowan built six new stations in New Jersey, and Edward Watts, a civil engineer in the Treasury Department, added another eight along the coast of Long Island. The following year, Lt. Joseph Noyes built new stations on Long Island and extended the service to Rhode Island. By 1854, the LSS was operating fifty-five stations and approximately eighty lifeboats and surfboats on the Atlantic Coast, Gulf Coast, and Great Lakes. By then, there were new stations on the beaches of the Carolinas, Georgia, Florida, and Texas. Unfortunately, the department assigned no crews to the new stations. It made a few lighthouse keepers responsible for the stations, and they depended on volunteers to care for the equipment and to respond to each crisis as it developed. As a result, most of the stations fell into disrepair. Service was spotty, at best, and a series of tragic disasters followed.[9]

One such disaster stimulated Congress to take action. On 16 April 1854, the *Powhattan* wrecked below Beach Haven, New Jersey, within six miles of an LSS station. More than 200 persons on board perished. Congress responded by appointing paid superintendents for the coasts of New York and New Jersey and assigned paid keepers to stations in those states, but it failed to appropriate money to pay for the keepers until 1857. According to Shoemaker, who worked with the LSS during many years of his career in the Revenue Cutter Service, even this legislation failed to bear fruit because appointments were made for political reasons and without regard for the good of the service. As a result, he states: "No one in the management evinced other than indifference to the service which was struggling into life, and so it floundered along, without organization, without regulations[,] without drive or discipline, or an effort to attain any of these, piling up year after year a record of utter worthlessness and inefficiency."[10]

Means pointed out, however, that "it is clear . . . that in spite of poor organization, mismanagement, general neglect, and scanty support, the early service accomplished noble work. Manned only by make-shift crews as each occasion of shipwreck demanded, the stations proved valuable in preserving life and property from storm and sea." In his annual report for 1872, Kimball, then superintendent of the Life-Saving Service, acknowledged that no records of disaster had been kept before 1855 and only irregular records after that, but he estimated that at least 4,163 lives and property valued at $716,000 had been saved by the service. The figures, he believed, would have been much higher had accurate records been kept.[11]

A victim of public indifference and neglect, the Life-Saving Service languished throughout the Civil War. The following year, Congressman Newall again prodded Congress into action. It appropriated $10,000 for new stations and equipment to be used on the same stretch of beach in New Jersey that had been protected as the result of Newall's original amendment. Three years later, the New Jersey legislature tried without success to convince Congress of the need for paid crews at the stations.

Congressman Charles Haight followed up with a compromise proposal, which became law in 1870, to man every other station with six surfmen. The next winter, several disasters caused Congress to appropriate $200,000 to enable the secretary to employ paid crews at any stations he chose for as long as he thought necessary. With this bill, Congress made the service respectable.[12]

Paid crews living at the stations were important because they could respond to shipwrecks without delay. Vessels that ran aground along the U.S. coast usually did not break up within the first few hours on shore, and timely responses offered opportunities for successful rescue operations.

More important than the bill for paid crews was the appointment of Sumner Increase Kimball to lead both the Revenue Cutter Service and the Life-Saving Service. Secretary of the Treasury George S. Boutwell offered Kimball the job in February 1871. This capable, dedicated public servant (see chapter 2) took a week to consider the offer. He told Boutwell that he would accept the job if Boutwell would promise to support efforts to reform the service. Also, Kimball warned Boutwell that pressure from politicians insisting that he was ruining the organization would be tremendous. Having been assured that Boutwell could take the pressure and would not interfere, Kimball accepted the position. He was in charge of both services until 1878; after that, he led the Life-Saving Service until 1915. According to Means, Kimball's acceptance of the job was the "most important event in the history of the Life-Saving Service."[13] It is hard to argue with that conclusion—by 1890, Kimball had made the service the model of its kind in the world.

He began by appointing Capt. John Faunce, a revenue cutter officer who had repaired old stations and built new ones for the LSS in the 1840s, to survey the condition of the stations. Lt. L. N. Geddis accompanied Faunce on his inspection tour. The two officers evaluated each station, its equipment, and the crew. On 9 August 1871, Faunce submitted a report of his findings to Kimball. Most stations, he wrote, were rundown and showed evidence of neglect and, in many cases, were too far apart. Equipment had rusted, deteriorated, or been stolen. Some stations lacked such basic supplies as shovels, powder, and rockets, and no station had all of the equipment it was supposed to have. Some keepers were too old and infirm to perform their duties. Others lived too far from their stations to be effective. Some keepers and surfmen who had been appointed for political reasons were incompetent. The practice of paying crews at every other station had been a grave mistake. There were paid crews at less important locations than those depending on volunteers for rescues. Resentment and discontent were the predictable products of this practice.[14]

Responding to Faunce's report, Kimball initiated reforms before the winter gales of 1871 hit the coast. He had revenue cutter officers supervise the dismantling of some of the worn-out stations, build new stations at more strategic locations, and repair stations that could be saved. They replaced equipment where it was needed and fired incompetent keepers and crewmen. The LSS also adopted a standard model for a station. During 1871 and 1872, Congress appropriated a total of $50,000 to erect new stations on the beaches of Rhode Island and Cape Cod.[15]

During 1871 and 1872, the LSS made major advances. It reduced the distance between stations to about three miles, developed a system of signaling that made it possible for a crew at one station to call nearby stations for help, and initiated a beach patrol that kept the coastline under surveillance in all kinds of weather. In May 1872, Kimball appointed a commission, with Capt. James H. Merryman in charge, to test and review lifesaving equipment used around the world. On 1 September, Merryman submitted a report to Kimball that led the LSS to adopt the breeches buoy and the cork life belt for rescues. Finding no satisfactory lifeboat, Kimball had one developed by making modifications to a cedar surfboat in general use along the New Jersey shore. The resulting success of the service in 1871–72 inspired widespread support in Congress.[16]

During 1872 and 1873, Congress appropriated a total of $30,000 to establish signal stations at lighthouses and LSS stations, where flags by day and rockets by night informed passing ships of danger and weather conditions.[17]

On 10 June 1872, Congress called for the construction of new stations under the supervision of two revenue cutter captains. Subsequently, Kimball appointed Captains Faunce and Merryman as superintendents of construction, and new stations were built on the coasts of Massachusetts, Rhode Island, New York, and New Jersey.[18]

Merryman, who was first appointed to serve with the LSS on 18 June 1872, also wrote a comprehensive set of regulations for the service, which the government promulgated on 11 January 1873. Those regulations established order and discipline in all of the service's operations. Merryman served the LSS, with the title, Inspector of Life-Saving Stations and Superintendent of Construction, until the late 1880s. His intelligence, leadership, and energy contributed greatly to the service's success and secured for him the confidence and trust of Sumner Kimball.[19]

In response to an act of Congress dated 3 March 1873, Kimball, Faunce, and Merryman surveyed the U.S. coast and sought information from the maritime community to determine where additional LSS stations should be erected. Subsequently, the service extended its reach to the beaches of Delaware, Maryland, Oregon, California, and the Great Lakes.[20] By 1878, the Life-Saving Service had expanded to a total of 148 stations on the Atlantic Coast, Pacific Coast, and Great Lakes.

Kimball divided those stations into the following eleven (later to be thirteen) districts:[21]

DISTRICT	AREA	NO. OF STATIONS
No. 1	Coast of Maine and New Hampshire	6
No. 2	Coast of Massachusetts	14
No. 3	Coast of Rhode Island and New York	36
No. 4	Coast of New Jersey	9
No. 5	Coast of Cape Henlopen, Delaware, to Cape Charles, Virginia	6
No. 6	Coast of Cape Henry, Virginia, to Cape Hatteras, North Carolina	10
No. 7	Eastern coast of Florida	5
No. 8	Lakes Erie and Ontario	9
No. 9	Lakes Huron and Superior	9
No. 10	Lake Michigan	12
No. 11	Pacific Coast	2

One hundred twenty-five of the stations were complete lifesaving stations, with a keeper and a regular crew of surfmen, that remained open from December until May. All were on the Atlantic Coast between Maine and Cape Hatteras. Sixteen of the stations on the Great Lakes and two on the Pacific Coast were lifeboat stations with a paid keeper and an enrolled crew of volunteers. The five stations on the coast of Florida were refuges, with a paid keeper but no crew, where shipwrecked mariners could find shelter and food.[22]

Shoemaker notes that between his appointment in 1871 and 30 June 1878, Kimball had raised the reputation of the LSS to a status "known for its deeds the world over." He had extended the service, limited in 1871 to the coast of New York and New Jersey, "to portions of the whole eastern seaboard, from Maine to Florida and upon the Great Lakes from Ontario to Michigan and Superior." Kimball had improved its lifesaving equipment by importing and improving the best foreign devices, such as the breeches buoy and self-righting and self-bailing boats from England, Shoemaker continues. The light and incomparable Lyle gun had replaced heavy and cumbersome lifesaving ordnance. In addition, Kimball had provided the new stations with capable keepers and surfmen who made good use of the new equipment, in part as a result of improved training drills developed by First Lt. Charles H. McLellan of the Revenue Cutter Service.[23]

Later, in 1899, McLellan assembled a motor lifeboat, powered by an internal combustion engine, that led to establishment of a commission to develop a motorboat suitable for the LSS. By 1915, the service was operating 80 motor lifeboats and about 150 power surfboats.[24]

During the seven years that Kimball ran both the LSS and the cutter service, the latter detailed nineteen officers (six captains and thirteen lieutenants) to serve with the Life-Saving Service. They supervised the construction of stations; inspected the stations and their crews and equipment; drilled the crews in the use of boats in the surf and in the use of lifesaving apparatus; and examined the stations' keepers and surfmen. Two revenue cutter officers and one Marine Hospital Service officer made up a board of examiners that inspected lifesaving stations for the department. The report of the Life-Saving Service for 1877 outlines the board's objectives. It held the examination as early in the season as possible, in part to eliminate unworthy men and motivate the stations' crews for the coming season.

In 1877, within one district, five of eight keepers and one fifth of the surfmen examined were found to be incompetent and unequal to their duties. The examiners found clear evidence of neglect. Many stations had failed to arrange the new apparatus provided by Kimball in a usable manner. The board tried to impress on the men in the district their grave responsibility to improve their lifesaving skills and sought to discover the cause of the problem. The examiners concluded that it had resulted from the district superintendent's misunderstanding of his job. Local politicians had skillfully worked on the superintendent's fears to convince him to appoint and retain unqualified men whom they wanted employed. They had succeeded in their effort by making the superintendent believe that they spoke for the department and that his job was in jeopardy if he failed to take their advice. Of course, none of this was true.[25]

Other cutter officers delivered examiners, supplies, boats, lifesaving equipment, and inspectors to LSS stations. In seven years, their cutters sailed nearly 130,000 miles to perform these services.[26]

Cutter officers continued these duties for the Life-Saving Service after the separation of the two services in 1878. By 1892, the cutters had sailed more than 400,000 miles while working for the Life-Saving Service. The entire cost of officers and cutters serving the lifesavers was borne by the Revenue Cutter Service.[27]

Two maritime disasters threatened the LSS with a takeover by the U.S. Navy, but Kimball's accomplishments between 1871 and 1878 made it possible for supporters in Congress to beat off the assault and to establish the service as an independent agency in the Treasury Department. On 24 November 1877, the navy's 541-ton, barkentine-rigged screw steamer *Huron* ran aground in a gale and broke up within 2½ miles of Station No. 7 at Nags Head, North Carolina. Ens. Lucian Young fired five rockets and burned over one hundred Coston flares, all that were on board, in an effort to attract attention to the wreck. The nearby, inactive lifesaving station failed to respond. A few fishermen went down to the shore, but they either did not know how to use the station's equipment or did not dare to break into the station to get it. Receiving no help from shore, 98 of 132 men on board perished.[28]

Two months later, on 31 January 1878, the aging wooden steamer *Metropolis*, which never should have put to sea with passengers on board, ran aground on Currituck Beach, a short distance from the site of the *Huron* disaster. She struck ground four and a half miles from Station No. 5, commanded by keeper John G. Chappell. With his six-man crew, Chappell responded to the emergency, but far too many errors were made both on board the *Metropolis* and on shore. Chappell tried to fire a line to the steamer without success; then, he made the decision that no lifeboat could reach the wreck under the existing conditions. As a result, 85 of 248 persons on board perished. The local press, civic leaders, and government officials condemned the lifesavers. Some called them scandalously inefficient; others suggested they must be in cahoots with local wreckers.[29]

In response to the *Metropolis* disaster, Senator Aaron A. Sargent of California introduced legislation on 19 February 1878 to transfer the LSS to the navy, where proper discipline could be instilled in the service. Earlier, Congressman Samuel S. Cox of New York had filed a bill in the House of Representatives to strengthen and expand the LSS. At the time, he had praised Kimball for having organized the service in just seven years from nothing to the best lifesaving service in the world. Months of debate, some of it testy, followed. When the talking ended, Congress voted to establish the LSS as a separate organization in the Treasury Department. Revenue cutter officers generally lobbied for the legislation that passed and opposed the proposal to transfer the LSS to the Navy Department. On 18 June 1878, President Rutherford B. Hayes signed the bill into law and nominated Sumner Kimball to serve as general superintendent of the Life-Saving Service. The Senate unanimously approved the appointment.[30]

Subsequently, Secretary of the Treasury John Sherman appointed William D. O'Connor as Kimball's assistant general superintendent and cutter captains who patrolled the first, second, seventh, ninth, and tenth districts as assistant inspectors. Officers stationed in the third, fourth, fifth, sixth, and eleventh districts who had been assistant inspectors for the previous two years continued to serve.[31]

During discussions about Senator Sargent's proposal, Congress had praised Kimball for his accomplishments of the previous eight years. Congressman Omar D. Conger of Michigan had said that Kimball, "the little black-eyed man" from Maine, had made the stations efficient. Congressman Cox had praised Kimball for doing "what nobody else thought worth doing. . . . He organized what he had." Cox continued:

> With skill, with patience, with perseverance, with energy that never faltered, with foresight that saw the end in the beginning, and judgment that discerned in small and scattered sources the amplest possibilities, he made the service what it is today. Hampered by legislative restrictions and slender appropriations, he has contrived to set barriers against the measureless destruction of the sea. . . . He has linked our exposed beaches on seaboard and lake with improved stations. He has filled them with selected crews, . . . he has stocked them with the best boats, wreck-ordnance and life-saving appliances of every kind that modern skill has been able to devise; he has trained his heroic gangs with constant discipline until, from simple fishermen, they have become soldiers of surf and storm and the defense of imperiled seafarers. He has by skill and patience far outdone my most sanguine expectations of 1870; for he has brought into existence that system of patrol which puts the American life-saving establishment in advance of any in the world."[32]

Captain Merryman noted that 578 disasters involving 6,287 persons had occurred within reach of an LSS station between November 1871 and the end of June 1878. The LSS saved 5,981 of those persons and provided 3,716 days of relief to the survivors. By comparing the loss of life on the beaches of New York and New Jersey for equal periods before and after Kimball's reforms, Merryman estimated that the service had reduced the loss of life by 87 percent.[33]

On 22 November 1889, over eleven years after he took charge of the LSS as an independent agency, Kimball read a paper, "Organization and Methods of the United States Life-Saving Service" (later published), before an international marine conference. At that time, there were 227 lifesaving stations located at points of danger for merchant shipping in the U.S.: 165 on the Atlantic Coast, 8 each on the Pacific Coast and the Gulf of Mexico, 45 on the Great Lakes, and 1 at the falls of the Ohio River in Louisville, Kentucky.[34] On some stretches of the coast, according to Kimball, they were "placed at long intervals, while upon others they form[ed] chains of contiguous posts within communicating distance of each other."[35]

Kimball explained where the stations were located and the thinking that had led to their distribution. Sixteen stations stood between Eastport, Maine, and Race Point on Cape Cod. Just ten of these guarded the dangerous stretches of the Maine and New Hampshire coasts; although the distance was great (415 miles) and the coast rugged, the northern stretches of the area offered many harbors of safe refuge and, along the dangerous sandy beaches to the south, the Massachusetts Humane Society manned its own stations.

Ten stations, located an equal distance from one another, stood guard on the eastern end of Cape Cod, where the cape's extended forearm had been waving mariners onto its treacherous shifting sand bars for centuries. "From Monomoy—the elbow of the Cape—to Montauk Point [New York], a distance of 110 miles," there were just nine stations, Kimball explained, because the coast was "again somewhat similar to that of Maine."[36]

Seventy-nine stations protected the shipping along the 250 miles of sand beaches in New York and New Jersey, for they took the full brunt of eastern storms and an enormous amount of shipping skirted those beaches to enter the ports of New York, Philadelphia, and Wilmington, Delaware. The port of New York was the busiest in the nation. Northeast storms posed a serious danger for this shipping. Ships sailed into the funnel-like Ambrose Channel to enter the harbor there, with the Long Island

and New Jersey shores on the border. Similar considerations led Kimball to place sixteen stations between Cape Henlopen and Cape Charles, a distance of 116 miles, and twenty-three stations between Cape Henry and Cape Hatteras, a distance of 121 miles. Some of the shipping into Philadelphia transited those waters, along with all of the shipping into Baltimore and Norfolk.

An additional six stations protected the commerce of Beaufort and Wilmington, North Carolina, along 175 miles of coastline between Cape Hatteras and Cape Fear. Between Cape Fear and Florida just one station stood guard, at the entrance to Charleston Harbor, because the coastline south of Cape Fear swung off to the west and away from the shipping lanes of the area.

Ships sailing along the coast of Florida usually stranded close to the beach, so shipwrecked sailors generally were able to wade ashore. Because there were few inhabitants along the beach, however, ten houses of refuge were located there to provide water, and one fully equipped station stood guard at Jupiter Point.

Storms in the Gulf of Mexico, blowing out of the north, drove vessels offshore, rather than onshore, except where the coast of Texas ran north and south. Ships were driven on shore there when the storms were "quartering from the east," according to Kimball.[37] The LSS had established four stations along that stretch of beach and had located three additional stations at unusually exposed points, including one at the entrance to Galveston Harbor.

Just eight stations guarded the entire Pacific Coast. Most of them stood at the entrance to important ports. Because of the bland climate between the southern border and San Francisco, shipwrecks were rare, and the weather along the entire Pacific Coast was predictable.

Forty-five stations stood guard on the nearly 2,500 miles of coastline on the shores of the Great Lakes. Most were at the entrances to ports, for that was where most vessels stranded in the Lakes, usually during concentrations of storms in early spring and late fall. The Lakes, according to Kimball, could turn treacherous in a short time.

There were a few more stations at particularly dangerous locations, and one floating station protected shipping at the falls of the Ohio River at Louisville, Kentucky. Station No. 276 was established there on 3 November 1881. (By 17 January 1937, lifesavers at that station had saved 5,896 lives and $6 million in property and had recovered 797 bodies.[38]

When Kimball made his presentation in 1889, the LSS was building eight additional stations and had plans to build twenty more. Once those were completed, Kimball thought that protection would be adequate for the conditions then existing.[39]

The LSS located stations along the coast back from the beach to protect them from the surf, and it built them solidly so that they could be moved without damage if the sea encroached upon them. Essentially, the stations housed the surfmen and their equipment and provided space for rescued mariners.

Between the construction of the first station at Spermacetti Cove, New Jersey, and the erection of the last stations built before Kimball's 1889 speech, the stations had evolved from simple huts into sophisticated buildings. Tracing their development, York notes that eight stations built under the Newall Act were "little more than crude one-and-a-half story frame boathouses, 16 feet wide by 28 feet long. . . . [A] single room on the first floor housed the surf-boat and other rescue equipment while a small loft above was used for storage."[40] The outside of each station "was covered with two or three layers of shingles on the walls and roof and painted or whitewashed."

As the service built additional stations, it increased their size, but kept them simple in design and plain in appearance. New stations for Long Island and New Jersey, built in 1871–72, measured forty-two feet by eighteen feet. Like the first stations, they were "shingled on their roofs and sides," York says, "and were often referred to as 'red houses' since many were painted that color."

Not until 1874, according to York, was the first serious consideration given to architectural style. The "elaborate detailing" of exterior trim on stations built that year led him to conclude that an architect had designed them. They were carried out, he writes, in the "stick" style popular in home construction of the day: "Such buildings were highlighted by functional appearing decorative wood bracketing in the roof gable and under the eaves, diagonal boards applied over horizontal or vertical siding, and the occasional use of vertical battens. All worked to symbolize the structural skeleton within. Over hanging eaves, steeply pitched gable roofs, towers, and pointed dormers were also characteristic features."

With variations, more than one hundred of these stations were built during the 1870s before Kimball separated the lifesaving and revenue cutter services. Shortly thereafter, in 1882, the LSS built a new type of sta-

The Big Sandy Station in New York was one of the 1874 stick-style stations.

tion that was similar in appearance to the 1874 stations. It was the first station built with an enclosed lookout tower, and it had nearly a full second story. A large dormer protruded on one side and sometimes on both sides of the roof.

John J. Pelz, architect for the Library of Congress, designed stations in the Queen Anne style, popular at the time, for Bay Head, New Jersey, and Brenton Point in Newport, Rhode Island, in 1882. York notes that they "were characterized by asymmetrical massing and the use of a variety of forms, textures, materials, and colors. The [Bay Head] station's extremely high peaked tower topped with ornamental ironwork, and massive cross-gable roof ending in a large projecting bay window typifies this style." Pelz designed other Queen Anne–style stations. According to York, this revealed the Life-Saving Service's concern about the design of lifesaving stations.

York's opinion is confirmed by the service's employment of Albert B. Bibb to make alterations to old stations and to provide designs for new ones. Bibb modified 1871–72 and 1874 stations by adding lean-tos to either side of the original building, carrying the original roof over the lean-tos, and

The Deal Station in New Jersey, designed by Paul J. Pelz, was an example of Queen Anne–style architecture.

shingling the whole. The result was a shingle-style station. In 1886, Bibb designed a new station in the shingle style that looked much like a summer home. By 1891, the LSS had built fifteen of these stations. In 1889, the LSS built a unique Bibb station at Cuttyhunk, Massachusetts, that, York correctly notes, looked "more like a large summer cottage than a life-saving station."[41] In 1928, Henry Beston, an author and naturalist then living near the Nauset lifesaving station on Cape Cod, describes the station as "a white wooden building built snug and low like a Cape Cod cottage; indeed, it rather resembles a Cape Cod cottage in design."[42]

Kimball notes that in most stations the first floor was divided into four rooms: "a boat room, a mess room (also serving for a sitting room for the men), a keeper's room, and a store room. Wide, double-leafed doors and a sloping platform extending from the sills to the ground permit the running out of the heavier equipment from the building."[43]

The second floor was divided into two rooms, one a bedroom for the crew and the other a bedroom for rescued mariners and for storage. Bigger

The Orleans Station on Cape Cod is similar to the "red houses" in New Jersey. Built in 1872, it was remodeled by Albert B. Bibb in 1885. The lean-tos on each side transform it into a shingle-style building.

stations had two additional rooms—a kitchen and a spare room. At locations without good water, cisterns caught water from the roof. Each station had a lookout where its crew stood watch. The service usually painted the roofs of stations that could be seen from the sea a dark red, so that mariners could pick them out at a great distance. A sixty-foot-high flag staff was also provided for signaling passing vessels.

By 1889, the service had developed three types of stations, and Kimball describes the equipment in each (see Appendix B for details).

Telephone lines connected all of the stations on Long Island and between Cape Henry and Cape Hatteras Inlet. Most of the stations on the New Jersey coast were similarly connected.

The president appointed the general superintendent, who was confirmed by the Senate and served at the pleasure of the president for $4,000 a year. The secretary of the treasury appointed the assistant general superintendent, who received a salary of $2,500 a year. A "hand full" of clerks served as the general superintendent's staff. The Board of

Life-Saving Appliances evaluated proposals for equipment used in the work of the service.

The Revenue Cutter Service provided the general superintendent with an inspector, who made periodic inspections of the stations and their equipment. He operated out of New York, where nearly all of the self-bailing and self-righting lifeboats and most of the apparatus of the service were built or manufactured. The Revenue Cutter Service also assigned an assistant inspector for each district, who visited each station in his district when it opened for the year, once a month during the season, and following any accident involving loss of life. He inspected the stations, their crews, and all equipment. He evaluated the ability of each crew with the lifesaving apparatus, and filed a report on the circumstances surrounding all accidents involving loss of life.

A civilian "of good character" led each district as district superintendent. Requirements for appointment also included literacy in English and enough knowledge about accounts to transact the business of the district. The superintendent had to be between twenty-five and fifty-five years of age when appointed, be from the district he would serve, know the coast of the district, and be familiar with the service's equipment and its use. His responsibilities included paying the surfmen, supervising maintenance and repair of the stations, acting as collector of customs, and visiting each station in the district once a quarter. For these duties, he received from $1,000 to $1,800 a year.

The district superintendent nominated the keeper of each station. The most important man at the station, the keeper had to be between twenty-one and forty-five years of age when appointed. He had to be of good character, a capable leader, and in good health—a surgeon in the Marine Hospital Service administered a rigorous physical examination before appointment. Usually, the keeper came from the area he served, and, almost always, he was drawn from the surfmen at the station. According to Kimball, the keeper led the men in all rescues, took the steering oar when boats were used, and directed all operations with the apparatus. He assumed responsibility for wrecked property until it was turned over to its owner. He kept a daily log, wrote a report on any disaster that occurred near his station, and sent a transcript of his log to the general superintendent each week. For these duties, the keeper of a lifesaving stations usually received $700 a year and the keeper of a refuge, $400; some keepers of great reputation or at isolated stations received $800.

The LSS kept stations open, according to need, either all or part of the year. Stations on the Atlantic Coast and the Gulf of Mexico stayed open from 1 September to 1 May; those on the Pacific Coast were open at the direction of the general superintendent, who kept four of those on the Pacific Coast and the one at Louisville open all year. Around the turn of the century, the LSS kept most of the stations open almost year round.

The size of a station's crew was determined by the maximum number of men required to row the rescue boats. Thus, there were some five-man stations on the Atlantic Coast, but most were six-man stations. In December, an additional man was added to stay on shore and help to launch and recover the boat. There were many eight-man crews on the Great Lakes, where self-righting and self-bailing boats were used.

Each keeper selected his own crewmen. When political patronage seriously threatened the efficiency of the service during its early years, Kimball fought against it, and Congress sanctioned his views in 1882.[44] Some historians have argued that this ended the patronage problem, but Shoemaker disputes this conclusion. He explains that, shortly after passage of the 1854 legislation providing for paid keepers and crews, politicians closest to the stations came to dominate both the selection of the keepers and their choices of surfmen. It did not matter which major party was in power. Both wanted the spoils of office and, according to Shoemaker, got them. The problem was compounded, Shoemaker states, by the appointment of district superintendents by the secretary of the treasury, who was himself a political appointee. Thus, the superintendents became part of the problem, rather than a source of the solution. According to Shoemaker, examiners tried to eliminate such influences but failed, and relief was sought from Congress. In 1882, Congress passed legislation stating that the appointment of district superintendents, inspectors, keepers, "and crews of life-saving stations shall be made solely with reference to their fitness, without reference to their political or party affiliations." Thereafter, Shoemaker claimed, keepers who failed to cooperate with local politicians came in for serious criticism. Of course, the political leaders who made the complaints put their criticism in the context of great concern for the good of the service, but the real message was clear to any keeper who received it. Shoemaker, who observed the process firsthand, also understood the reality.[45]

Shoemaker recounts the case of the district on the coast of Long Island, New York, one of the oldest in the system. He traces the abuse of political power in the district from 1876 to 1885 and demonstrates how the abuse continued after 1882, and ended, eventually, in 1885:

> The superintendent of this district was personally a very respectable man: he was also a very ardent and an exceedingly bitter partisan. His political creed governed his official acts in the conduct of affairs in his district to the extent that he so organized the service under his control that it became a complete and perfect political machine, and was worked as such in the interest of his party. Every station keeper, with two exceptions, was a member of the political organization to which the superintendent belonged. Through these keepers, of whom there were thirty-seven, every man employed as a surfman was either of that party, or taken on because of a promise to "vote the ticket" while retained. A violation of this rule, by a keeper, was met with instructions from the district superintendent to discharge the man or men, "not in harmony with the administration and employ others who are" so flagrant has this condition of things obtained from the date of appointment of the superintendent of the district, now under consideration, that the people on the coast took it up and preferred charges against him. These charges were investigated by a Board composed of a Special Agent of the Treasury Department and an officer of the Revenue Marine appointed for the purpose in the winter of 1877.[46]

Shoemaker states that he knew the conditions were as reported, but the superintendent had covered his tracks and got off with a reprimand, plus strict new guidance from the treasury secretary. Within a brief time, according to Shoemaker, "he was again as deep in the mud, as he had before been in the mire." Even after the reform legislation of 1882, conditions remained unchanged. "This district, under the same supervision of the same superintendent, was found in 1885 to be as thoroughly organized a political machine as it was eight years before."[47]

Once again, charges were brought against the superintendent. An exhaustive investigation was conducted, and, finally, the man was removed from office, along with twelve to fifteen keepers, who were replaced with competent surfmen. All involved were then forcefully informed that no person would be appointed to or removed from a position because of his political affiliation. The reform in the district, Shoemaker writes, "was genuine and far reaching." Proof of this was found in the fact that for five years between the winter of 1886 and the spring of 1891, "not a single complaint for any cause against anybody connected with the service in the district was filed, and not a single case of dereliction of duty was reported or discovered."[48]

Shoemaker gave revenue cutter officers credit for making the 1882 legislation work as Congress had intended. After 1885, he writes, the Treasury Department required district superintendents to gain the approval of assistant inspectors before recommending a person to become the keeper of a station. This was not a legal requirement, but it was followed and proved to be the salvation of the LSS. According to Shoemaker, it "practically assured the selection of men with sole reference to fitness, and in utter disregard of their political affiliations." In addition, it relieved district superintendents, who wanted to be relieved, of the problem of listening to pleas from political friends.[49] Revenue cutter officers who had life tenure during good behavior and who rotated from district to district served as assistant inspectors. They were free to be impartial and to recommend keepers for fitness alone in a way that district superintendents could not. As a result, they looked out for the public's best interests. This, Shoemaker concludes, eliminated political considerations from the LSS to the extent that politics was eliminated from the system.[50]

District superintendents, Shoemaker notes, did not enjoy the same independence as cutter officers: they were subject to removal with each new administration. He knew of only one exception to the rule that district superintendents were approved because of their political affiliation with the party in power. It was true that they had more secure tenure after 1882, but even under the reform legislation of that year, he writes, the Republican superintendent of the seventh district, in Florida, was removed by the Cleveland administration and replaced with a Democrat. Similarly, the Harrison administration had just replaced the Democratic superintendent of the sixth district, in North Carolina, with a Republican. "The 'pull' that secures the appointment of the district superintendent influences him in the selection of the Keepers in his district," Shoemaker writes, "and so on down to the men in the crews." Only the voices of the assistant inspectors prevented this abuse. Shoemaker was sure that if the assistant inspectors were removed from the districts, the system would revert immediately to its old, politically corrupt ways.[51]

The assistant inspectors chose the keepers for their ability, then assured them that they not only could, but must, appoint surfmen for their ability. Finally, they assured the keepers that they could not be removed for acting in the best interest of their station. This was the system that finally freed the stations of the evils of political influence and disregard for the saving of lives.[52]

Surfmen had to be under forty years of age when appointed and of good character and health. They were required to reside at the station during the active season, for which they were paid $50 a month. During the off-season, they were expected to be available for rescues and were paid $3 per occasion of service. Out of their pay, they supplied their own food and clothing. The LSS prohibited them from having any interest in a wrecking company, and they could not claim salvage rights for any of their work. If injured on the job, a surfman or keeper received his salary for a maximum of two years. If he was killed, his widow and children under sixteen years of age received the same consideration.[53]

From the station, a surfman kept watch over the station's patrol limits from sunup to sundown. If he could not see the limits from the station, he went far enough along the beach to see them at least three times each day. During periods of fog and stormy weather, a complete watch was kept. The station kept a record of each passing vessel every day.

At night, two men stood one of three watches together: 2000 to 2400, 2400 to 0400, or 0400 to sunup. At the beginning of their patrol, the men split up and walked in opposite directions along the beach to a midpoint from neighboring stations, where they exchanged (with a surfman from the neighboring station) a metal check with their number on it. The following night they got back their own check. At isolated stations, the surfman punched a clock at the outer reaches of his station with a key fixed to a post. The marked dial proved that he had walked his route.

Each patrolman carried a lantern and several red Coston flares. If he discovered "a wreck, a vessel in distress, or one running dangerously near the shore," he ignited a flare, Kimball writes, which burned with a "brilliant red flame." This served "the double purpose of warning the people on the vessel of their danger and of assuring them of succor if they [were] already in distress.[54]

Every station followed a regular weekday routine. On Mondays and Thursdays, the men practiced with the beach apparatus; on Mondays, they also overhauled all of their equipment. The rest of the week was devoted to practice: Tuesdays with the boats; Wednesdays, international code signals; and Fridays, methods of "restoring the apparently drowned." On Saturdays, they cleaned the station.[55]

If a crew could not simulate a successful rescue with the breeches buoy apparatus in 5 minutes, Kimball notes, "it is considered that they have been remiss in drilling, or that there are some stupid men among them" It was common for a crew to be able to make a rescue in 2½ minutes. The real object of the drill was to have the crew become so successful and familiar with the stowage of the materials in the cart that they could do it in the dark. Indeed, they could. During a storm on 3 February 1880, in utter darkness on a sleeting night that wreaked havoc along the New Jersey coast, three LSS crews saved every crew member of four wrecked vessels.[56]

The LSS used three types of surfboats: Beebe, Higgins and Gifford, and Beebe-McLellan. They were constructed of white cedar with white oak frames and measured 25 to 27 feet in length; 6½ to 7 feet, beam; 2 feet 3 inches to 2 feet 6 inches, depth amidships, and 1 foot 7 inches to 2 feet 1 inch, sheer of gunwale. Flat-bottomed, with little or no keel, they drew 6 or 7 inches of water, and weighed between 700 and 1,100 pounds. In addition to its crew, each boat could carry up to fifteen rescued persons. Each cost between $210 and $275. In the hands of an experienced crew of six oars, they were marvelously maneuverable in the surf.[57]

The safety record of the boats was favorable. Kimball records that in their first eighteen years of use by LSS crews, they had "been launched 6,730 times in actual service, and landed 6,735 persons from wrecked vessels. In all this service they capsized but 14 times." Forty-one lives were lost on six of these occasions, twenty-seven lifesavers and fourteen shipwrecked people.[58]

The LSS used two guns and a rocket to throw a line to a stranded ship: the Lyle gun, developed by Capt. David A. Lyle of the U.S. Army Ordnance Department; the Hunt gun, developed by Edmund S. Hunt of Massachusetts; and the Cunningham rocket, developed by Patrick Cunningham of Massachusetts. The service preferred a gun to the rocket for general use because it was easier and less expensive to use and was usually more accurate. The rocket had to be fired at a considerable elevation, with more exposure to the wind and a greater chance of its falling wide of the mark. The service preferred the Lyle gun to the Hunt gun because it could throw a stronger line and reduce the necessity of using an intermediate line for hauling the whip line on board. It was also less expensive to use because the projectile was reusable, whereas the projectile for the Hunt gun had to be returned to the factory for reloading after each firing. Both the rocket and the Hunt gun had one advantage over the Lyle gun. They could throw a line farther, but the range of the Lyle gun, 695 yards under favorable circumstances, was about as far as the beach apparatus could be used effectively.[59] The range of the Hunt gun was an additional 40 yards, and the Cunningham rocket could throw a line 700 to 1,000 yards.

The Lyle gun was bronze, with a smooth 2½-inch bore. The gun and its carriage together weighed only 185 pounds. It fired a solid elongated shot, 14½ inches in length and 17 pounds in weight. An eyebolt in the base of the shot received the line, which protruded beyond the muzzle of the gun. When the gun was fired, the projectile reversed from the weight and inertia of the line. Three shot lines, varying from $\frac{7}{32}$-inch to $\frac{9}{32}$-inch diameter, were used, but the service preferred the heaviest line to avoid using an intermediate line to haul the whip line on board a stranded vessel. The smaller lines, however, could be fired a greater distance and were used when necessary.[60]

Lyle developed the gun after Captain Merryman recommended the development of a new line-throwing gun following the wreck of the Italian bark *Giovanni* near Provincetown, Cape Cod, on 4 March 1875. Fourteen men had drowned in the disaster because the lifesavers' ordnance could not reach the stranded vessel and heavy surf prevented the launching of a surfboat. The U.S. Army ordnance department began work on the project almost immediately, but progress seemed to stall until 1877, when Lyle was made a special project officer. Giving full time and attention to the matter, he first reviewed all previous line-carrying ideas, including mortars, rockets, kites, and even bows and arrows. After eliminating ideas that he considered flawed in some way, he concentrated on developing a line-throwing gun. He solved problem after problem as he struggled to gain accuracy, as well as adequate range. The result was the incomparable Lyle gun, which soon became standard ordnance of the LSS.[61]

Once a ship's crew had a line from shore on board the vessel, the lifesavers tied a whip line to it and the ship's crew hauled it on board. The whip line, threaded through a block, was tied as high up on the ship's mast as possible, while the lifesavers held onto both ends of the whip line. They then anchored a hawser, which the ship's crew had hauled on board and tied to the mast above the whip line, in the sand and raised it up by wedging a cross beam in the shape of a giant X under it. Using the whip line, they ran equipment, such as a breeches buoy, lifecar, life vest, or life belt, back and forth between the ship and the shore.

Once the hawser was stretched taut, the LSS, as did most lifesavers around the world, usually accomplished the rescue with a breeches buoy. This was a simple ring buoy with a pair of short leather pants sewn into the ring's opening. A person climbed into the pants and was hauled through the surf. Although the ride to shore was likely to be uncomfortable, it was usually safe. Under some conditions, a life car proved to be more useful. On 20 February 1893, the captain of the stranded three-masted schooner *Nathan Esterbrook, Jr.*, failed to tie the whip line high enough on his ship's mast. This caused the death of the first member of his crew hauled ashore by the lifesavers at the Little Kinnakeet Station on the coast of North Carolina. As they dragged the man through the surf, he swallowed water and suffered blows from floating wreckage. Before he died, he was able to relate his ordeal to the LSS crew. On four subsequent runs, the crew sent a lifecar to the schooner and successfully rescued the rest of her nine-man crew.[62]

As those familiar with the sea would expect, lifesavers often had to improvise in response to unusual conditions. Lifesavers from the station at Oak Island, North Carolina, discovered the Norwegian bark *Ogir* aground on an outer bar on the morning of 11 October 1894. Keeper Dunbar Davis and his crew rowed a surfboat three miles to reach the *Ogir* and her eleven-man crew. Floating wreckage and downed masts and rigging surged and pounded with each wave. Making a rescue attempt would be treacherous but not impossible. The spanker boom had toppled overboard on the port side, but it lay by itself with one end on the deck. Between breakers, Davis and his men rowed to the end of the spar, grabbed a man who had crawled to its outer reaches, and dashed away from the wreck. They successfully repeated this process nine times. Two of the crew refused to chance such a dangerous rescue and chose to take their chances with the vessel. Davis returned to shore with the nine brave men, and, fortunately, was able to return for the last two the next morning after the winds had died down. The *Ogir* was left to her fate in the surf.[63]

In 1899, a devastating hurricane destroyed seven vessels along the North Carolina coast, drove the Diamond Shoals lightship aground, obliterated six ships at sea, killed more than fifty people, and flooded hundreds of coastal homes. The 643-ton barkentine *Priscilla* had departed Baltimore on 12 August and was bound for Rio de Janeiro with general cargo. Her captain, Benjamin E. Springsteen, was sailing with a twelve-man crew, including himself and his son William who served as mate, and his wife and twelve-year-old son as passengers. The *Priscilla* survived the hurricane but was severely damaged. On 18 August, she ran aground near the Gull Shoal Station on the outer banks. With breakers rolling over the vessel, the crew cut her rigging. The masts soon went overboard. A wave swept the younger Springsteen boy from his father's arms and carried him away, along with his mother and a young cabin boy.

At this point, Rasmus Midgett of the LSS station discovered the wreck, but he had no time to go for help. Between waves, he ran to the *Priscilla*, shouted instructions to the ten men still on board, and ran back to shore. On the next series of waves, he ran back to the vessel, took hold of a crewman who had climbed down a rope to the ground, and dragged him to the safety of the beach. Midgett repeated this feat seven times. There were three men left on the *Priscilla*, who were too exhausted or injured to climb down the rope on their own. Midgett again dashed between the breakers and climbed up the rope to the *Priscilla*'s sloping deck. He crossed the deck, hoisted a crewman onto his back, descended to the ground, then dashed into shore with his burden. He made this back-breaking scramble for life three times. For his unbelievable rescue of the *Priscilla*'s crew, he received the Gold Lifesaving Medal, the highest peacetime award for saving lives.[64]

The 393-ton three-masted schooner *E. S. Newman* of Stonington, Connecticut, had departed Providence, Rhode Island, in October 1896 and was bound for Norfolk in ballast. Just short of her destination, she ran into a storm that disabled her. She drifted about one hundred miles before washing up on the beach at Pea Island, North Carolina, about two miles north of the lifesaving station. Capt. Stephen A. Gardiner burned a red flare to alert the lifesavers; keeper Richard Etheridge had been forced to discontinue beach patrols, but he had ordered surfman Theodore Meekins to keep watch from the station's tower. At the height of the storm, Meekins thought he saw a rocket. In response, he burned a Coston flare and called the keeper. Both Meekins and Etheridge were certain that they saw a second red light. Immediately, they headed down the beach with a pair of mules pulling their apparatus cart, but progress was nearly impossible through the tide sweeping over the beach. When they arrived opposite the wreck, they could not use the beach apparatus because they could not secure an anchor in the flooded sand.

Keeper Etheridge had an idea. He called for his two strongest lifesavers. They tied a line around their bodies and, connected to one another and to the line held by their mates, they forged ahead into the surf with a second line in their hands. When they reached the *Newman*, one of the ship's crew climbed down a ladder and they tied the second line around him. Wading through the surf, they dragged him to shore. In turn, various members of the lifesavers, two at a time, rescued all nine persons on board the schooner, including Captain Gardiner's wife and three-year-old daughter.[65]

The rescuers of those on board the *Newman* were indeed heroic, but they were also unusual, in that Etheridge and the entire crew of the Pea Island Station were black. When the Life-Saving Service built the station in 1870, it assigned an all-white crew. Eight years later, a crew of both whites and blacks served together. The following year, after the station had reverted to an all-white crew, the *M & S Henderson* wrecked near the station. Because four persons died in the tragedy, the LSS assigned Shoemaker to investigate it. Discovering that neglect of duty had played a role in the loss of life, Shoemaker recommended removal of keeper George C. Daniels for lying about the case, discharge of two surfmen for failing to perform their duty, reassignment of the remaining crew, and appointment of Etheridge as the new keeper. He reported, "I examined this man, and found him to be 38 years of age, strong, robust physique, intelligent and able to read and write. He is reputed one of the best surfmen on this part of the coast of North Carolina." Shoemaker's recommendation carried great weight with Kimball. On 24 January 1880, he appointed Etheridge to be the first black LSS keeper in the nation. Subsequently, to avoid placing white men under Etheridge's command, the entire crew was made up of African Americans.[66]

The service had another unusual crew at a station on Lake Michigan. The crew at Evanston, Illinois, was made up extensively of Northwestern University students. Like its counterpart at Pea Island, it was a successful crew.[67]

Communications were important to rescue efforts. Information about how a ship's crew could assist the LSS crew in the use of the rescue equipment was conveyed to a stranded ship on a tally board attached to the whip line. The tally board, which looked like a fraternity paddle, had instructions on one side in English and on the other in French. In addition, Kimball published a small booklet of instructions for mariners that also provided the location of each station along the U.S. coast.[68]

Telephone lines stretched along much of the coast, and telephone

calls could summon nearby station crews to a rescue site. Kimball recounts the story of a rescue made near Cape Henlopen in a great storm of
10–12 September 1889. The storm, he writes, was "one of the most de-
structive that has ever visited our coast, when the crews of three stations,
under the leadership of Captain Clampitt, of the Lewes Station, rescued
the crews of 22 stranded vessels—194 persons—by the use of every form
of rescuing appliance; 23 being landed with the surf-boats, 16 with the
self-righting life-boat, 135 with the breeches-buoy, and 20 with the lifecar—not a life being lost."[69] By use of the telegraph and railroad systems,
the LSS had transported equipment as far as 240 miles to make the rescues. Use of the railroads was possible because they skirted the shore
along much of the U.S. coast and at many of the lakes.

In 1888, Kimball notes, the LSS saved 282 ships, with 1,552 persons
on board, worth (with cargoes) $3,666,050. The service saved 194 of
these vessels unassisted; they had 898 persons on board, and their worth
(with cargoes) was $1,495,550. The following year, the LSS saved 257
ships, with 1,446 persons on board, worth $3,241,830; of these, the ser-
vice saved unassisted 172 ships, with 823 persons on board, worth
$1,127,295. An additional 253 ships received minor assistance from the
LSS. In addition to direct assistance, the LSS telephoned marine exchanges and underwriters who often called in tugs to assist ships before
they were damaged or destroyed, and, of course, the LSS crews warned
ships of danger before they got into serious trouble. Although there was
no way to know the number of persons or the value of property thus
saved, Kimball notes that 217 warnings were given in 1889 and not fewer
than 200 in each of the previous six years.[70]

A total of 378 disasters to documented vessels occurred within the
scope of the Life-Saving Service in 1888. According to Kimball, 38 of the
3,106 persons on board those vessels were lost, 63 of the vessels were totally lost, and $1,348,750 of their total estimated monetary value of
$6,343,880 was lost. An additional 150 smaller craft wrecked near the
stations, which saved 316 of 320 persons on board and all but $13,585
worth of property out of the total estimated value of $59,310. The total
cost of operations for the LSS in 1888 was $965,907.18.[71]

In 1892, Shoemaker notes that the efficiency of the service for the
purpose of saving lives and property from wrecks was perfect. The morale
of the men who filled the ranks, he adds, could not have been better.
Somewhat surprising for a revenue cutter officer, he understood and

praised the less than spit-and-polish lifesavers. They had respect for authority and obeyed orders, which was necessary. Beyond that, he says: "A strictly military discipline could never be successfully inaugurated and maintained in this service, simply because the restraints incident thereto, would disgust the men who fill its ranks and drive them out, and they cannot be replaced by any other class." The fewer ceremonies and forms required of these hardy Americans, Shoemaker added, "the better will be the results. It is unquestionable that no amount of drill, no amount of restrictions imposed could ever instill into their hearts and consciences, the utter abnegation of self, which has heretofore prompted the men of this great service to the performance of the deeds of heroic daring, which have made the Life-Saving Service of the United States a household word among the nations of the earth."[72]

Joshua James was the kind of man described by Shoemaker. He was born in Hull, Massachusetts, on 22 November 1826 and went to sea at an early age on his father's boat, which carried paving stones from Hull to Boston. Blessed with keen senses and a scientific aptitude, James was an excellent navigator. By the time he was in his mid-twenties, he had command of his own ship. In 1889, the LSS appointed him keeper of the Point Allerton lifesaving station. He was then sixty-two years old, with more than forty years of experience in the Massachusetts Humane Society. He had rescued more than two hundred persons from drowning in the surf, twenty-nine of them during a hurricane on 25 and 26 November 1888.[73]

James was seventeen years past the maximum age for receiving a keeper's assignment and had to apply for a waiver. During his tenure at Point Allerton, 86 ships wrecked near the station. He and his crew saved 540 of 556 persons on the wrecked ships and 75 percent of the property involved. All 16 persons lost within reach of the Point Allerton station died during the hurricane of 26–27 November 1898, perhaps the worst storm ever to hit the East Coast. It sank the steamer *Portland* off Cape Cod with all hands, 129 persons.

Kimball writes of that night: "The terrors and suffering which the surfmen endured as they maintained their patrols throughout that dreadful night are beyond description. The force of the wind was so great as to literally take away their breath, so that they were frequently compelled to turn their backs and crouch close to the earth for relief, while the great seas rolling far up the rock-strewn beaches constantly threatened to overwhelm them and repeatedly forced them to flee with all speed to higher ground."

Keeper Joshua James (front row, second from left) of the Point Allerton Station in Massachusetts with his crack crew and lifesaving equipment.

On 17 March 1902, then seventy-five years of age, James drilled his boat crew in the surf, stepped ashore, and then fell dead on the beach. Thus ended fifty-three years of rescue work by the best-known surfman in the nation.

Shoemaker's lavish praise of the LSS might be considered pure hyperbole except for the fact that it is backed up by impartial, competent observers. Congressman William Charles Adamson of Georgia said that it was "the best life-saving service in the world." Emile Cacheux, secretary general of the Fifth International Congress of Life-Saving at Toulon, France, in April 1890, pronounced it the best and most complete: "Nearly all civilized nations have established life-saving stations along their coasts. The most complete is, as shown by the documents which we have received, that of the United States, directed with so much devotion by General Superintendent Kimball."[74]

Senator John Sherman of Ohio thought that Kimball's "wonderful success in developing the Life-Saving Service [had] been his early and

The lifesaving station crew and rescue gear at Salisbury Beach, Massachusetts, circa 1900.

unswerving resolution to conduct it upon non-partisan lines." Kimball fought for that end even before taking the job as general superintendent. On 4 May 1882, Congress passed legislation declaring that "The appointment of district superintendents, inspectors, and keepers and crews of life-saving stations shall be made solely with reference to their fitness, and without reference to their political or party affiliations." This was the first law of its kind ever enacted by Congress, but Kimball went beyond it and convinced the president to place the life savers within the classified civil service by executive decree.[75] Although political patronage did not end with passage of this legislation, it did end as a result of the legislation and the efforts of Sumner Kimball, who deserves all the praise he has received for making the U.S. Life-Saving Service the best in the world.

The LSS changed little during its last twenty-five years. More stations were added. Motor lifeboats and surfboats, which increased the reach of the lifesavers, were built and put into service, but the system of saving lives described above remained much the same and continued to work well. By 1915, when the LSS joined with the Revenue Cutter Service to form the U.S. Coast Guard, the LSS had saved 181,449 lives and 28,000 vessels, thus making it one of the greatest humanitarian services ever operated by the U.S. government.

CHAPTER ELEVEN

The Birth of the U.S. Coast Guard

C ommandant Worth G. Ross retired from the Revenue Cutter Service on 1 May 1911 and recommended that Capt. John C. Cantwell succeed him. A senior captain in the service, Cantwell had graduated from the Revenue Cutter School of Instruction in 1882 and had a distinguished record of accomplishment in the waters of the Pacific and Arctic oceans. His record also bore some blemishes. As commander of the *McCulloch* in 1905, he had taken his wife and some friends on a short trip from California to Oregon without getting permission from headquarters to have guests on board; he also failed to record their presence in the ship's logbook. Two years later, he ran the *Manning* aground in Prince William Sound. Although an investigation revealed that he was blameless, again he had failed to record the events accurately in the logbook.[1]

Such handicaps might not have proved fatal to Cantwell's candidacy under other circumstances and in another era. Under legislation passed in 1908, Congress had granted the commandant of the Revenue Cutter Service the same rank and pay as a captain in the U.S. Navy, and other captains decided to compete with Cantwell for the position. One of his competitors was Ellsworth P. Bertholf, who, like Cantwell, had personal problems on his record. He had been expelled from the U.S. Naval Academy for hazing; as an upperclassman on the U.S. practice ship *Constellation*, he was involved with other upperclassmen who made fourth-class cadets (freshmen) turn out of their hammocks and

Capt. Ellsworth P. Bertholf. Courtesy of U.S. Coast Guard
Academy Museum.

stand on their heads on the berth deck. The fourth classmen were dressed in
their nightshirts, and standing on their heads caused them to expose themselves. For his failure to stop this hazing, Bertholf received a letter of dismissal from Earl English, acting secretary of the navy. Subsequently, he
gained admission to the Revenue Cutter School of Instruction and graduated in the class of 1889, seven years behind Cantwell. Bertholf was also
junior to Cantwell in rank. He stood twenty-third on the 1911 list of captains and Cantwell stood third. Along with his problems, however, Bertholf
also had great assets. Congress had unanimously awarded him a gold
medal for his role in the Overland Expedition in 1897–98 (see chapter 6),
and he had held important commands, including that of the venerable *Bear.*
In addition, he was willing to use political influence from outside the service
to get the job, which apparently had not been done by his predecessor.[2]

On 22 January 1909, Bertholf wrote to Capt. Godfrey L. Carden and asked if Carden was going to make a run for the commandant's job. He stated that he thought Carden was an excellent candidate and could probably get the backing he needed if he chose to run. Bertholf added that he would support Carden if he ran and would not run if Carden did; if Carden was not going to run, however, Bertholf requested his support. Bertholf also said that he did not plan to make a "service campaign," as Ross had done; his efforts would be entirely outside the service. In a letter to Bertholf dated 6 March, Carden did not commit himself and told Bertholf to campaign for the job without regard for what he himself should do. He also concurred with Bertholf's assessment that help must come from outside, not inside, the service. Bertholf succeeded in impressing Secretary of the Treasury Franklin MacVeagh with his qualifications. MacVeagh recommended Bertholf's appointment to President Taft, who submitted Bertholf's name to the Senate for confirmation.[3] Taft had not been swayed by Cantwell's personal attempts to influence his decision. Cantwell had visited the White House in an unsuccessful attempt to meet with the president. When that effort failed, he wrote a personal letter, dated 8 May 1911, seeking the president's support.[4]

On 19 June 1911, Bertholf succeeded Worth G. Ross as commandant of the Revenue Cutter Service. Four years later, he would be reappointed, but as commandant of the new U.S. Coast Guard.

The same year that Bertholf took charge of the service, the Treasury Department divided it into six administrative divisions: operations, engineering, construction, ordnance, supply, and law, and assigned a captain to headquarters, under direct control of the commandant, to head each division. The following year, Bertholf established two divisions on each coast, with headquarters at San Francisco and Port Townsend on the Pacific Coast and New York and Boston on the Atlantic Coast. Gradually, the division commanders assumed operations authority over the cutters in their districts. Cutters and functions operating outside of those divisions were responsible directly to the commandant. These changes finally established a military chain of command in the Revenue Cutter Service and eliminated the collectors of customs from the chain of command.[5] Unfortunately, the service itself was nearly eliminated at the same time.

Frederick A. Cleveland, Taft's economic advisor, presented Congress with the "Report of the Commission on Economy and Efficiency" on 17 November 1911. This document, with its innocent-sounding title, reopened a threat, long dormant, to the existence of the Revenue Cutter Service. Six men had signed the report: Cleveland, commission chairman, gave his name to the group, to be known thereafter as the Cleveland Commission.

The Cleveland Commission broke with earlier groups that had studied the question of what to do with the Revenue Cutter Service. For nearly a century, various groups had recommended moving the service into the navy. The Cleveland Commission did not study that possibility nor even investigate the service's operations to determine how effectively the service was run. It acknowledged that such a study would be informative but declared that the question was "not whether the Revenue-Cutter Service is or is not being efficiently operated." The commission assumed that it was run competently. "The question," it declared, "is a much larger one, namely, whether such a service should be maintained at all as a separately organized branch of the Government." After what it described as a careful study, the commission concluded that there was "not a single duty or function that can not be performed by some other existing service, and performed by the latter at much smaller expense." Therefore, the commission recommended abolishing the service and distributing its duties and equipment to other existing branches of government.[6]

The commission reported that the service annually spent about $2,500,000. It expected net savings from the abolition of the service to total about $1,000,000 a year and was convinced that the services performed by the Revenue Cutter Service would be carried out as well as, or better than, the cutter service had done.[7]

According to the commission, the Revenue Cutter Service had the special characteristic of having no specific duties of its own.[8] It had originally been created to enforce customs laws against smuggling, the report noted, but since its origins in the eighteenth century, it had grown considerably in many maritime areas. It had come to exist to assist other governmental agencies, such as the Life-Saving Service, Lighthouse Service, Steamboat Inspection Service, Bureau of Navigation, and Department of Commerce and Labor, but it did not, in assisting those agencies, eliminate their jobs. For example, the Department of Commerce and Labor still needed its own boats to enforce the navigation laws, and all of the agencies helped by the cutter service still had their own administrative organizations. The result, the commission claimed, was duplication, confusion about obligations, and excessive cost.

The commission noted another special characteristic of the cutter service. It was a military service with armed ships, a corps of military officers, and military duties—it served with the navy in time of war. The commission questioned (and by the manner of questioning, answered itself negatively) whether it was not extremely uneconomical to maintain two naval establishments; as well as to have a military organization perform purely civil duties. The report stated that, for years, various secretaries of the navy had maintained that the navy could carry out the functions of the cruising cutters at great savings to the government. It quoted at length from former Secretary of the Navy Benjamin Tracy to document the commission's case.

The commission argued that to evaluate the duties of the service, it had to break them down into those performed on the high seas and those performed in harbors or on shore, and it proceeded to do so with long lists. According to the report, the lists of duties looked impressive, but a number of them were, in fact, "practically nonexistent in so far as they may impose any real work upon the service." Included in this category were suppressing the slave trade, suppressing piracy, and enforcing neutrality laws. The commission added that it was "doubtful whether the service performs any work of importance at the present time in respect to the suppression of illegal traffic in firearms, ammunition, and liquor with natives of Alaska, or in protecting timber reserves."

The report stressed what the commission considered the important fact: the navy could perform all necessary naval duties and suppress the slave trade, protect merchant ships, enforce neutrality laws, suppress mutinies, assist vessels in distress, protect wrecked property, and destroy derelicts. If the Revenue Cutter Service turned over to the navy the ships it used to carry out its Alaskan duties and to protect the fisheries, there was no reason why the navy could not perform those duties as well. The Forest Service could protect the nation's timber reserves.

This left the question of protecting the revenue. Was it necessary to cruise the high seas to protect the revenue, the commission asked, and if so, could the navy do it? Answering its own questions, the commission admitted that the nation had needed revenue cutters to stop smuggling and collect duties at the nation's beginning, but it argued that the population spread along the coast, good communications systems, and a navy resulted in much less need for a coastal patrol, and the navy could provide any that was necessary. Some might argue that a military establishment should not carry out such a civil duty, the commission conceded; but it pointed out that the Revenue Cutter Service had always claimed to be a military service and was recognized as such.

Regarding its duties in harbors, the commission saw no reason for a military organization to perform such duties and employing an expensive type of organization to carry them out resulted in poor economy and bad administration. As an example, the commission pointed out that revenue cutter captains filled positions as superintendents of construction and repair for lifesaving stations and for construction of lifeboats and lifesaving apparatus. In addition to their pay as military officers, they received additional payment for travel, quarters, and other allowances. Their salaries were appropriated for the Revenue Cutter Service; such permanent assignments of revenue cutter officers to Life-Saving Service duties, the commission argued, was indefensible and resulted in divided responsibility; conflict of authority and jurisdiction; confusion of accounts, which prevented proper allocation of expenses to the Life-Saving Service; and other administrative difficulties. Such details were likely to lead to temporary assignments. Men trained to do another job would want to do the other job, would see the temporary assignment as a problem, and would not perform their duty as well as men trained for it, for whom it was their only duty.

The reason for assigning revenue cutter officers to Life-Saving Service duty was historical. Because it had long been a distinct organization with its own personnel, the commission saw no reason to continue the practice. Initially, the drilling of lifesaving crews by revenue cutter officers had been beneficial because the surfmen had had no experience with disciplined organization. By now, the commission declared, the keepers of the stations had come up through the ranks and were well suited to drilling the surfmen. Also, they knew the surf and lifesaving equipment better than anyone else. A letter from Sumner Kimball to the secretary of the treasury, dated 25 March 1911, was quoted to document this last argument. Then, the commission, without much documentation, made similar cases for navigation, immigration, and quarantine services and recommended that revenue cutters used for harbor duties be turned over to those services.

Congress had not specified that the Revenue Cutter Service must suppress the slave trade, enforce neutrality laws, protect the merchant marine from pirates, assist vessels in distress, protect the seal fisheries, enforce immigration laws, suppress illegal arms and liquor traffic to Alaska, and protect game in Alaska, the commission claimed. The Treasury Department had assigned those duties to revenue cutters. Because there was no legislative mandate for cutters to be assigned those tasks, other agencies could perform them legally.

The commission stressed that its recommendation differed from all previous studies. It did not recommend moving the Revenue Cutter Service from one department to another. It recommended its total abolition as a separate service:

> In concluding this report the commission desires again to make it clear that its recommendation is essentially different in purpose from the various efforts made in the past affecting the status of the Revenue Cutter Service. The recommendation of the commission is that the service be abolished as a separate service, and that its duties be taken over by other services—not that a transfer of the service in toto be made. The position of the commission is, not that the service as at present organized and conducted should be in one department instead of another, but that there is no need for such a service at all; that the duties performed by it can be performed by other existing services at much less cost.[9]

The commission concluded by recommending the transfer of the cruising cutters to the navy and the harbor cutters to other appropriate agencies. It made no recommendation about revenue cutter personnel but left that issue until a decision was made on its other recommendations.

Congress distributed the commission's report to the Treasury Department, the Navy Department, and the Department of Commerce and Labor for comment. In reply, it received three definite arguments against the commission's recommendations and a response from Charles Nagel, secretary of commerce and labor, that could be interpreted as either for or against the proposed changes, depending on the section of his response on which one chose to concentrate.

Nagel responded to the report in a letter to the president dated 10 January 1912. He wrote that his department required the use of vessels from outside its own fleet to enforce the laws for which it was responsible, and it was "customary" to use some of the revenue cutters. He agreed with the commission's argument that many duties could be best performed by the departments charged with them. It would be more economical and efficient, he wrote, to transfer the cruising cutters to the navy, which could deliver the services needed by other departments. For example, cutters patrolling the Bering Sea to protect seal herds for the Department of Commerce and Labor could continue to carry out that duty under the navy just as well as under the Revenue Cutter Service. Many duties performed in smooth waters, such as enforcing navigation, steamboat inspection, anchorage, and motorboat laws and rules to prevent collisions and patrolling regattas, could be done more economically by vessels smaller than cutters.[10]

The more difficult question, in Nagel's mind, involved aiding vessels in distress along the U.S. coast, and he believed that revenue cutters detailed to that job should not be placed under the Navy Department. Economy and efficiency, he wrote, would be served by uniting under one administrative director the Life-Saving Service, Lighthouse Service, and Revenue Cutter Service. He did not indicate where that administration should be located, except to emphasize that it should not be in the Navy Department.[11]

Whereas Secretaries of the Navy William E. Chandler and Tracy had been anxious to absorb the Revenue Cutter Service in the 1880s and early 1890s, when they needed ships for naval officers and recent graduates of the Naval Academy, the secretary of the navy in 1912, George von Lengerke Meyer, considered the prospect of absorbing some of the service in 1912, after years of naval growth, a problem for the navy. "The functions of the two services are not similar," as the commission had argued, he wrote. The Revenue Cutter Service existed to assist vessels in distress, to protect seal fisheries, and to destroy derelicts. The navy existed to protect U.S. citizens abroad and to defend U.S. security in war. Naval vessels could perform the major duties of revenue cutters, but not, Meyer said, "as stated in the Cleveland report (p. 13) in the regular performance of their military duties. All duties which interfere with the training of the personnel for war are irregular and in a degree detrimental to the efficiency of the fleet." The navy did not want the personnel of the Revenue Cutter Service. It had just recently overcome personnel problems of its own. Taking into the navy the 390 (actually 290) officers and cadets and the 1,390 enlisted men of the Revenue Cutter Service would raise questions about pay, precedence, and privileges. Meyer emphasized that if the navy had to take over revenue cutter jobs, it would need both revenue cutters and enlisted personnel, but it did not want the officer corps. The ratio of officers to enlisted men in the navy was one to sixteen, in the Revenue

Cutter Service, one to four. Absorption of those officers into the navy, which had just solved its personnel problems, would just cause trouble.[12]

Secretary of the Treasury MacVeagh was completely surprised by the recommendations of the commission. He had not even known that such a study was being considered. No one connected with the Treasury Department had known of Cleveland's study until the report was finished. MacVeagh, of course, was aware of past proposals to transfer the service into the navy, but no one had ever thought of abolishing it. "It came at a time when the service was performing conspicuous and heroic work . . .," MacVeagh argued in a letter to President Taft.[13]

The public response to the proposal, he wrote, "was a salve to the wounded pride of the officers and men." The public had given a good deal of attention to it, "and no newspaper, no commercial organization, and no individual in Washington or throughout the country, so far as I am advised, has approved the suggestion."[14]

MacVeagh wrote that the service had been both efficient and indispensable since 1790 and was now more important than ever before. It was also more efficient than in the past, and performed more honorably. "To abolish a service with such a record and such present significance would be unprecedented," he argued.[15]

The commission's recommendation implied that a service was misplaced if it did "not exclusively act for a single department," but "at the same time" it "proposed to have the Navy Department do the same work . . . for other departments, including the Treasury." Economy, which was the motive for the recommendation, MacVeagh declared, "is not treated by the commission with any detail or even with any calculations. Only general expectations of savings are expressed. In point of fact, there would be no hope of economy. The captain commandant [of the Revenue Cutter Service] claims, on the basis of careful study and calculation, that it would cost about 50 per cent more to do the work through other departments."[16]

MacVeagh agreed with that calculation, and he was on solid ground when he challenged the economic claims of the commission. By its own admission, the commission had not investigated the efficiency of revenue cutter operations.

MacVeagh wrote that he knew that the navy needed more men and ships, and was in no position at that time to take on the work of the cutters without receiving additional vessels and personnel. If naval vessels performed cutter duties, it would cost more to do the job than it cost the Revenue Cutter Service to do it. He also noted that the work might be suspended if there were a war.[17]

No one was dissatisfied with the way the navy was employed, nor with its competence in doing the jobs assigned. No one wanted to divert it "from its purely naval occupations." The navy, MacVeagh wrote, "could never give the kind and degree of attention that is required of the Revenue Cutter Service and its officers and men trained in their particular duties for 120 years. The work is alien to the work of the Navy, alien to the spirit of the Navy, and alien, I think, to its professional capacities and instincts—alien certainly to its training and its tastes."[18]

MacVeagh added a few comments on the relationship between the Revenue Cutter Service and the Life-Saving Service. From the inside, he insisted, it was obvious that the two services should work more closely together, not be further separated. The Revenue Cutter Service, with its military character, offered precisely that training that the Life-Saving Service needed: "To disassociate the Life-Saving Service and the Revenue Cutter Service would be disastrous. We have been working to secure a closer relationship between the two services; and that is the line of progress; that is the line of development. I say this without any hesitation or doubt whatever. It would be the greatest mistake in the world to add any separation between these two great services. Indeed, I think it might be very well a little later to make the Life-Saving Service a part of the Revenue Cutter Service, and I believe that will be done."[19] MacVeagh had suggested the line of development that would, in fact, come out of the Cleveland Commission's initiative.

The secretary concluded his letter to the president by declaring that the notion that the Revenue Cutter Service should not have a military character was a misconception. The president of the United States and the governors of the states were not military officers, but they had military organizations under their control. City mayors introduced as much military discipline into their police and fire departments as they could. Within the Treasury Department, there were organizations with military characteristics. The Life-Saving Service was as military in character as the department had been able to make it. The Public Health Service and Marine Hospital Service were on a "military footing." These three military-type organizations always had been associated with the civilian Treasury Department and were, according to MacVeagh, "among the most conspicuously successful and admired branches of the Federal Government."[20]

With his letter, MacVeagh sent the president a copy of a speech he had given at the commissioning of the cutters *Unalga* and *Miami* on 10 February 1912 and a prepared statement, in the form of a letter from Commandant Bertholf of the Revenue Cutter Service to MacVeagh.

MacVeagh's speech retraced the history of the service and emphasized some of its more impressive accomplishments since the turn of the century, including its heroic service during the Spanish-American War, the Overland Expedition, impressive rescues involving both lives and property, the destruction of derelicts, patrolling of regattas, protection of seal herds in Alaska, and the enforcement of quarantines. He had concluded his speech on an effusive note, expressing the nation's pride in the service:

> The officers and men of this service are proud of it; proud of its history; proud of its over 120 years of achievement; and they have a right to be. The Treasury Department is proud of this service, and it has a right to be. The whole Government is proud of it, and has a right to be. And the people are proud of it—the people know well that they have a right to be proud of it. For in the course of the years it has come to be one of the most beneficent governmental agencies in the world. With the changing times this service, while always enlarging its useful duties to the Government in peace and war, has also become a protector of the helpless of the seas. This ever-alert fleet is the ever-vigilant friend and defender of those for whom there is no other help; and no more fearless vessels and no more gallant men ever patrolled the oceans in any part of the world. They are an honor to their country. They carry their lives in their hands; and when they are at rest in a harbor they stand at attention—listening for the cries for help.
>
> My friends, wherever a man sees a revenue cutter he ought to take off his hat to it.[21]

Bertholf's prepared statement was all business. He gave a survey of the service's duties, addressed the question of how efficient the organization was, asked if any other department could perform the duties with existing equipment, and evaluated the economic consequences of the commission's proposals. Beginning with the well-known origins of the service to prevent smuggling and to protect the seacoast during the years before the new nation had a navy, he explained that the government had understandably turned to the service to perform duties for departments that had no seagoing capability. Thus the service had assumed duties for several departments, notably the Departments of Commerce and Labor, Interior, Justice, and, to a limited degree, Agriculture. There was no disagreement between Bertholf and the commission about what those duties were. Bertholf contended that the commission did fail to appreciate that there was a need for an armed patrol to prevent smuggling. Smuggling was under control, he wrote, because "of the accumulated deterrent effect of years of vigilant patrol. . . . [Lawlessness was] kept in check only by physical force or the presence of such force, and it is clear that without an armed coast patrol smuggling would soon spring into existence along our many miles of seacoast."[22]

Although the commission had not studied the efficiency of the Revenue Cutter Service, Bertholf addressed the issue because, he said, "all investments are judged by the dividends paid," and it was therefore appropriate to evaluate the output of the service.[23] It was obviously difficult to judge the return to the nation for the money expended on the service because much of the benefit was in lives saved and nonmonetary rewards, but Bertholf compared the amounts spent on the service and the property saved by it. Between 1908 and 1912, the government had spent $9,192,670 to support the service and the service had saved floating property worth $40,689,494. Thus, an investment of $1 had saved $4.43. In contrast, for the years 1898 through 1901, the service had saved $2.39 worth of property for each dollar spent. In citing these figures, Bertholf's obvious points were that the nation received more value from the services of the cutters than it cost to operate them and that the service was becoming more efficient with the passage of time. For its support of the Revenue Cutter Service, the nation also received a very good naval auxiliary in time of war.

Bertholf's statement reviewed the duties performed by the service for the various government departments, and asserted that they could not be performed by the "existing equipment of other departments." For example the navy would have to save lives, assist vessels in distress, destroy derelicts, prevent smuggling, and patrol the Bering Sea. The secretary of the navy had already written that he did not have the vessels and personnel on hand to perform those duties. The Departments of Justice, Interior, and Agriculture would have to acquire and maintain vessels to perform the many duties carried out for them by the Revenue Cutter Service, including those in Alaska and Hawaii.

Finally, Bertholf declared that there would be no savings if the government distributed the vessels of the Revenue Cutter Service to the navy and civil departments to perform the work then being done by the cutters. He used specific cost figures to illustrate the validity of his case. For example, the navy would have to use vessels equivalent to first-class cutters to patrol the Bering Sea and to destroy derelicts. Because the navy did not have vessels of its own to spare, it would have to operate first-class cutters for those purposes. In a comparison of costs for the last three years, Bertholf demonstrated that the navy spent an average of $134,445 a year to operate a vessel comparable in size and characteristics to a first-class cutter, which the Revenue Cutter Service operated for an average of $84,552 a year. Put another way, the navy spent $127 to operate one ton of displacement versus the cost to the Revenue Cutter Service of $83.

Bertholf concluded: "This shows that the cost of maintenance and operation is 53.2 per cent greater in the Navy than in the Revenue Cutter Service for vessels of similar size and type." Thus, if the navy were to take over and operate twenty first-class cutters, "as proposed by the commission, . . . there would be an annual increase in cost of $840,000." Bertholf assumed that the Treasury Department could operate second- and third-class cutters and launches as economically as did the Revenue Cutter Service. The department would need all of the service's vessels for its duties. There would be no increase or decrease in cost to the government for services performed by the department if that proved to be the case. The Department of Commerce and Labor, would need at least fifteen small vessels, with a cost of at least $15,000 a year for maintenance, to perform the duties it would have to take over. This would increase the cost of the commission's proposal by $225,000 a year, not counting the cost of new vessels that would be required for the department to fulfill its obligations. The Departments of Interior, Justice, and Agriculture also had no vessels of their own, and they would have to purchase and maintain small craft for the duties currently performed by the Revenue Cutter Service. Not less than $20,000 a year for maintenance would be required for each of these departments, Bertholf asserted. This would add another $60,000 per year to the costs of $840,000 for the navy and $225,000 for the Department of Commerce and Labor. The total increase in the cost of government under the commission's plan would be at least $1,125,000, in addition to administrative expenses and the cost of acquiring the vessels that would be needed.[24]

Clearly, Bertholf stated, it was most reasonable to allow the Revenue Cutter Service, with its 122 years of experience, to continue to serve departments requiring the use of ships and boats to fulfill their obligations to the nation. The cutter service had grown to serve the nation at sea in a most reasonable way. It efficiently served the needs of the nation by using its vessels where and when they were needed.

Bertholf's statement concluded:

> To disband this organization and distribute its duties and equipment among the several departments, as proposed by the Commission on Economy and Efficiency, would inevitably result in the establishment of several services, each under a separate organization and administration, with all the confusion and expense incident to the formation of any organization as it passes through the transitory stage necessary for the perfection of the system. Each of these services would require as many vessels as the Revenue Cutter Service now periodically uses for that particular class of duty, if the same results are to be obtained. As none of these services could use the vessels or do the work of another service (otherwise the object sought in the proposed distribution would be lost), this would necessitate a far greater number of vessels in the several services than is now needed by the Revenue Cutter Service for the accomplishment of all these duties. All this would result in confusion and lack of coordination, which means inefficiency and duplication of equipment and administration, entailing under the most conservative estimate an additional annual expense of at least $1,125,000.[25]

The Cleveland Commission report and reports from opponents of the commission's findings were sent to President Taft. Not surprisingly, Taft supported his own economic adviser, Frederick Cleveland, and, on 4 April 1912, recommended that the Congress enact legislation to implement the commission's recommendations. Treasury Secretary MacVeagh, who remained convinced that the commission's recommendations were pure folly, ordered Bertholf and Kimball to draft a bill to unite the Life-Saving Service and the Revenue Cutter Service. MacVeagh sent the results of their labors—the bill to create the Coast Guard—to Congress, where it and

Taft's recommendation vied for attention with other important legislation, an internal struggle between conservatives and progressives for control of the Republican party, and a presidential election.

In the 1912 election, the people replaced President Taft with Woodrow Wilson, whose administration would ultimately act on the bill drawn up by Bertholf and Kimball. Secretary of the Treasury William G. McAdoo, MacVeagh's successor, was a strong supporter of the bill, as was President Wilson.

The bill to create the Coast Guard by uniting the Life-Saving Service and Revenue Cutter Service, accompanied by McAdoo's endorsement, was referred to the Committee of Commerce in the Senate and the Committee on Interstate and Foreign Commerce in the House of Representatives. The package for the Senate committee also included an account of the accomplishments of the Life-Saving Service and Revenue Cutter Service for fiscal year 1913. Both committees recommended passage of the bill.[26]

Provisions for retirement and longevity pay for members of the Life-Saving Service were written into the bill, under which they could ask to be retired at 75 percent of their pay after thirty years of service. This was essential, McAdoo wrote, for the life of a surfman was extremely dangerous. Between the organization of the Life-Saving Service and 1 January 1914, there had been 320 deaths in the service directly related to exposure and hazardous duty. An average of 11.7 deaths had occurred each year during the last decade, mostly from drowning. McAdoo explained that men injured on the job in the Life-Saving Service were paid two years' wages and their employment was terminated. When this happened, they were usually elderly and became dependent on others for their lives. Naturally, men were reluctant to serve under those conditions—eleven and one half percent of the men in the Life-Saving Service were let go or refused to continue in the service in fiscal year 1912. Several districts, he wrote, were finding it difficult to recruit new surfmen, which had resulted in employing temporary personnel, who were "too frequently of the ne'er-do-well, shiftless, and incompetent type, unable or unwilling to qualify for regular enlistment." Their presence demoralized the crews, and increased the danger of rescue attempts.[27]

The union of the Life-Saving Service and Revenue Cutter Service would provide better protection for life and property at sea, McAdoo wrote, and serve as a "valuable auxiliary to the Navy in time of war, as the Coast Guard, with its more than 4300 trained officers and enlisted men, would constitute a . . . naval auxiliary of no small proportions."[28]

An estimate of the increased annual cost of the Coast Guard under the provisions of bill S. 2337 accompanied each package to the House and Senate. Total increased costs of $397,700 were expected, $357,700 for the Life-Saving Service and $40,000 for the Revenue Cutter Service. Most of the increase would pay for retirement and longevity pay for the lifesavers. McAdoo, who agreed with the estimate, thought that it was "inconsiderable in comparison with the hundreds of lives and millions of dollars' worth of property saved annually by these two services."[29]

McAdoo also provided an abstract of the Life-Saving Service's 1913 annual report and a statistical survey of the rescue work performed by the two services. Each documented significant accomplishments. "In a total of 1,743 casualties," reported within range of the Life-Saving Service's stations, "but 69 vessels were totally lost." Of the 9,041 persons on board these vessels, 87 were lost. The vessels involved in the rescues were worth $13,080,380, the cargoes another $2,542,770. Of the total property value of $15,623,150, only $1,763,150 was lost. At the service's 279 stations, 437 persons were provided food and shelter for a total of 736 days. The Life-Saving Service alone had rescued 4,096 persons from peril and assisted vessels and cargoes worth $6,032,935. In the other rescues, they were assisted by revenue cutters, wrecking vessels, and others. Annual maintenance of the Life-Saving Service had cost $2,246,306 in 1913. That same year, the Revenue Cutter Service operated forty-four vessels (twenty-five seagoing ships and nineteen harbor tugs and launches), with an authorized complement of 1,838 men, at a cost of $2,471,532. It had rescued 327 persons and assisted vessels and cargoes worth $10,626,610.[30]

Both services agreed that Coast Guard was an appropriate name for their new organization. According to the report of the House Committee on Interstate and Foreign Commerce, the Coast Guard would continue its humanitarian service in time of peace but "have a military status, and become a first Naval Reserve in time of war." The committee reported the "principal advantages to be derived from the consolidation" as "increased efficiency in the saving of life and property, . . . simplification of the administrative functions, . . . a retired list for the highly deserving men of the Life-Saving Service, . . . and the creation of a first Naval Reserve of approximately 4,100 trained and experienced men." Total costs of the Coast Guard were expected to be about $5,000,000 a year. The committee report concluded: "The total cost of the Army and Navy, exclusive of pensions, is approximately $250,000,000 annually. In the opinion of this committee the expenditure of only one-fiftieth as much for saving life and property as we now expend for preparing to destroy them is, to say the least, warranted. The committee therefore recommends the passage of this bill at the earliest practicable time."[31]

The committee failed to get the full Senate to act on its recommendation to pass the bill in 1913. The Senate passed it on 12 March 1914.

The following year, on 20 January, the House of Representatives debated the bill. Even those who spoke against it, represented most significantly by Republican Congressman James Robert Mann of Illinois, acknowledged that the two U.S. services were the best organizations of their kind in the world. Their opposition to the bill was based on a desire to prevent an escalation in the costs of government. By granting longevity and retirement pay to the Life-Saving Service, they argued, the bill would increase government spending. They believed that lifesavers were paid more than adequately, when compared with men serving in the army and navy, and they feared that other civil servants would use any gains by the Life-Saving Service to support arguments for a further expansion of pension rights. Congressmen opposed to the civil service system argued that the Life-Saving Service could attract plenty of young men, if it would allow them to be hired without civil service examinations.[32] Even its proponents agreed that the bill would increase the cost of government by about $400,000 a year.

Congressman William C. Adamson, Democrat from Georgia, was the bill's strongest supporter. He responded to the economic argument for the bill's advocates: "If we are to be met at every juncture with the cry of economy when we come in to support the institutions of the Government, we can not get along decently. It is all right to spend $40,000,000 for a railroad, $300,000,000 for the Post Office, $35,000,000 for rivers and harbors, $30,000,000 for public buildings, two or three hundred millions for the support of the Army and the Navy, but when you come to talk about the organization which supports the civil system, collects the customs, defeats the pirates, catches the smugglers in time of peace, as well as saving the lives and property of the people, and fights our battles in time of war, they say you must not increase the expenses of the Government by $400,000." The House broke into applause.[33]

Opponents of the bill had other concerns, including the prospect, as they read and understood the bill, of revenue cutter officers receiving the same pay as naval officers, which they opposed. Congressmen who supported the legislation assured its opponents that the bill did not alter revenue cutter officers' pay. They would continue to be paid under an act of 1902 that stipulated that a revenue cutter captain would receive pay equal to that of a major in the army and a lieutenant commander in the navy; a first lieutenant, equal to captain in the army and lieutenant in the navy; a second lieutenant, equal to first lieutenant in the army and lieutenant (junior grade) in the navy; and a third lieutenant, equal to second lieutenant in the army and ensign in the navy. That issue agreed to, the House proceeded with its deliberations.[34]

Debate about the retirement of Sumner Kimball followed opposition to his retirement. This opposition was withdrawn when the opponent learned that Kimball was almost eighty years of age, but the issue offered those who knew Kimball and his work an opportunity to comment on his service. Congressman John Humphrey Small, a Democrat from North Carolina, said that he understood that Kimball was originally from the State of Maine and that "in sympathy he was a Republican." Small wanted his audience to know that he spoke without partisan motive: "Mr. Kimball deserves well of his country. He was at the head of the Life Saving Service at its inception. As a man he has the qualities which make for genuine manhood, in character, in sincere devotion to duty, in loyalty to the Government which he represents, and in fostering the service at the head of which he has been general superintendent he is a model of civic virtue. Mr. Chairman, whatever the Life Saving Service is today, the pride of our country and the pride of the world, in the saving of life and property, is due to the genius and the consecration to duty of Sumner I. Kimball."[35]

Small's tribute to Kimball evoked applause from the House. Finally, on 20 January 1915, the House passed S. 2337 to create the Coast Guard by a vote of 212 to 79, with 3 congressmen answering present and 130 not voting.[36] On that day, the service had forty-four vessels, twenty-five seagoing cutters and nineteen harbor tugs and launches, and 270 stations. The bill authorized a total of 4,093 officers, warrant officers, and enlisted men.[37] The service also consisted of one headquarters, in Washington, D.C., seventeen regional commands, four depots, and one academy.

Eight days later, President Wilson signed the bill into law. On 30 January, the union of the Life-Saving Service and the Revenue Cutter Service occurred to give birth to the U.S. Coast Guard.

The organizations replaced by the Coast Guard had served the nation very well indeed. In their last full fiscal year of life, ending on 30 June 1914, the two services had destroyed thirty-one derelicts, rescued 5,238 persons from peril, and assisted 2,147 vessels, with a total of 10,983 persons on board and a combined value (vessels and cargo) of $24,386,191. The cost of operating both services had been $4,781,949.[38]

Epilogue

The decision of Congress to retain the Coast Guard as an independent seagoing service in the Treasury Department was vindicated by the service's contribution to the success of the Allies during World War I. Coast Guard cutters supplemented naval destroyers on escort duty in the Atlantic Ocean and Mediterranean Sea during the critical months of the tonnage war of 1917–18. As captains of the nation's major ports, Coast Guardsmen stopped losses from sabotage and the careless handling of explosives. Coast Guard officers helped to alleviate the shortage of experienced seagoing professionals needed to command U.S. Navy combat ships, and the always important work of saving lives in U.S. waters became even more important when German U-boats began to take a toll on shipping along the Atlantic Coast during the summer of 1918. The Coast Guard would continue to serve with the U.S. Navy in future conflicts, including World War II, the Vietnam War, and the Persian Gulf War.

In peacetime, the Coast Guard continued to perform as a servant that met the nation's changing maritime needs. To its duties in preventing smuggling, it added liquor and drug interdiction, along with its efforts to stop illegal migrants during the 1980s and 1990s.

The Coast Guard absorbed the Lighthouse Service and the Bureau of Marine Inspection and Navigation during World War II.

After the war, it increased its obligation to protect those in peril on the sea, the world's environment, and the nation's natural resources.

Whenever the nation faces a new challenge on the high seas, it turns with confidence to the U.S. Coast Guard, which continues to expand into new frontiers as they are discovered.

Appendixes, Notes, and Bibliography

Summary of Cutter Operations,

YEAR	COST OF MAINTENANCE OF THE SERVICE, INCLUDING REPAIRS (IN DOLLARS)	NUMBER OF OFFICERS, CADETS, AND MEN	NUMBER OF VESSELS IN THE SERVICE	MILES CRUISED BY VESSELS	LIVES SAVED OR RESCUED FROM DROWNING	VESSELS ASSISTED
1880	845,333			265,263	65	114
1881	846,791	930	36	282,027	141	148
1882	846,423	999[C]	37	303,562	111	147
1883	853,553	1,002[C]	38	300,880	60	224
1884	851,311	950[D]	38	317,843	63	246
1885	819,807	1,027	39	312,569	60	274
1886		995	38	344,681	154	313
1887	890,000	1,046	38	351,395	42	207
1888	912,000			303,311	60	526
1889	965,000	1,062	37	274,287	26	122
1890	937,033	1,062	36	282,112	43	80
1891	934,995	1,063	36	301,416	26	123
1892	975,551	1,065	36	335,512	50	84
1893	920,342	984	34	305,807	29	119
1894	927,445	937	37	308,682	78	70
1895	925,000	937	26	310,661	43	122
1896	935,000			307,133	60	67
1897	945,180	1,257[E]	36	300,762	70	88
1898	1,066,478				27	92
1899	1,040,594	280[F]	42	239,061[G]	18[G]	111[G]
1900	1,229,337	292[F]	38	312,091	55	77
1901	1,256,550	293[F]	41	297,810	187	107
1902	1,203,637	282[F]	37	294,173	55	101
1903	1,441,614	300[F]	40		19	71
1904	1,524,763	293[F]	40		24	154
1905	1,610,812	300[F]	40		18	521
1906	1,469,595	299[F]	39		17	131
1907	1,795,000	311[F]	37		41	138
1908	1,814,155	326[F]	39		50	146
1909	2,418,481	331[F]	44		56	156
1910	2,545,361	373[F]	44		25	156
1911	2,455,041	363[F]	43		55	173
1912	2,458,246	1,808	43		106	260
1913	2,471,532	1,818	44		327	179
1914	2,472,632	1,906	43		476	210

[A] The average fines and penalties incurred by vessels for violating laws between 1881 and 1885 was $645,000.
[B] The average number of persons on board vessels assisted between 1881 and 1885 was 2,783.
[C] These numbers are based on the approximate number of 800 enlisted men in the service in 1882 and 1883.
[D] There were approximately 950 officers, cadets, and enlisted men in the service in 1884.

1880–1914

PERSONS ON BOARD VESSELS ASSISTED	VALUE OF VESSELS ASSISTED (IN DOLLARS)	VESSELS BOARDED AND PAPERS EXAMINED	VESSELS SEIZED OR REPORTED FOR VIOLATION OF LAWS	FINES AND PENALTIES INCURRED BY VESSELS VIOLATING LAWS (IN DOLLARS)	DERELICTS AND OBSTRUCTIONS TO NAVIGATION MOVED OR DESTROYED	REGATTAS PATROLLED
	2,011,509	36,318	3,556			
2,688[B]	2,776,882	29,101	3,163	645,614[A]		
2,688[B]	2,254,716	24,008	1,042	645,614[A]		
2,688[B]	4,885,175	25,587	2,240	645,614[A]		
3,310	7,015,572	26,282	2,270	683,642		
2,542	5,568,043	24,481	1,425	604,515		
2,888	6,738,569	28,304	1,688	651,199		
3,106	4,969,450	31,586	1,282	393,961		
4,041	7,328,793	25,552	1,026	311,844		
1,021	2,500,000	22,893	1,127	445,196		
	2,500,000	23,161	915	396,616		
	2,806,056	26,962	1,042	334,046		
570	2,417,745	37,521	1,233	363,173		
945	2,838,250	30,502	675	160,814		
658	1,709,105	29,727	482	98,335		
	1,081,592	23,726	451	176,433		
694	1,011,807	20,250	645	210,994		
623	1,217,213	18,549	536	149,007		
679	1,640,280	23,172	548	242,695		
946[G]	1,735,762[G]	18,039[G]	142[G]	28,970[G]		
3,520	4,923,095	20,089	309	54,860		
1,581	2,697,825	22,563	178	29,285		
645	2,224,089	22,567	191	45,182		
799	2,648,549	21,404	230	34,680		
1,217	2,714,072	16,738	494	131,620		
2,730	7,815,925	17,483	262	46,350		
1,664	5,012,955	17,344	378	67,410		
2,937	9,196,097	14,122	319	53,732	17	
3,269	6,858,918	13,252	242	54,700	18	
5,050	13,940,709	14,826	330	39,175	25	
1,801	10,247,535	18,799	647	160,569	28	
4,343	9,488,562	20,083	992	185,701	21	
2,212	10,545,573	24,918	1,208	224,210	45	31
2,755	10,626,610	25,079	850	180,470	31	39
1,687	9,056,551	28,787	968	204,310	31	50

[E] This is the number of authorized personnel for 1897.

[F] These numbers are the numbers of officers, cadets, and warrant officers in the service.

[G] These figures are exclusive of services with the army and navy in the Spanish-American War. The Revenue Cutter Service was without the services of fourteen vessels for part of the year while they were repaired as a result of their participation in the Spanish-American War.

Note: Blank spaces indicate that figures are not available

Source: author

Equipment in Stations
of the Life-Saving Service

66 **T**he stations (other than the house of refuge) are generally
equipped with two surf-boats (supplied with oars, life-boat
compass, and other outfits), a boat-carriage, two sets of
breeches-buoy apparatus (including a Lyle gun and acces-
sories), a cart for the transportation of the apparatus, a life-car,
twenty cork jackets, two heaving sticks, a dozen Coston signals, a
dozen signal rockets, a set of the signal flags of the International
Code, a medicine-chest with contents, a barometer, a thermome-
ter, patrol lanterns, patrol checks or patrol clocks, the requisite
furniture for rude housekeeping by the crew and for the succor of
rescued people, fuel and oil, tools for the repair of the boats and
apparatus and for minor repairs to the buildings, and the necessary books and stationery. At some of the stations, the Hunt gun
and projectiles are supplied, and at a few the Cunningham rocket
apparatus. To facilitate the transportation of boats and apparatus
to scenes of shipwreck a pair of horses is also provided at stations
where they can not be hired, and to those stations where the supplies, mails, etc., have to be brought by water a supply boat is furnished.

"The few lake stations located upon the sand beaches are similar in all respects to those upon the sea-coast, but those situated
at the harbors differ from them in that room is provided for a
heavy life-boat and for a small boat for quick work in the immediate vicinity of the station. The buildings are usually located not
far from the water's edge, behind one of the piers of crib-work
forming the sides of the harbor entrance. An inclined platform,
on which are laid two tramways for the launching of the boats,
extends from the boat room down to the water through an open-

ing cut in the pier. Cradles or cars are provided, on which the boats are kept mounted and by which they can be put afloat with the men at their oars in half a minute. Exit for the surf-boat wagon and apparatus cart is also provided in the rear of the building, in case it should be necessary to transport them along the shore. These stations usually have telephone connection with the systems of the adjacent towns.

"The houses of refuge on the Florida coast are simple dwellings, not unlike those common at the south, with capacity sufficient for the residence of a family, and for the temporary shelter of as many as are likely to need it. The distance between them averages 26 miles, and at each mile along the coast are placed guide posts indicating the distance and direction to the nearest station. The houses are supplied with cots and provisions sufficient to succor twenty-five persons for ten days. No boats or apparatus are provided, except a small galvanized iron boat for the use of the keeper."

Source: Quoted from Sumner I. Kimball, *Organization and Methods of the United States Life-Saving Service,* Washington, D.C.: Government Printing Office, 1890, 7–8.

Notes

CHAPTER ONE

1. George S. Boutwell, *Reminiscences of Sixty Years*, 2:129–30; Devereux, *Report of Chief of Revenue Marine*, 3–5.

2. Devereux, *Report of Chief of Revenue Marine*, 5.

3. George S. Boutwell, "Letter of Secretary of the Treasury," 1–12.

4. Devereux, *Report of Chief of Revenue Marine*, 4–8.

5. Ibid., 7.

6. Ibid., 4–8.

7. Boutwell, "Letter of Secretary of the Treasury," 5.

8. Ibid.

9. Devereux, *Report of Chief of Revenue Marine*, 8.

10. Ibid., 8, 15, 17–18.

11. Kimball, *Annual Report of Chief of Revenue Marine Bureau, 1872*, 20–21, 23, quotation on 23.

12. Ibid., 15, 17, 19; Chandler, *Annual Report of Secretary of the Navy*, 274–75; Boutwell, "Letter of Secretary of the Treasury," 4, 8.

13. Evans, *United States Coast Guard*, 91–92.

14. Emery, *History of Sanford, Maine*, 472–74.

15. Kimball, *Annual Report of Chief of Revenue Marine Bureau, 1872*, 21–22.

16. Ibid., 21; Clark, *Report of Operations of Revenue Marine Service*, 42–45; Boutwell, *Reminiscences of Sixty Years*, 2:129–30.

17. Kimball, *Annual Report of Chief of Revenue Marine Bureau, 1872*, 21, 23.

18. Kimball, *Annual Report of Chief of Revenue Marine Bureau, 1873*, 15–16.

19. Leonard D. White, *The Republican Era*, 110–33, especially 110, 116, 123, 129–33.

20. Clark, Report of Operations of Revenue Marine Service, 28; Evans, *United States Coast Guard*, 93–95; Johnson and Earle, "U.S. Coast Guard Academy," 2.

21. Kimball, *Annual Report of Chief of Revenue Marine Bureau, 1872*, 15–17.

22. Ibid., 1–3.

23. Ibid., 15–16.

24. Ibid., 15–16; Boutwell, "Letter of Secretary of the Treasury," 6.

25. Kimball, *Annual Report of Chief of Revenue Marine Bureau, 1872,* 16–17; Boutwell, "Letter of Secretary of the Treasury," 4–5.

26. Kimball, *Annual Report of Chief of Revenue Marine Bureau, 1873,* 15–16.

27. Clark, *Report of Operations of Revenue Marine Service,* 3–4, 7; *Register of Officers Vessels of Revenue Marine,* 16–23.

28. Clark, *Report of Operations of Revenue Marine Service,* 6–7.

29. Ibid., 5–7.

30. Chandler, *Annual Report of Secretary of the Navy, 1882,* 269.

31. Clark, *Report of Operations of Revenue Marine Service,* 4–5.

32. Ibid., 4–5, 7.

33. Kimball, *Annual Report of Chief of Revenue Marine Bureau, 1872,* 14, 15, 20.

34. Ibid., 15; Clark, *Report of Operations of Revenue Marine Service,* 12; Boutwell, "Letter of Secretary of the Treasury," 9.

35. Kimball, *Annual Report of Chief of Revenue Marine Bureau, 1872,* 19; Kimball, *Annual Report of Chief of Revenue Marine Bureau, 1873,* 15; Devereux, *Report of Chief of Revenue Marine,* 17–20; Boutwell, "Letter of Secretary of the Treasury," 8.

36. Kimball, *Annual Report of the Chief of the Revenue Marine Bureau, 1872,* 4, 14.

37. Ibid., Kimball, 14, 23.

38. Clark, *Report of Operations of Revenue Marine Service,* 12–13.

39. Kimball, *Annual Report of Chief of Revenue Marine Bureau, 1872,* 18; Kimball, *Annual Report of Chief of Revenue Marine Bureau, 1873,* 16–17.

40. Kimball, *Annual Report of Chief of Revenue Marine Bureau, 1872,* 23–25; Kimball, *Annual Report of Chief of Revenue Marine Bureau, 1873,* 17–18, 41.

41. Clark, Report of Operations of Revenue Marine Service, 52–54, 61–65.

42. Ibid., 47–52, 54, quotation on 51.

CHAPTER TWO

1. Evans, *United States Coast Guard,* 106–10; Bell, *Always Ready,* 127; Clark, *Report of Operations of Revenue Marine Service,* 54.

2. Morris, *Report upon Alaska Territory,* 103–4.

3. Ibid., 98, 99.

4. The information in this and the next two paragraphs is from Morris, *Report upon Alaska Territory,* 90–153.

5. Quoted in Evans, *United States Coast Guard,* 111–12.

6. Evans, *United States Coast Guard,* 110–14.

7. Albion, *Five Centuries of Famous Ships,* 273.

8. Morris, *Report upon Alaska Territory,* 56–57, 64–65.

9. Ibid., 64–66.

10. Ibid., 2, 13, 22–25.

11. Ibid., 27.

12. The information in this and the next three paragraphs is from Morris, *Report upon Alaska Territory,* 27–40, 126–27.

13. J. W. White, report reprinted in Morris, *Report upon Alaska Territory*, 127–28.

14. J. M. Selden, report reprinted in Morris, *Report upon Alaska Territory*, 128.

15. Morris, *Report upon Alaska Territory*, 131–32.

16. Quoted in Morris, *Report upon Alaska Territory*, 22–25.

17. Morris, *Report upon Alaska Territory*, 12.

18. Ibid., 22–25.

19. Killey, "Opening the Door to Alaska; 23–27; U.S. Coast Guard, Office of Assistant Commandant, *Record of Movements*, 1:193–96.

20. Muir, *The Cruise of the* Corwin, xii; Hooper, *Cruise of the* Corwin, *1880.*

21. Quoted in Noble and Voulgaris, "Alaska and Hawaii," 13.

22. Clark, *Report of Operations of Revenue Marine Service*, 58.

23. Reed, "Contribution of Coast Guard to Development of Alaska," 408; Hooper, *Cruise of the* Corwin, *1880,* 14, 52–54.

24. Hooper, *Cruise of the* Corwin, *1881,* 9, 14, 24–25, 27–28, 36, 46, 57–61.

25. Ibid., 5, 7, 8, 15, 20, 51–55, 64–71, 132; Muir, *Cruise of the* Corwin, 172, 177; Reed, "Contribution of Coast Guard to Development of Alaska," 408; Ross, "Our Coast Guard," 913–14.

26. Hooper, *Cruise of the* Corwin, *1881,* 13.

27. Allard, "To the North Pole," 60–61; Muir, *The Cruise of the* Corwin, ix–xvii, xxi–xxii.

28. Allard, "To the North Pole," 60–61.

29. Hooper, *Cruise of the* Corwin, *1880,* 19–23, 42–44; Hooper, *Cruise of the* Corwin, *1881,* 8–18.

30. Hooper, *Cruise of the* Corwin, *1880,* 10–12, 42–44, 62–64; Hooper, *Cruise of the* Corwin, *1881,* 9, 22–23.

31. Hooper, *Cruise of the* Corwin, *1880,* 42–44, 62–64.

32. Hooper, *Cruise of the* Corwin, *1881,* 113.

33. Hooper, *Cruise of the* Corwin, *1880,* 44–45, 63–64.

34. Ibid., 56.

35. Ibid., especially 13, 17–19, 29–30, 32, 34, 37, 40–41, 48, 65–68, 69–71; Hooper, *Cruise of the* Corwin, *1881,* 35, 44; Ross, "Our Coast Guard," 914–15.

36. U.S. Congress, House of Representatives, *Cruise of Revenue-Steamer* Corwin, *in Alaska,* 3–120; Muir, *Cruise of the* Corwin, ix–xiii, xvii, xxi–xxii, 18; Hooper, *Cruise of the* Corwin, *1881,* 22, 31, 33, 37, 38, 66, 75, 86, 135–46.

37. Evans, *United States Coast Guard,* 121.

38. *New York Sun,* 28 January 1894.

39. Morris, *Report upon Alaska Territory,* 25; quotation in Evans, *United States Coast Guard,* 107–8.

40. Reed, "Contribution of Coast Guard to Development of Alaska"; Wilkinson, "Reporter at Large," 110–12.

41. Evans, *United States Coast Guard,* 107–8; Reed, "Contribution of Coast Guard to Development of Alaska."

42. Wilkinson, "Reporter at Large," 111–12.

43. Account of the *Corwin*'s 1884 cruise is from Healy, *Cruise of Revenue Marine Steamer* Corwin, *1884,* 10–26, 53–74.

44. Ibid., 19.
45. Evans, *United States Coast Guard;* Murphy, *Cutter Captain,* 22–38.
46. Murphy, *Cutter Captain,* 24.
47. Cantwell's report of 1884 expedition in Healy, *Cruise of the* Corwin, *1884,* 51, 55–57, 60, 64–65, 68, 72, 74; quotation, 64.
48. Healy, *Cruise of Revenue Marine Steamer* Corwin, *1885,* 7, 23.
49. Ibid., 25–26.
50. Quoted in Healy, *Cruise of Revenue Marine Steamer* Corwin, *1885,* 34.
51. Quoted in Healy, *Cruise of Revenue Marine Steamer* Corwin, *1885,* 70.
52. Healy, *Cruise of Revenue Marine Steamer* Corwin, *1885,* 3, 3–102.
53. U.S. Coast Guard, Office of Assistant Commandant, Record of Movements, 1:284–85.
54. Account of the 1889 cruise of the *Rush* is from Shepard, *Cruise of the* Rush, 9–15, 72.
55. Shepard, *Cruise of the* Rush, *1889,* 189–90.
56. Ibid., 240–41.
57. Ibid.
58. Robert Erwin Johnson, *Guardians of the Sea,* 9; Evans, *United States Coast Guard,* 112–14; Hunt, *Arctic Passage,* 224–47.
59. Shoemaker, *Report of Chief of Division of Revenue Cutter Service,* 22–23.
60. G. L. Carden to D. P. Foley, Commanding Bering Sea Fleet, 22 June 1910; Carden to Foley, 25 September 1910; Bering Sea Memoranda (1910 cruise), 1–6; Memorandum, Japanese Sealing Vessels; J. C. to Lt. P. H. Brereton, 25 October 1910; all at U.S. Coast Guard Academy Library.
61. Bell, *Always Ready,* 143–44; Berry, *You Have to Go Out,* 103.

CHAPTER THREE

1. Chandler, *Annual Report of Secretary of the Navy,* 29, 31.
2. Ibid., 29.
3. The material in this and the next three paragraphs is from Chandler, *Annual Report of Secretary of the Navy,* 29–30.
4. The account of Clark's rebuttal is from Clark, "Report of Chief of Revenue Marine Division, 326–35.
5. Clark, *Report of Chief of Revenue Marine Division,* 328–29.
6. Forward quoted in Clark, *Report of Chief of Revenue Marine Division,* 335.
7. U.S. Congress, "History of Efforts Looking to Transfer of Service," 302–3.
8. Ross, "Our Coast Guard," 916.
9. U.S. Congress, "History of Efforts Looking to Transfer of Service," 337–38, 342.
10. Ibid., 339–41.
11. Ibid., 341–42.
12. Ibid., 342–49.
13. Shoemaker, *Report of Chief of Division of Revenue Cutter Service,* 9.
14. "List of Officers and Vessels in the United States Revenue-Cutter Service.

January 1, 1891"; "Register of the Officers and Vessels of the United States Revenue Marine, July 1, 1892." Both in Hamlet, *Register Revenue Cutter Service*, 3, 4.

15. U.S. Congress, *House Documents*, 62d Cong., 2d sess., vol. 116, 356.

CHAPTER FOUR

1. In Appendix A, a sample average was used for the cost of maintenance of the service; the number of officers, cadets and men; the number of vessels; the number of persons on board vessels assisted; and the fines and penalties incurred by vessels violating laws.

2. Clark, *Report of Operations of Revenue Marine Service*, 11.

3. Ibid., 15–17, 22–23.

4. Ibid., 24–28.

5. Hough, *Disaster on Devil's Bridge*, 3–7, 123; Forbes, *Notes on Some Few Wrecks and Rescues*, 66–67; *The Boston Daily Globe*, 19 January 1884, 1.

6. Hough, *Disaster on Devil's Bridge*, 3–7, 123; Forbes, *Notes on Some Few Wrecks and Rescues*, 67; *The Boston Daily Globe*, 5 February 1884, 6 February 1884, 1.

7. *The Boston Sunday Globe*, 20 January 1884, 1; 5 February 1884, 1; 6 February 1884, 1.

8. *The Boston Daily Globe*, 19 January 1884; 5 February 1884, 1; 6 February 1884, 1; 7 February 1884, 1.

9. Hough, *Disaster on Devil's Bridge*, 26–30.

10. Hammond and O'Leary quoted in *The Boston Daily Globe*, Saturday Evening, 19 January 1884, 1, 6.

11. Hough, *Disaster on Devil's Bridge*, 38–39; *The Boston Daily Globe*, 19 January 1884, 1; 5 February 1884, 1; 6 February 1884, 1.

12. *The Boston Daily Globe*, Saturday Evening, 19 January 1884, 1.

13. Hough, *Disaster on Devil's Bridge*, 41–42.

14. *The Boston Daily Globe*, 21 January 1884, 1.

15. Ibid.; quotation in Forbes, *Notes on Some Few Wrecks and Rescues*, 71.

16. Howe, *Humane Society of Massachusetts*, 238–39.

17. Ibid., 240; Howe reports that the crew transferred thirteen persons to the *Dexter*. An officer from the *Dexter*, in *The Boston Sunday Globe*, 27 January 1884, reports that the crew transferred twelve persons to the *Dexter*.

18. Hough, *Disaster on Devil's Bridge*, 52–57.

19. Ibid. 59–60, 66; quotation, 59–60; *The Boston Daily Globe*, Saturday Evening, 19 January 1884, 1.

20. Hough, *Disaster on Devil's Bridge*, 59–60, 107.

21. *The Boston Daily Globe*, Saturday Evening, 19 January 1884, 1.

22. Hough, *Disaster on Devil's Bridge*, 63; *The Boston Daily Globe*, Saturday Evening, 19 January 1884, 1.

23. Hough, *Disaster on Devil's Bridge*, 67, 69–70, 124–27. An officer of the *Dexter* wrote that six of the persons rescued by the *Dexter* lived. See *The Boston Sunday Globe*, 27 January 1884, 1; *The Boston Daily Globe*, 19 January 1884, 1.

24. Hough, *Disaster on Devil's Bridge*, 79–82; *The Boston Sunday Globe*, 20 January 1884, 1.

25. Ibid.

26. Forbes, *Notes on Some Few Wrecks and Rescues*, 71; Hough, *Disaster on Devil's Bridge*, 78, 85–93; *The Boston Daily Globe*, 6 and 7 February 1884, 1.

27. *Annual Report of Secretary of the Treasury, 1884*, LI.

28. Manning, *Annual Report of Secretary of the Treasury, 1885*, XLVIII.

29. Manning, *Annual Report of Secretary of the Treasury, 1886*, LVI.

30. U.S. Congress, "Economy and Efficiency," 293.

31. Windom, *Annual Report of Secretary of the Treasury, 1889*, LXXXIV; Congdon, "Newspaper Clippings."

32. Windom, *Annual Report of Secretary of the Treasury, 1890*, LV.

33. Manning, *Annual Report of Secretary of the Treasury, 1886*, LIII, LIV.

34. Fairchild, *Annual Report of Secretary of the Treasury, 1887*, XXXVIII, XXXIX.

35. Ibid., XXXVIII–XXXIX.

36. Fairchild, *Annual Report of Secretary of the Treasury, 1888*, XXXIX.

37. Windom, *Annual Report of Secretary of the Treasury, 1889*, LXXXIV.

CHAPTER FIVE

1. Chandler, *Annual Report of Secretary of the Navy*, 277; Ross, "Our Coast Guard," 916; King, *Coast Guard under Sail*, x, 84, 88, 110–42, 155, 156.

2. *List of Officers and Vessels*, 1892, 4; U.S. Congress, *House Documents*, 62d Cong., 2d Session, 356.

3. Congdon, "Newspaper Clippings."

4. U.S. Treasury, Revenue Cutter Service, *Annual Report, 1891*, 2–3.

5. Ibid.

6. Congdon, "Newspaper Clippings."

7. Windom, *Annual Report of Secretary of the Treasury, 1890*, LV–LVI.

8. Foster, *Annual Report of Secretary of the Treasury, 1891*, LI. Also, see Shoemaker, *Report of Chief of Division of Revenue Cutter Service*, 11.

9. Foster, *Annual Report of Secretary of the Treasury, 1891*, LI.

10. Foster, *Annual Report of Secretary of the Treasury, 1892*, XLIII.

11. Carlisle, *Report of Secretary of the Treasury, 1893*, XXXIX.

12. Shoemaker, *Report of Chief of Division of Revenue Cutter Service*, 11.

13. Carlisle, *Annual Report of Secretary of the Treasury, 1894*, XXXIII.

14. Carlisle, *Annual Report of Secretary of the Treasury, 1895*, XXXI–XXXII; Windom, *Annual Report of Secretary of the Treasury, 1889*, LXXXIV–LXXV; Windom, *Annual Report of Secretary of the Treasury, 1890*, LV.

15. Evans, *United States Coast Guard*, 157.

16. Windom, *Annual Report of Secretary of the Treasury, 1890*, LVI; Foster, *Annual Report of Secretary of the Treasury, 1891*, XLIX; Foster, *Annual Report of Secretary of the Treasury, 1892*, XLIX; Carlisle, *Annual Report of Secretary of the Treasury, 1893*, XXXIX; Carlisle, *Annual Report of Secretary of the Treasury, 1894*, XXXIII; Carlisle, *Annual Report of Secretary of the Treasury, 1895*, XXXII.

17. Carlisle, *Annual Report of Secretary of the Treasury, 1894*, XXXIII.

18. Congdon, "Newspaper Clippings."

19. U.S. Congress, *House Documents*, 62d Cong., 2d sess., 356.

20. Carlisle, *Annual Report of Secretary of the Treasury, 1895*, XXXII–XXXIII.

21. Evans, *United States Coast Guard*, 151–56; Murphy, *Cutter Captain*, 69–72.

22. Congdon, "Newspaper Clippings."

23. Shoemaker, *Report of Chief of Division of Revenue Cutter Service*, 11, 12; Bertholf, *Annual Report of Revenue Cutter Service, 1914*, 15.

24. Shoemaker, *Report of Chief of Division of Revenue Cutter Service*, 12.

25. Ibid., 13; Bertholf, *Annual Report of Revenue Cutter Service, 1914*, 15.

26. Baker, "Seamanship Notes"; Bertholf, *Annual Report of Revenue Cutter Service, 1914*, 15.

27. Shoemaker, *Report of Chief of Division of Revenue Cutter Service*, 8, 9, 18; Carlisle, *Annual Report of Secretary of the Treasury, 1895*, 32–33.

28. Carlisle, *Annual Report of Secretary of the Treasury, 1896*, XLI; Gage, *Annual Report of Secretary of the Treasury, 1897*, XLI–XLIII; Shoemaker, *Report of Chief of Division of Revenue Cutter Service*, 18–19, 23.

CHAPTER SIX

1. Albion, *Five Centuries of Famous Ships*, 271–72; Bell, *Always Ready*, 134; Bixby, *Track of the* Bear, 89; Ross, "Our Coast Guard," 915.

2. Quoted in Burroughs, *The Great Ice Ship* Bear, 42.

3. Albion, *Five Centuries of Famous Ships*, 271–72.

4. Ibid., Burroughs, *The Great Ice Ship* Bear, 9–19.

5. Schley, *Forty-Five Years under the Flag*, 146–57.

6. Ibid., Schley, 146–57, 158–69, 170–81; Noble and Strobridge, "Arctic Adventures of the *Thetis*," 3–4.

7. Burroughs, *The Great Ice Ship* Bear, 40.

8. General Court, testimony taken at the investigation into the conduct of Capt. M. A. Healy of the Revenue Cutter *Bear*, San Francisco, California, 10 March 1896, Entry 184, Record Group 26, Records of the U.S. Coast Guard, National Archives. This collection is hereafter cited as RG 26.

9. Ibid.

10. Ibid.

11. L. J. Gage, Secretary, to Capt. Francis Tuttle, R. C. S., Treasury Department, Office of the Secretary, Washington, D.C., 15 November 1897, *Report of the Cruise of the Revenue Cutter* Bear *and the Overland Expedition for the Relief of the Whalers in the Arctic Ocean, from November 27, 1897, to September 13, 1898*, 5.

12. Burroughs, *The Great Ice Ship* Bear, 47.

13. Ibid., 45–47; Bixby, *Track of the* Bear, 207–12.

14. Burroughs, *The Great Ice Ship* Bear, 48–49.

15. Ibid., 49.

16. Healy, *Cruise of Revenue Marine Steamer* Corwin, *1885*, 88.

17. Cantwell, "Captain Healy's Reindeer," 27.

18. Ibid., 28–29, 58–59.

19. Ibid., 59.

20. Burroughs, *The Great Ice Ship* Bear, 54–56; Evans, *United States Coast Guard*, 132–33; Jackson, *Introduction of Domesticated Reindeer into Alaska*, 21.

21. Burroughs, *The Great Ice Ship* Bear, 54–56.

22. Account of the introduction of reindeer is from Jackson, *Introduction of Domesticated Reindeer into Alaska*, 14, 16–18, 21, 31.

23. Jackson, *Twelfth Annual Report on Domestic Reindeer, 1902*, 35; Hunt, *Arctic Passage*, 176–82, 194, 200–201.

24. Jackson, *Introduction of Domesticated Reindeer into Alaska*, 11–14.

25. Ibid., 22.

26. Anderson and Eels, *Alaska Natives*, 197.

27. James T. White, "Diary of Cruise of Revenue Steamer *Bear* in 1889, 10 June–28 Sept. 1889, 23 June 1889." Also, see Bixby, *Track of the* Bear, 232–33.

28. James T. White, "Diary of Cruise of Revenue Steamer *Bear* in 1889, 28 June, 3 July, and 25–26 July."

29. General Court, Capt. M. A. Healy, RG 26.

30. Ibid., quotation is in Paul H. Johnson, "Captain Michael A. Healy, Part III," 26–30.

31. *The New York Times*, 10 Jun 1896, 1; Bixby, *Track of the* Bear, 232–33.

32. Gage's letter quoted in U.S. Revenue Cutter Service, *Report of Cruise of* Bear *and Overland Expedition*, 5.

33. U.S. Revenue Cutter Service, *Report of Cruise of* Bear *and Overland Expedition*, 5–10; Bixby, *Track of the* Bear, 154.

34. U.S. Revenue Cutter Service, *Report of Cruise of* Bear *and Overland Expedition*, 9–10.

35. Ibid., 139–40.

36. Ibid., 11; Wead, *Gales, Ice and Men*, 148.

37. Account of Jarvis's trip north is from U.S. Revenue Cutter Service, *Report of Cruise of* Bear *and Overland Expedition*, 29–79, 104, 143–44.

38. U.S. Revenue Cutter Service, *Report of Cruise of* Bear *and Overland Expedition*, 33–34.

39. Ibid., 35, 104; Bixby, *Track of the* Bear, 160.

40. David H. Jarvis, letter to Secretary of the Treasury, mailed from Andreaofski, Alaska, 24 December 1897.

41. U.S. Revenue Cutter Service, *Report of Cruise of* Bear *and Overland Expedition*, 43; Bixby, *Track of the* Bear, 162–64.

42. Gaw, "Tilton's Walk," 19–21; Tilton, *Cap'n George Fred Himself*, 164–208; D. H. Jarvis, letter to Secretary of the Treasury, mailed from Norton Sound, 3 January 1898.

43. Tilton, *Cap'n George Fred Himself*, 205, 207.

44. Bixby, *Track of the* Bear, 165–66.

45. Account of Jarvis's trip from Point Clarence to Cape Prince of Wales is from U.S. Revenue Cutter Service, *Report of Cruise of* Bear *and Overland Expedition*, 47–57, 143–44; quotations, 47–48.

46. U.S. Revenue Cutter Service, *Report of Cruise of* Bear *and Overland Expedition,* 55.

47. Ibid. 57–67; Jackson, *Twelfth Annual Report on Domestic Reindeer,* 4.

48. Account of remainder of trip to Point Barrow and the conditions at Point Barrow is from U.S. Revenue Cutter Service, *Report of Cruise of* Bear *and Overland Expedition,* 64–84, 87–90, 95, 119, 143.

49. U.S. Revenue Cutter Service, *Report of Cruise of* Bear *and Overland Expedition,* 79.

50. Ibid., 81.

51. Ibid., 82–83.

52. Quoted in U.S. Revenue Cutter Service, *Report of Cruise of* Bear *and Overland Expedition,* 117.

53. U.S. Revenue Cutter Service, *Report of Cruise of* Bear *and Overland Expedition,* 88.

54. Ibid., 95–101; Wead, *Gales, Ice and Men,* 164–65.

55. U.S. Revenue Cutter Service, *Report of Cruise of* Bear *and Overland Expedition,* 101–2, 120, 125.

56. Ibid., 128.

57. Account of the Alaskan gold rush and the *Bear*'s activities relating to the gold rush is from Bixby, *Track of the* Bear, 200–207.

CHAPTER SEVEN

1. Shoemaker, *Report of Chief of Division of Revenue Cutter Service,* 21.

2. Carlisle, *Annual Report of Secretary of the Treasury, 1895,* XXXI.

3. Carlisle, *Annual Report of Secretary of the Treasury, 1896,* XXXIX–XL.

4. Gage, *Annual Report of Secretary of the Treasury, 1897,* XXXIX.

5. U.S. Coast Guard, Office of Assistant Commandant, *Record of Movements,* 1:148; The President, "Transfer of the Cutters on the Great Lakes to the Navy," May 3, 1898, in correspondence concerning the operations of the Revenue Cutter Service in the Spanish-American War, 1898, Entry 175, RG 26.

6. *The New York Times,* 26 January 1896, 2.

7. "Vessels Recently Added to the Navy," 17.

8. Sargent, *Admiral Dewey and the Manila Campaign,* 17.

9. U.S. Coast Guard, Office of Assistant Commandant, *Record of Movements,* 2:370–73.

10. U.S. Congress, *United States Revenue Cutter Service in War with Spain,* 13–14.

11. Sargent, *Admiral Dewey and Manila Campaign,* 21–22; Vivian, *With Dewey at Manila,* 11; Wilson, *Downfall of Spain,* 122.

12. U.S. Congress, *United States Revenue Cutter Service in War with Spain,* 14.

13. Ibid.; Daniel B. Hodgsdon to Commodore George Dewey, 3 May 1898, "Operations of the Service in the Spanish-American War," 1898, Entry 175, RG 26.

14. Spears, *Our Navy in War with Spain,* 162–63.

15. U.S. Congress, *United States Revenue Cutter Service in War with Spain,* 10, 13, 15; quotation in Hodgsdon to Dewey, 3 May 1898.

16. Sargent, *Admiral Dewey and Manila Campaign*, 35–37.

17. Ibid., 34–35, 39; Spear, *Our Navy in War with Spain*, 172–79.

18. U.S. Congress, *United States Revenue Cutter Service in War with Spain*, 13, 15.

19. Sargent, *Admiral Dewey and Manila Campaign*, 104, 109; Spear, *Our Navy in War with Spain*, 186–87, 189.

20. Adelbert Dewey, *Life and Letters of Admiral Dewey*, 239; Ridgely, "Coast Guard Cutter *McCulloch* at Manila," 418; Sargent, *Admiral Dewey and Manila Campaign*, 104; U.S. Congress, *United States Revenue Cutter Service in War with Spain*, 15; Hodgsdon to Dewey, 3 May 1898.

21. Sargent, *Admiral Dewey and Manila Campaign*, 44, 51, 52; Trask, *War with Spain in 1898*, 369; U.S. Congress, *United States Revenue Cutter Service in War with Spain*, 10.

22. Trask, *War with Spain in 1898*, 402; U.S. Congress, *United States Revenue Cutter Service in War with Spain*, 16; McCutchenk, "Surrender of Manila," 935.

23. Spears, *Our Navy in War with Spain*, 118–19, 126, 127, 129, 130.

24. U.S. Congress, *House Documents*, 62d Cong., 2d sess., 386.

25. S. E. Maguire, "Reporting Part Taken by *Windom* in the Action at Cienfuegos, Cuba, May 11, 1898," in *Operations of the Service in the Spanish-American War*, 1898, Entry 175, RG 26; Spears, *Our Navy in War with Spain*, 141.

26. Maguire, "Reporting Part Taken by *Windom*"; Spears, *Our Navy in War with Spain*, 141–45.

27. Maguire, "Reporting Part Taken by *Windom*."

28. Spears, *Our Navy in War with Spain*, 145; Mead, "Rescue of the *Winslow*," 122; Goode, *With Sampson through the War*, 96–97.

29. Mead, "Rescue of the *Winslow*," 122; Frank H. Newcomb, "Report of Part Taken by *Hudson* in Recent Engagements at Cardenas," 31 May 1898, in *Operations of the Service in the Spanish-American War*, 1898, Entry 175, RG 26; U.S. Congress, *United States Revenue Cutter Service in War with Spain*, 20–21.

30. Wilson, *Downfall of Spain*, 184–85; Goode, *With Sampson through the War*, 99–102.

31. Spears, *Our Navy in War with Spain*, 150–51.

32. Mead, "Rescue of the *Winslow*," 126.

33. Mead, "Rescue of the *Winslow*," 126–28; U.S. Congress, *United States Revenue Cutter Service in War with Spain*, 10–11.

34. Newcomb, "Report of Part taken by *Hudson* in Recent Engagements at Cardenas"; Mead, "Rescue of the *Winslow*," 128–29; U.S. Congress, *United States Revenue Cutter Service in War with Spain*, 20–22.

35. Todd's remarks in Goode, *With Sampson through the War*, 102–3.

36. U.S. Congress, *United States Revenue Cutter Service in War with Spain*, 11; U.S. Congress, *Senate Report*, 57th Cong., 1st sess., Vol. 2, 11; Also see Frank H. Newcomb, "Supplementary Report of Part Taken by This Vessel *[Hudson]* in Late Engagement at Cardenas," 16 June 1898, in *Operations of the Service in the Spanish-American War*, 1898, File 175, RG 26.

37. U.S. Congress, *House Documents*, 62d Cong., 2d sess., 386.

38. W. E. Reynolds, "Report of Duties Performed in Cooperation with the

Navy—April 12, 1898, to August 26, 1898," in *Operations of the Service in the Spanish-American War, 1898,* File 175, RG 26. Also, see U.S. Congress, *United States Revenue Cutter Service in War with Spain,* 37–39.

39. U.S. Coast Guard, Office of Assistant Commandant, *Record of Movements,* 1:159; U.S. Congress, *United States Revenue Cutter Service in War with Spain,* 7.

40. F. M. Munger, four reports of duty performed by the *Manning* between 1 June 1898 and 22 August 1898, in *Operations of the Service in the Spanish-American War, 1898,* File 175, RG 26; quotation in U.S. Congress, *United States Revenue Cutter Service in War with Spain,* 11–12, 25–28, 31–34.

41. U.S. Congress, *United States Revenue Cutter Service in War with Spain,* 10, 16–17.

42. Ibid., 16.

43. Admiral Dewey quoted in U.S. Congress, *United States Revenue Cutter Service in War with Spain,* 10.

44. Sargent, *Admiral Dewey and Manila Campaign,* 67–70.

45. U.S. Congress, *United States Revenue Cutter Service in War with Spain,* 19–20.

46. Ibid.; Ridgely, "The Coast Guard Cutter *McCulloch* at Manila," 417–26.

47. U.S. Congress, United States *Revenue Cutter Service in War with Spain,* 9, 19, 28.

48. Gage, *Annual Report of Secretary of the Treasury, 1899,* LVI–LVIII; Gage, *Annual Report of Secretary of the Treasury, 1900,* LVIII–LIV; Gage, *Annual Report of Secretary of the Treasury, 1901,* 48–49.

49. U.S. Congress, Senate Committee on Commerce, *Efficiency of the Revenue Cutter Service,* 1–2.

50. Ibid., 8.

51. Shaw, *Annual Report of Secretary of the Treasury, 1902,* 40–41.

52. Ibid.

CHAPTER EIGHT

1. Murphy, *Cutter Captain,* 76–80.

2. Ibid., 80–81; Cantwell, *Report of Revenue Steamer* Nunivak, 9–12.

3. Account of the voyages of the *Nunivak,* 1899–1900, is from Cantwell, *Report of Revenue Steamer* Nunivak, 24–27, 35–37, 44–58, 61, 64, 67, 69–70, 74, 280–81.

4. *New Orleans Times-Democrat,* 21 July–27 October 1905, especially 29 July, 1, 3; 31 July, 1; 20 August, 8; 23 August, 1, 3, 5, 6; 24 August, 3; 25 August, 1, 7; 27 October, 1, 4. Also, see *The New York Times,* 16 August 1905; 20 August, 4; 30 August, 4.

5. *New Orleans Times-Democrat,* 7 August–27 October 1905, especially 29 July, 3; 28 July, 3; 7 August, 1; 16 August, 1, 3, 4; 19 August, 3, 4; 27 October, 1, 4.

6. As reported in *New Orleans Times-Democrat,* 20 August 1905, 8.

7. *New Orleans Times-Democrat,* 29 July 1905, 3; U.S. Coast Guard, Office of Assistant Commandant, *Record of Movements,* 1:160; U.S. Congress, *House Documents,* 62d Cong., 2d sess., 388; Shaw, *Annual Report of Secretary of the Treasury,*

1906, 35; correspondence relating to the Yellow Fever Patrol, 1905, Entry 177, RG 26.

8. *The New York Times*, 2 August 1905, 1; 5 August 1905, 1; 6 August 1905, 1, 3; U.S. Coast Guard, Office of Assistant Commandant, *Record of Movements*, 1:160; correspondence, Yellow Fever Patrol.

9. Correspondence, Yellow Fever Patrol; see especially the report by 2d Lt. John Boedeker, USRCS, and Eugene Wasdin, M.D., to Lt. Edmonds, 23 October 1905.

10. Wasdin to Edmonds.

11. Correspondence concerning the San Francisco fire, 1906, Entry 178, RG 26.

12. O. C. Hamlet to Chief of Division, Revenue Cutter Service, 3 May 1906; C. F. Goodrich, Rear Admiral, U.S. Navy, Commander-in-Chief, Pacific Squadron, to Hamlet, 2 May 1906, both in Entry 178, RG 26.

13. O. C. Hamlet to Secretary of the Treasury, 7 May 1906; John T. Bell to L. Shaw, 4 May 1906, both in Entry 178, RG 26.

14. John C. Berry to Secretary of the Treasury, 9 May 1906, Entry 178, RG 26.

15. Lt. F. G. Dodge to Secretary of the Treasury, 1 May 1906, Entry 178, RG 26.

16. G. W. Glover to O. C. Hamlet, 1 May 1906; C. C. McMillan to Capt. O. C. Hamlet, 1 May 1906; Hamlet to Secretary of the Treasury, 21 April 1906, all in Entry 178, RG 26.

17. J. C. Cantwell to Secretary of the Treasury, 18 April, 22 April, and 17 May 1906, Entry 178, RG 26.

18. O. C. Hamlet to Secretary of the Treasury, 22 April 1906; Lt. F. G. Dodge to Secretary of the Treasury, 22 April and 1 May 1906; M. H. Simons, report of admission into hospital of S. Ichiba of the revenue cutter *Bear*, 24 April 1906, all in Entry 178, RG 26.

19. C. F. Goodrich to O. C. Hamlet, 2 May 1906, Entry 178, RG 26.

20. Theodore Roosevelt to Hon. H. A. Taylor, Acting Secretary of the Treasury, 31 May 1906.

21. U.S. Congress, *House Documents*, 61st Cong., 2d sess., 6; *The Boston Daily Globe*, 26 January 1909, 7.

22. *The Boston Daily Globe*, 26 January 1909, 1, 4, 5; *The Boston Daily Globe*, 27 January 1909, 8.

23. *The Boston Sunday Globe*, 24 January 1909, 1, 13; *The Boston Daily Globe*, 25 January 1909, 5, 9.

24. *The Boston Daily Globe*, 23 January 1909, 5; *The Boston Sunday Globe*, 24 January 1909, 13; *The Boston Daily Globe*, 25 January 1909, 1; U.S. Congress, *House Documents*, 61st Cong., 2d Session, 6 et seq.

25. U.S. Congress, *House Documents*, 61st Cong., 2d sess., 6; *The Boston Daily Globe*, 26 January 1909, 7.

26. U.S. Congress, *House Documents*, 61st Cong., 2d sess., 6 et seq.

27. Ibid.

28. *The Boston Daily Globe*, 26 January 1909, 1, 4, 7.

29. U.S. Congress, *House Documents*, 61st Cong., 2d sess., 6 et seq.; *The Boston Daily Globe*, 26 January 7 and 27 January 1909, 7.

30. Quoted in *The Boston Daily Globe*, 27 January 1909, 7.

31. *The Boston Daily Globe*, 26 January 1909, 7.

32. U.S. Congress, *House Documents*, 61st Cong., 2d sess., 6 et seq.

33. *The Boston Daily Globe*, 23 January 1909, 1.

34. From statements of Gatchell and Marconi in *The Boston Sunday Globe*, 24 January 1909, 13, 14.

35. Reported in *The Boston Daily Globe*, 27 January 1909, 7.

36. *Portland Evening Express*, 15 January 1912, 1; MacVeagh, "Address Delivered by McVeagh," 387.

37. *Portland Evening Express*, 15 January, 1, and 16 January 1912, 2.

38. *Portland Evening Express*, 15 January 1912, 1, and 19 January 1912, 7.

39. Events of the rescue as reported in *Portland Evening Express*, 19 January 1912, 7, and *The New York Times*, 21 January 1912, 5; Bertholf, *Annual Report of United States Revenue Cutter Service*, 1912, 43.

40. *The New York Times*, 21 January 1912, 5; *Portland Evening Express*, 25 January 1912, 16.

41. MacVeagh, "Address Delivered by MacVeagh," 387.

42. U.S. Coast Guard, Office of Assistant Commandant, *Record of Movements*, 2:385–88; Bundy, *Maritime Association*, 65; U.S. Congress, *House Documents*, 62d Cong., 2d sess., 361; International Ice Patrol File, Box 1368, Entry 283A, RG 26.

43. U.S. Congress, *House Documents*, 62d Cong., 2d sess., 361; E. P. Bertholf to Franklin MacVeagh, January 18, 1913, International Ice Patrol File, Box 1368, Entry 283A, RG 26.

44. Morgan, "Coastal Shipping under Sail, 1880–1920," 17.

45. U.S. Coast Guard, Office of Assistant Commandant, *Record of Movements*, 2:385–88; Bundy, *Maritime Association*, 65; International Ice Patrol File, Box 1368, Entry 283A, RG 26.

46. Bertholf, *Annual Report of Revenue Cutter Service*, 1912, 43–46; Bertholf, *Annual Report of Revenue Cutter Service*, 1913, 42–44; Bertholf, *Annual Report of Revenue Cutter Service*, 1914, 77–78.

47. Bertholf, *Annual Report of Revenue Cutter Service*, 1912, 43.

48. Ibid.; Bertholf, *Annual Report of Revenue Cutter Service*, 1913, 42–44; Bertholf, *Annual Report of Revenue Cutter Service*, 1914, 77–78; *Annual Report of Secretary of the Treasury*, 1913, 67.

49. Treasury Department, *Methods of Searching for Derelicts*, 3–8.

50. *The New York Times*, 4 March, 1, and 7 March 1910, 6.

51. *Annual Report of Secretary of the Treasury*, 1914, 181.

52. Evans, *United States Coast Guard*, 147–48; Robert Erwin Johnson, *Guardians of the Sea*, 9–10.

53. *Annual Report of Secretary of the Treasury*, 1914, 180–81.

54. Account of the *Titanic* disaster is from Albion, *Five Centuries of Famous Ships*, 335–39.

55. Bertholf, *Annual Report of Revenue Cutter Service*, 1913, 46–48; Bertholf, "Reports of Vessels on Ice Patrol," 5–6; Williard U. Taylor, President, Maritime Association of the Port of New York, to Hon. William McAdoo, 13 March 1913; and

Meyer to Franklin MacVeagh, 28 February 1913, both in International Ice Patrol File, Box 1368, Entry 283A, RG 26.

56. Captain Commandant, memorandum to Mr. Allen, 4 January 1913; and E. P. Bertholf to Franklin MacVeagh, 18 January 1913, both in International Ice Patrol File, Box 1368, Entry 283A, RG 26.

57. Bertholf, *Annual Report of Revenue Cutter Service, 1913*, 48–49; Bertholf, "Reports of Vessels on Ice Patrol," 3–4; International Ice Patrol File, Box 1368, Entry 283A, RG 26.

58. C. E. Johnston to Secretary of the Treasury, 23 April 1913, in International Ice Patrol File, Box 1368, Entry 283A, RG 26.

59. Bertholf, "Reports of Vessels on Ice Patrol," 8–10.

60. Ibid., 10–16.

61. E. P. Bertholf, memorandum to Mr. Allen, 24 June 1913; and Bertholf to Hydrographer, Navy Department, 1 July 1913, both in International Ice Patrol File, Box 1368, Entry 283A, RG 26.

62. Account of Johnston's observations, with quotations from his report, is in Bertholf, "Reports of Vessels on Ice Patrol," 20–24.

63. President, New York Maritime Exchange, letter to Secretary of the Treasury, 8 July 1913, in International Ice Patrol File, Box 1368, Entry 283A, RG 26; Bertholf, *Annual Report of Revenue Cutter Service, 1913*, 49–50.

64. McAdoo, *Annual Report of Secretary of the Treasury, 1914*, 181–82; Instructions to the *Scotia*'s master and testimony of E. P. Bertholf before House Committee on Appropriations on Deficiency Bill for fiscal year 1913; William Simmons to William G. McAdoo, 24 March 1913, in International Ice Patrol File, Box 1368, Entry 283A, RG 26; Robert Erwin Johnson, *Guardians of the Sea*, 26–27.

65. Quotations from *Seattle Post-Intelligencer*, 5 September 1890.

66. Bertholf, *Annual Report of Revenue Cutter Service, 1912*, 49.

67. Curtis, *Annual Report of Secretary of the Treasury, 1912*, 20.

68. MacVeagh, "Report of Secretary of the Treasury, 1910. Revenue Cutter Service"; *Annual Report of Secretary of the Treasury, 1910*, 65–66.

69. Pettus, *Medical Handbook*.

70. MacVeagh, "Report of Secretary of the Treasury, 1910, Revenue Cutter Service," 369.

71. Curtis, *Annual Report of Secretary of the Treasury, 1912*, 74.

72. Bertholf, *Annual Report of Coast Guard, 1915*, 94–95, 114–18; quotation, 27–28; Robert Erwin Johnson, *Guardians of the Sea*, 28–29; Record of Proceedings, Board of Inquiry, on loss of the *Perry*.

CHAPTER NINE

1. King, *Coast Guard under Sail*, 47; Joseph Whipple to Albert Gallatin, 10 November 1800; 28 November 1801; 4 August, 27 September, and 31 December 1802; 18 March, 15 April, and 31 December 1803; 16 October 1804; 24 February 1805; 10 February, 9 April, 11 October, 25 November, and 23 December 1808, Treasury Secretary correspondence, Roll 26, National Archives.

2. King, *Coast Guard under Sail,* 140; Evans, *United States Coast Guard,* 70.

3. King, *Coast Guard under Sail,* 172–73.

4. Ross, "Our Coast Guard," 909–22; Clark, *Report of Operations of Revenue Marine Service,* 37.

5. Clark, *Report of Operations of Revenue Marine Service,* 28.

6. Ibid., 29–35, quotations, 34; Ross, "Our Coast Guard," 917.

7. Clark, *Report of Operations of Revenue Marine Service,* 34; Prout, "Investigation of Coast Guard Academy History," 20; *Changes in U.S. Revenue Cutter Service, 1911,* 15, Entry 149, RG 26.

8. Clark, *Report of Operations of Revenue Marine Service,* 34.

9. Johnson and Earle, "U.S. Coast Guard Academy," 4.

10. Ross, "Our Coast Guard," 917.

11. Ibid., 37; Clark, *Report of Operations of Revenue Marine Service,* 37–42.

12. Johnson and Earle, "U.S. Coast Guard Academy," 4, quotation, 4; Clark, *Report of Operations of Revenue Marine Service,* 41–42.

13. Ross, "Our Coast Guard," 918.

14. Clark, *Report of Operations of Revenue Marine Service,* 41–42.

15. Wyman, Cruise on the *S. P. Chase,* 9, 12–13.

16. Ross, "Our Coast Guard," 918, 920; Clark, *Report of Operations of Revenue Marine Service,* 37.

17. Ross, "Our Coast Guard," 918, 920.

18. Ibid., 918.

19. Ibid., 920.

20. Wyman, Cruise on the *S. P. Chase,* 113, 221–27.

21. Ibid., 173–77, quotation, 174, 177; Murphy, "Cutter Captain," 7 (insert 1).

22. Congdon, "Newspaper Clippings."

23. "Letters from Cadets at Brest."

24. John Cantwell, "Life on Board the *Chase,*" *New Bedford Chronicle,* 1 November 1887.

25. Ibid.

26. Ross, "Our Coast Guard," 917.

27. Clark, *Report of Operations of Revenue Marine Service, 1881,* 42.

28. Ibid., 44.

29. Ibid., 13.

30. Shoemaker, *Report of Chief of Division of Revenue Cutter Service,* 9.

31. Information about the schoolship *Chase* is from Congdon, "Newspaper Clippings."

32. U.S. Congress, *House Documents,* 62d Cong. 2d sess., 356.

33. Shoemaker, *Report of Chief of Division of Revenue Cutter Service,* 9.

34. William J. Wheeler, letter to A. A. Lawrence, 2 August 1938, 3.

35. Ibid., cover letter and pages 1 and 9 of letter.

36. Ibid., 1.

37. Ibid., 1–2.

38. Ibid., 2–3; Hamlet, Records and Papers.

39. Wheeler to Lawrence, 5–6.

40. Ibid., 4–8.

41. Ibid., Wheeler to Lawrence, 7.

42. Johnson and Earle, "U.S. Coast Guard Academy," 10.

43. Ibid.

44. Ibid., 10–11; Daniel B. Hodgsdon to Commodore George Dewey, 3 May 1898, "Operations of the Service in the Spanish-American War, 1898," File 175, RG 26; Wheeler to Lawrence, 9.

45. Hall, Records and Papers.

46. Johnson and Earle, "U.S. Coast Guard Academy," 11.

47. Ibid.

48. Ibid., 11–12.

49. Ibid., 12.

50. Account of the class of 1909 and Gray's quotations are from Gray, "Schooldays on a Sailing Ship," 2.

51. Johnson and Earle, "U.S. Coast Guard Academy" 17–18.

52. Gray, "Schooldays On a Sailing Ship," 2.

53. Hall, Records and Papers; Capt. W. E. Reynolds, letter to Secretary of the Treasury, 29 March 1919, in Reynolds, Records and Papers.

54. MacVeagh, *Information Relative to Appointments to Cadetships*, 4. This pamphlet was also published by the Treasury Department in 1910, signed by Charles D. Hill, and in 1913, signed by Secretary of the Treasury Sherman Allen.

55. Ibid.; U.S. Congress, *House Documents*, 62d Cong., 2d sess., 364.

56. *Annual Report of Secretary of the Treasury, 1914*; Capron, *U.S. Coast Guard*, 117; Johnson and Earle, "U.S. Coast Guard Academy," 14; Newton, *Regulations for Academy*, 8.

57. Shaw, *Annual Report of Secretary of the Treasury, 1904*, 40; Shaw, *Annual Report of Secretary of the Treasury, 1905*, 35; Cortelyou, *Annual Report of Secretary of the Treasury, 1907*, 41.

58. Johnson and Earle, "U.S. Coast Guard Academy," 14–15; Capron, *U.S. Coast Guard*, 117; Cortelyou, *Annual Report of Secretary of the Treasury, 1907*, 41; Sweetman, *U.S. Naval Academy*, 113.

59. Gray, "Schooldays on a Sailing Ship," 2.

60. Johnson and Earle, "U.S. Coast Guard Academy," 15.

61. Johnson and Earle, "U.S. Coast Guard Academy," 15–17.

62. Barrett, "Seamanship Notebook"; U.S. Practice Cutter *Itasca* Weekly Hull-Board Reports; Stewart, "Diary on *Itasca* Cruise."

63. Stewart, "Diary on *Itasca* Cruise," 26 May 1908 (he meant 1909).

64. Ibid., 27 May, 5 July 1909.

65. Ibid., 6, 7, 8, 9, 10, and 11 June 1909.

66. Ibid., 3, 13, and 16 June and 8 July 1909.

67. Ibid., 29 May, 12, 18, and 24 June, 1, 6, 12, 17, 23, and 29 July, and 1 and 6 August 1909.

68. Ibid., 24, 25, and 27 June 1909.

69. Ibid., 29 June and 1 July 1909.

70. Ibid., 4 July 1909.

71. Ibid., 8, 12, 21, 23, 24, and 29 July 1809.

72. Ibid., 28 May and 1, 3, 5, and 26 June 1909.

73. "Changes in U.S. Revenue Cutter Service, 1908," 3, Entry 198, RG 26; Cortelyou, *Annual Report of Secretary of the Treasury, for the Fiscal Year 1906,* 78–79; MacVeagh, "Report of Secretary of the Treasury, 1910, Revenue Cutter Service," 370–71; Gray, "Schooldays on a Sailing Ship," 2.

74. MacVeagh, "Report of Secretary of the Treasury, 1910, Revenue Cutter Service," 24.

75. Gray, "Schooldays on a Sailing Ship," 2.

76. Jacobs, Records and Papers; "Changes in U.S. Revenue Cutter Service, 1908," 2; "Changes in U.S. Revenue Cutter Service, 1909," 16; "Changes in U.S. Revenue Cutter Service, 1910," 4–5; all in Entry 198, RG 26.

77. Johnson and Earle, "U.S. Coast Guard Academy," 20; MacVeagh, "Report of Secretary of the Treasury, 1910, Revenue Cutter Service," 370–71.

78. Johnson and Earle, "U.S. Coast Guard Academy," 20–21.

79. Admirals' comments in Johnson and Earle, "U.S. Coast Guard Academy," 21–22.

80. Curtis, *Annual Report of Secretary of the Treasury, 1911,* 64.

81. Ibid.

82. Curtis, *Annual Report of Secretary of the Treasury, 1912,* 74; Bertholf, *Annual Report of Revenue Cutter Service, 1912,* 55–56.

83. Curtis, *Annual Report of Secretary of the Treasury, 1912,* 73–74.

84. Bertholf, *Annual Report of Revenue Cutter Service, 1914,* 93; *Annual Report of Secretary of the Treasury, 1913,* 76–77; *Annual Report of Secretary of the Treasury, 1914.*

85. Johnson and Earle, "U.S. Coast Guard Academy," 22–23; Capron, *U.S. Coast Guard,* 118; Hughes, *Our Coast Guard Academy,* 59; Jacobs, Records and Papers.

86. MacVeagh, *Information Relative to Appointments to Cadetships,* 1–3; "Changes in U.S. Revenue Cutter Service, 1908," 19–22, 24–25, 40, 43, Entry 198, RG 26.

87. MacVeagh, *Information Relative to Appointments to Cadetships,* 4.

88. MacVeagh, *Information Relative to Appointments to Cadetships,* 4.

89. Newton, *Regulations for Academy,* 18–19.

90. Account of the academy through the rest of this chapter is from Newton, *Regulations for the Academy,* 7–21, 23–24, 36–37, 51–52.

91. Newton, *Regulations for the Academy,* 19–21.

CHAPTER TEN

1. Albion, *Square Riggers on Schedule,* 227; York, "Architecture of U.S. Life-Saving Stations," 3.

2. Albion, *Square Riggers on Schedule,* 226–27.

3. Shoemaker, "Evolution of Life-Saving System," 3–4; Evans, *United States Coast Guard,* 36–37; Leonard D. White, *The Jacksonians,* 38–39; Bennett, *Surfboats, Rockets, and Carronades,* 3.

4. York, "Architecture of U.S. Life-Saving Stations," 3.

5. Shoemaker, "Evolution of Life-Saving System," 4.

6. Kimball, *Organization and Methods,* 24; Shoemaker, "Evolution of Life-Saving Systems," 4.

7. Kimball, *Organization and Methods,* 24.

8. Forbes, *Notes on Some Few Wrecks and Rescues,* 180–81.

9. Shoemaker, "Evolution of Life-Saving Systems," 4–7; Leonard D. White, *The Jacksonians,* 438–39; Dennis R. Means, "A Heavy Sea Running," 225–26.

10. Shoemaker, "Evolution of Life-Saving Systems," 9–10; Means, "A Heavy Sea Running," 225–26.

11. Means, "A Heavy Sea Running," 225–27, 239 (note 24); Kimball, *Annual Report of Chief of Revenue Marine Bureau, 1872,* 26–27; Shoemaker, "Evolution of Life-Saving Systems," 9–10.

12. Means, "A Heavy Sea Running," 226–27; Shoemaker, "Evolution of Life-Saving Systems," 9–12.

13. Means, "A Heavy Sea Running," 227. Also, see Leonard D. White, *The Republican Era,* 10.

14. Shoemaker, "Evolution of Life-Saving System," 12–14; Means, "A Heavy Sea Running," 227–28.

15. Shoemaker, "Evolution of Life-Saving Systems," 15–17; Means, "A Heavy Sea Running," 228.

16. Means, "A Heavy Sea Running," 228–29; Shoemaker, "Evolution of Life-Saving Systems," 15–17; Kimball, *Annual Report of Chief of Revenue Marine Bureau, 1873,* 27–31.

17. Means, "A Heavy Sea Running," 229.

18. Shoemaker, "Evolution of Life-Saving Systems," 17.

19. Ibid., 17–19.

20. Means, "A Heavy Sea Running," 229.

21. Shoemaker, "Evolution of Life-Saving Systems," 27.

22. Ibid., 29.

23. Ibid., 36–37, 55–56.

24. Evans, *United States Coast Guard,* 187–88.

25. Shoemaker, "Evolution of Life-Saving Systems," 24–26, 29–30.

26. Ibid., 29–30.

27. Ibid., 56–69.

28. Stick, *Graveyard of the Atlantic,* 73–85.

29. Ibid., 86–105; Means, "A Heavy Sea Running," 230–33.

30. Means, "A Heavy Sea Running," 230–37; Shoemaker, "Evolution of Life-Saving Systems," 30–33.

31. Shoemaker, "Evolution of Life-Saving Systems," 34–35.

32. Quoted in Emery, *History of Sanford, Maine,* 477–78.

33. Merryman, *United States Life-Saving Service,* 27–28.

34. Information on numbers and specific locations of lifesaving stations is from Kimball, *Organization and Methods,* 3–6, 8.

35. Ibid., 3.

36. Ibid., 3.

37. Ibid., 5.

38. Platt, "Saving 5,896 Lives."

39. Kimball, *Organization and Methods*, 6.

40. Descriptions of architectural styles and York's quotations relating to these styles are from York, "Architecture of U.S. Life-Saving Stations," 3–10.

41. Ibid., 10–13.

42. Beston, *The Outermost House*, 134, 136–39.

43. Quotation and descriptions of stations, equipment, and personnel that follow are from Kimball, *Organization and Methods*, 6–12.

44. Kimball, *Organization and Methods*, 13; Stick, *Graveyard of the Atlantic*, 105.

45. Shoemaker, "Evolution of Life-Saving Systems," 39–44.

46. Ibid., 45–46.

47. Ibid., 45–48.

48. Ibid.

49. Ibid., 49–50, 60.

50. Ibid., 49–50, 56–57.

51. Ibid., 50–52.

52. Ibid., 52–53.

53. Description of surfmen's responsibilities and duties is from Kimball, *Organization and Methods*, 12–15.

54. Kimball, *Organization and Methods*, 15.

55. Ibid., 15. Some of the language in this paragraph is close to the original source. It has been paraphrased for clarity.

56. Kimball, *Organization and Methods*, 16–17.

57. Ibid., 17–18.

58. Ibid., 18.

59. Ibid., 22–24.

60. Ibid., 22.

61. Means, "A Heavy Sea Running," 229; Shoemaker, "Evolution of Life-Saving Systems," 36–37, 55–56; Barnett, *Lifesaving Guns of David Lyle*, 3–7; Nalty, Noble, and Strobridge, *Wrecks, Rescues, and Investigations*, 23–24; Lyle, *Report on Life-Saving Ordnance*, 21–29; *Annual Report of Operations of Life Saving Service, 1880*, 273.

62. Stick, *Graveyard of the Atlantic*, 129–32.

63. Ibid., 150–51.

64. Account of the *Priscilla* is from Stick, *Graveyard of the Atlantic*, 161–69.

65. Account of the *Newman* rescue is from Stick, *Graveyard of the Atlantic*, 155–58.

66. Benson, "Romance and Story of Pea Island Station"; Strobridge, *History of Blacks in the Coast Guard*, 15–17; Noble, *That Others Might Live*, 52–53.

67. Noble, *That Others Might Live*, 54; Noble and Strobridge, "You Have to Go Out," 12–20.

68. Kimball, *Organization and Methods*, 26; Noble, *That Others Might Live*, 91–93.

69. Kimball, *Organization and Methods*, 26.

70. Ibid., 28–29.

71. Ibid.

72. Shoemaker, "Evolution of Life-Saving Systems," 37–39.

73. Account of keeper Joshua James is from Kimball, *Joshua James*, 1–75, 85, 90–91, 97–102; quotation, 90–91.

74. *Congressional Record*, 63d Cong., 3d sess., 52, pt. 2:1952, 1968; Emery, *History of Sanford, Maine*, 479.

75. Emery, *History of Sanford, Maine*, 479.

CHAPTER ELEVEN

1. "Changes in U.S. Revenue Cutter Service, 1911," 15, Entry 198, RG 26; Murphy, *Cutter Captain*, 130, 135–36, 138, 141.

2. Bertholf, Records and Papers; Secretary of the Treasury L. M. Shaw to 1st Lt. David H. Jarvis, 13 August 1904.

3. E. P. Bertholf to Godfrey Carden, 22 January 1909, and G.L. C. to E.P. Bertholf, 6 March 1909; Carden, Records and Papers; Bertholf, Records and Papers.

4. John C. Cantwell to the President of the United States, 8 May 1911 (U.S. Coast Guard Academy Library).

5. Evans, *United States Coast Guard*, 204–5.

6. Cleveland, "Report of Commission on Economy and Efficiency," 269–70.

7. Ibid., 269.

8. Details of the Cleveland Commission report, including quotations, are from Cleveland, "Report of the Commission on Economy and Efficiency," 271–82.

9. Cleveland, "Report of Commission on Economy and Efficiency," 383–84.

10. Charles Nagel, "Letters to the President, 10 January 1912, 8 February 1912," in U.S. Congress, *House Documents*, 62d Cong., 2d sess., vol. 116, 378–81.

11. Ibid.

12. U.S. Congress, *House Documents*, 62d Cong., 2d sess., vol. 116, 381.

13. Franklin MacVeagh, letter to the President, 26 February 1912, in U.S. Congress, *House Documents*, 62d Cong., 2d sess., vol. 116, 382.

14. Ibid.

15. Ibid.

16. Ibid., 382–83.

17. Ibid., 383–84.

18. Ibid., 384.

19. Ibid., 386.

20. Ibid., 384–85.

21. MacVeagh, "Address Delivered by MacVeagh," 385–89, quotation, 389.

22. E. P. Bertholf, letter to Secretary of the Treasury, 17 February 1912, in U.S. Congress, *House Documents*, 62d Cong., 2d sess., vol. 116, 389–91.

23. Duties of Revenue Cutter Service for other government departments and comparative cost figures for its service are from Bertholf to Secretary of the Treasury, February 17, 1912, 391–96.

24. Bertholf, Letter to Secretary of the Treasury, February 17, 1912, 394–96.

25. Ibid., 396–97.

26. "To Create the Coast Guard," 1:1–10; McAdoo, "To Create the Coast Guard," 2:1–14.

27. "To Create the Coast Guard," 1:2–3; McAdoo, "To Create the Coast Guard," 2:2–3; *Congressional Record*, 63d Cong., 3d sess., 52, pt. 2: 1951–1952.

28. "To Create the Coast Guard," 1:3; McAdoo, "To Create the Coast Guard," 2:3.

29. "To Create the Coast Guard," 1:3–8; McAdoo, "To Create the Coast Guard," 2:3–8.

30. "To Create the Coast Guard," 1:8–10; McAdoo, "To Create the Coast Guard," 2:8–11.

31. McAdoo, "To Create the Coast Guard," 2:11–14.

32. *Congressional Record*, 52, pt 2:1949–1959, 1967–1969, 1973–1974, 1976.

33. Ibid., 1968.

34. Ibid., 1969–1973.

35. Ibid., 1977–1978.

36. Ibid., 1978–1997.

37. Ibid., 1964.

38. Ibid., 1952.

Bibliography of Works Cited

PRIMARY SOURCES

Annual Report of the Operations of the United States Life Saving Service for the Fiscal Year Ended June 30, 1880. Washington, D.C.: Government Printing Office, 1880.

Annual Report of the Secretary of the Treasury on the State of the Finances for the Year 1884. Washington, D.C.: Government Printing Office, 1884.

Annual Report of the Secretary of the Treasury on the State of the Finances for the Fiscal Year Ended June 30, 1910. Washington, D.C.: Government Printing Office, 1910.

Annual Report of the Secretary of the Treasury on the State of the Finances for the Fiscal Year Ended June 30, 1913. Washington, D.C.: Government Printing Office, 1913.

Annual Report of the Secretary of the Treasury on the State of the Finances for the Fiscal Year Ended June 30, 1914. Washington, D.C.: Government Printing Office, 1915.

Bertholf, E. P. *Annual Report of the United States Coast Guard for the Fiscal Year Ended June 30, 1915.* Washington, D.C.: Government Printing Office, 1915.

———. *Annual Report of the United States Revenue Cutter Service for the Fiscal Year Ended June 30, 1912.* Washington, D.C.: Government Printing Office, 1913.

———. *Annual Report of the United States Revenue Cutter Service for the Fiscal Year Ended June 30, 1913.* Washington, D.C.: Government Printing Office, 1913.

———. *Annual Report of the United States Revenue Cutter Service for the Fiscal Year Ended June 30, 1914.* Washington, D.C.: Government Printing Office, 1914.

———. Letter to the Secretary of the Treasury, 17 February 1912. In *House Documents*, 62d Cong., 2d sess., vol. 116.

Beston, Henry. *The Outermost House.* New York: Viking Press, 1976.

Boutwell, George S. Letter of the Secretary of the Treasury communicating a report of the special commission appointed to consider and report upon the character of vessels best adapted for the Revenue Marine Service. In *Senate Documents*, 41st Cong., 2d sess. Washington, D.C.: Government Printing Office, 1870.

———. *Reminiscences of Sixty Years in Public Affairs.* 2 vols. New York: McClure, Phillips, 1902.

Cantwell, J. C. *Report of the Operations of the U.S. Revenue Steamer* Nunivak *on the*

Yukon River Station, Alaska, 1899–1901. Washington, D.C.: Government Printing Office, 1902.

Carlisle, J. G. *Annual Report of the Secretary of the Treasury on the State of Finances for the Year 1893.* Washington, D.C.: Government Printing Office, 1893.

———. *Annual Report of the Secretary of the Treasury on the State of Finances for the Year 1894.* Washington, D.C.: Government Printing Office, 1894.

———. *Annual Report of the Secretary of the Treasury on the State of Finances for the Year 1895.* Washington, D.C.: Government Printing Office, 1895.

———. *Annual Report of the Secretary of the Treasury on the State of Finances for the Year 1896.* Washington, D.C.: Government Printing Office, 1896.

Chandler, William. *Annual Report of the Secretary of the Navy for the Year 1882,* vol. 1. Washington, D.C.: Government Printing Office, 1882.

Clark, E.W. "Report of Chief of Revenue Marine Division, January 27, 1883." In *House Documents,* 62d Cong., 2d sess., vol. 116, 1912.

———. *Report of the Operations of the Revenue Marine Service, 1881.* Washington, D.C.: Government Printing Office, 1881.

Cleveland, Frederick A. "Report of the Commission on Economy and Efficiency." *House Documents,* 62d Cong., 2d sess., vol. 116, 1912.

Congressional Record. 63d Cong., 3d sess., vol. 52, pt. 2, 1915.

Cortelyou, George B. *Annual Report of the Secretary of the Treasury on the State of the Finances for the Fiscal Year Ended June 30, 1907.* Washington, D.C.: Government Printing Office, 1907.

———. *Annual Report of the Secretary of the Treasury on the State of the Finances for the Fiscal Year Ended June 30, 1908.* Washington, D.C.: Government Printing Office, 1908.

Curtis, W. E. *Annual Report of the Secretary of the Treasury on the State of the Finances for the Fiscal Year Ended June 30, 1911.* Washington, D.C.: Government Printing Office, 1911.

———. *Annual Report of the Secretary of the Treasury on the State of the Finances for the Fiscal Year Ended June 30, 1912.* Washington, D.C.: Government Printing Office, 1912.

Devereux, N. Broughton. *Report of the Chief of Revenue Marine, of the Steamboat Inspection, Marine Hospitals, and of Life-Saving Stations.* Washington, D.C.: Government Printing Office, 1869.

Fairchild, Charles S. *Annual Report of the Secretary of the Treasury on the State of Finances for the Year 1887.* Washington, D.C.: Government Printing Office, 1887.

———. *Annual Report of the Secretary of the Treasury on the State of Finances for the Year 1888.* Washington, D.C.: Government Printing Office, 1888.

Foster, Charles. *Annual Report of the Secretary of the Treasury on the State of Finances for the Year 1891.* Washington, D.C. Government Printing Office, 1891.

———. *Annual Report of the Secretary of the Treasury on the State of Finances for the Year 1892.* Washington, D.C.: Government Printing Office, 1892.

Gage, Lyman J. *Annual Report of the Secretary of the Treasury on the State of Finances for the Year 1897.* Washington, D.C.: Government Printing Office, 1897.

————. *Annual Report of the Secretary of the Treasury on the State of Finances for the Fiscal Year Ended June 30, 1899.* Washington, D.C.: Government Printing Office, 1899.

————. *Annual Report of the Secretary of the Treasury on the State of Finances for the Year 1900.* Washington, D.C.: Government Printing Office, 1901.

————. *Annual Report of the Secretary of the Treasury on the State of Finances for the Year 1901.* Washington, D.C.: Government Printing Office, 1901.

Goode, W. A. *With Sampson through the War.* New York: Doubleday & McLure, 1898.

Hamlet, O. C. *Register Revenue Cutter Service of the United States, 1882–1904* (n.d.; no publication information appears in this work).

Healy, M. A. *Report of the Cruise of the Revenue Marine Steamer* Corwin *in the Arctic Ocean in the Year 1884.* Washington, D.C.: Government Printing Office, 1889.

Healy, Michael. *Report of the Cruise of the Revenue Marine Steamer* Corwin *in the Arctic Ocean in the Year 1885.* Washington, D.C.: Government Printing Office, 1887.

Hooper, C. L. *Report of the Cruise of the U.S. Revenue Steamer* Corwin *in the Arctic Ocean, 1880.* Washington, D.C.: Government Printing Office, 1881.

————. *Report of the Cruise of the U.S. Revenue Steamer* Corwin *in the Arctic Ocean, 1881.* Washington, D.C.: Government Printing Office, 1884.

Jackson, Sheldon. *Report on Introduction of Domesticated Reindeer into Alaska.* Washington, D.C.: Government Printing Office, 1894.

————. *Twelfth Annual Report on Introduction of Domesticated Reindeer into Alaska, 1902.* Washington, D.C.: Government Printing Office, 1903.

Kimball, S. I. *Annual Report of the Chief of the Revenue Marine Bureau for the Fiscal Year Ending June 30, 1872.* Washington, D.C.: Government Printing Office, 1872.

————. *Annual Report of the Chief of the Revenue Marine Bureau for the Fiscal Year Ending June 30, 1873.* Washington, D.C.: Government Printing Office, 1873.

Kimball, Sumner I. *Joshua James Life-Saver.* Boston: American Unitarian Association, 1909.

————. *Organization and Methods of the United States Life-Saving Service.* Washington, D.C.: Government Printing Office, 1890.

List of Officers and Vessels in the United States Revenue Cutter Service, 1882–1904 (n.d.; no publication information appears in this work).

Lyle, David A. *Report on Life-Saving Ordnance.* Washington, D.C.: Government Printing Office, 1878.

MacVeagh, Franklin. "Address Delivered by the Hon. Franklin MacVeagh . . . February 10, 1912, on the Occasion of the Launching of the Revenue Cutters *Unalga* and *Miami*." In *House Documents,* 62d Cong., 2d sess., vol. 116.

————. Letter to the President, 26 February 1912. In *House Documents,* 62d Cong. 2d sess., vol. 116.

————. "Report of the Secretary of the Treasury, FY 1910, regarding the Revenue Cutter Service." In *House Documents,* 62d Cong., 2d sess., vol. 116.

Manning, Daniel. *Annual Report of the Secretary of the Treasury on the State of the*

Finances for the Year 1885. Washington, D.C.: Government Printing Office, 1885.

———. *Annual Report of the Secretary of the Treasury on the State of the Finances for the Year 1886*. Washington, D.C.: Government Printing Office, 1886.

McAdoo, William G. *Annual Report of the Secretary of the Treasury on the State of the Finances for the Fiscal Year Ended June 30, 1914*. Washington, D.C.: Government Printing Office, 1915.

Morris, William Gouverneur. *Report upon the Customs District, Public Service, and Resources of Alaska Territory*. Washington, D.C.: Government Printing Office, 1879.

Muir, John. *The Cruise of the* Corwin: *Journal of the Arctic Expedition of 1881 in Search of DeLong and the* Jeannette. Boston: Houghton Mifflin, 1917.

Nagel, Charles. "Letters to the President, 10 January 1912, 8 February 1912." *House Documents*. 62d Cong., 2d sess., vol. 116.

Newton, Byron R. *Regulations for the Academy of the United States Revenue Cutter Service*. Washington, D.C.: Government Printing Office, 1914.

Pettus, W. J. *Medical Handbook for the Use of the Revenue Cutter Service*. Washington, D.C.: Government Printing Office, 1912.

Register of the Officers and Vessels of the United States Revenue Marine. Washington, D.C.: Government Printing Office, 1881.

Sargent, Nathan. *Admiral Dewey and the Manila Campaign*. Washington: Naval Historical Foundation, 1947.

Schley, Winfield Scott. *Forty-Five Years under the Flag*. New York: D. Appleton, 1904.

Shaw, Leslie M. *Annual Report of the Secretary of the Treasury on the State of the Finances for the Fiscal Year Ended June 30, 1902*. Washington, D.C.: Government Printing Office, 1902.

———. *Annual Report of the Secretary of the Treasury on the State of the Finances for the Fiscal Year Ended June 30, 1904*. Washington, D.C.: Government Printing Office, 1904.

———. *Annual Report of the Secretary of the Treasury on the State of the Finances for the Fiscal Year Ended June 30, 1905*. Washington, D.C.: Government Printing Office, 1905.

———. *Annual Report of the Secretary of the Treasury on the State of the Finances for the Fiscal Year Ended June 30, 1906*. Washington, D.C.: Government Printing Office, 1906.

Shepard, Isabel S. *The Cruise of the U.S. Steamer* Rush *in Behring Sea, Summer of 1889*. San Francisco: The Bancroft Company, 1889.

Shoemaker, C. F. *Report of the Chief of Division of Revenue Cutter Service, 1897*. Washington, D.C.: Government Printing Office, 1897.

Records of the United States Coast Guard, Record Group 26, National Archives, Washington, D.C.

Tilton, George Fred. *Cap'n George Fred Himself.* New York: Doubleday, Doran, 1928.

U.S. Coast Guard, Office of Assistant Commandant. *Record of Movements: Vessels of the United States Coast Guard*. 2 vols. Washington, D.C.: U.S. Coast Guard, 1933.

U.S. Congress. "Economy and Efficiency." In *House Documents*, 62d Cong., 2d sess., vol. 116.

U.S. Congress. "Efficiency of the Revenue Cutter Service," with official record of Revenue Cutter Service in War with Spain. In *Senate Reports*, 57th Cong., 1st sess., 1901–02.

U.S. Congress. "History of Efforts Looking to the Transfer of the Service from the Treasury Department to the Navy Department." In *House Documents*, 62d Cong., 2d sess., vol. 116.

U.S. Congress. *House Documents*. 61st Cong., 2d sess.

U.S. Congress. *House Documents*. 62d Cong., 2d sess., vol. 116.

U.S. Congress, House of Representatives. *Cruise of the Revenue-Steamer* Corwin *in Alaska and the N.W. Arctic Ocean in 1881*. 47th Cong., 2d sess., 1883, 3–120.

U.S. Congress. *The United States Revenue Cutter Service in the War with Spain, 1898*. 57th Cong., 1st sess., 1899, S. Rept. 172.

U.S. Department of the Treasury, U.S. Revenue Cutter Service. *Annual Report for the Year 1891*. Washington, D.C.: Government Printing Office, 1892.

U.S. Revenue Cutter Service. *Report of the Cruise of the U.S. Revenue Cutter* Bear *and the Overland Expedition for the Relief of the Whalers in the Arctic Ocean, from November 27, 1897 to September 13, 1898*. Washington, D.C.: Government Printing Office, 1899.

U.S. Congress. Senate. Committee on Commerce. "Efficiency of the Revenue Cutter Service." 57th Cong., 1st sess., S. Rept. 172, 1902.

Vivian, Thomas. *With Dewey at Manila*. New York: R. F. Feno, 1898.

Windom, William. *Annual Report of the Secretary of the Treasury on the State of the Finances for the Year 1889*. Washington, D.C.: Government Printing Office, 1889.

———. *Annual Report of the Secretary of the Treasury on the State of the Finances for the Year 1890*. Washington, D.C.: Government Printing Office, 1890.

Wyman, Walter. *A Cruise on the U.S. Practice Ship* S. P. Chase. New York: Grafton Press, 1910.

SECONDARY SOURCES

Albion, Robert G. *Five Centuries of Famous Ships*. New York: McGraw-Hill, 1978.

———. *Square Riggers on Schedule*. Princeton, N.J.: Princeton University Press, 1938.

Anderson, H. Dewey, and Walter C. Eels. *Alaska Natives*. Stanford, Calif.: Stanford University Press, 1935.

Barnett, J. P. *The Lifesaving Guns of David Lyle*. Plymouth: Town and Country Press, 1974.

Bell, Kensil. *Always Ready*. New York: Dodd, Mead, 1943.

Bennett, Robert F. *Surfboats, Rockets, and Carronades*. Washington, D.C.: Government Printing Office, n.d.

Berry, Erick. *You Have to Go Out*. New York: David McKay, 1964.

Bixby, William. *Track of the* Bear. New York: David McKay, 1965.

Bundy, C. Lynn. *The Maritime Association of the Port of New York.* New York: Press of Andrew H. Kellogg, 1923.

Burroughs, Polly. *The Great Ice Ship* Bear. New York: Van Nostrand Reinhold, 1970.

Capron, Walter C. *The U.S. Coast Guard.* New York: Franklin Watts, 1965.

Dewey, Adelbert. *The Life and Letters of Admiral Dewey.* New York: The Woolfall Campaign, 1899.

Emery, Edwin. *History of Sanford, Maine.* Fall River, Mass.: The Compiler, 1901.

Evans, Stephen H. *The United States Coast Guard, 1790–1915.* Annapolis, Md.; U.S. Naval Institute, 1949.

Foley, Albert S. *Bishop Healy: Beloved Outcast.* Dublin, Ireland: Clonmore and Reynolds, 1956.

Forbes, R. B. *Notes on Some Few of the Wrecks and Rescues during the Present Century.* Boston: Little, Brown, 1889.

Hough, George A. *Disaster on Devil's Bridge.* Chester, Conn.: The Pequot Press, 1977.

Howe, M. A. DeWolfe. *The Humane Society of the Commonwealth of Massachusetts.* Boston: The Riverside Press, 1918.

Hughes, Riley. *Our Coast Guard Academy.* New York: The Devin-Adair Company, 1944.

Hunt, William R. *Arctic Passage, the Turbulent History of the Land and People of the Bering Sea 1697–1975.* New York: Scribner's Sons, 1975.

Johnson, Paul, and Bill Earle. "U.S. Coast Guard Academy—The First 100 Years." *The Bulletin* of the U.S. Coast Guard Academy Alumni Association. Centennial Issue.

Johnson, Robert Erwin. *Guardians of the Sea: History of the U.S. Coast Guard, 1915 to Present.* Annapolis, Md.: Naval Institute Press, 1987.

King, Irving H. *The Coast Guard under Sail.* Annapolis, Md.: Naval Institute Press, 1989.

Merryman, J. H. *The United States Life-Saving Service—1880.* Golden, Colo.: Outbooks, 1981.

Nalty, Bernard, Dennis Noble, and Truman Strobridge, eds. *Wrecks, Rescues, and Investigations.* Wilmington, Del.: Scholarly Resources, 1978.

Noble, Dennis L. *That Others Might Live, the U.S. Life-Saving Service, 1878–1915.* Annapolis, Md.: Naval Institute Press, 1994.

Rankin, Robert H., and H. R. Kaplan. *Immortal* Bear. New York: G. P. Putnam's Sons, 1970.

Smith, Darrell, and Fred Wilbur Powell. *The Coast Guard: Its History, Activities and Organization.* Washington, D.C.: The Brookings Institution, 1929.

Spears, John. *Our Navy in the War with Spain.* New York: C. Scribner's Sons, 1898.

Stick, David. *Graveyard of the Atlantic.* Chapel Hill: University of North Carolina Press, 1952.

Sweetman, Jack. *The U.S. Naval Academy.* Annapolis, Md.: Naval Institute Press, 1979.

Trask, David. *The War with Spain in 1898.* New York: Macmillan, 1981.

Wead, Frank. *Gales, Ice and Men.* New York: Dodd, Mead, 1937.
White, Leonard D. *The Jacksonians.* New York: The Free Press, 1965.
————. *The Republican Era.* New York: The Free Press, 1958.
Wilson, H.W. *The Downfall of Spain.* Boston: Little, Brown, 1900.

ARTICLES AND PAMPHLETS

Allard, Dean C. "To The North Pole." U.S. Naval Institute *Proceedings* 113 (September 1987): 56–65.
Allen, Sherman. *Information Relative to Appointments to Cadetships in the Line of the United States Revenue Cutter Service, 1913.* Washington, D.C.: Government Printing Office, 1913.
Bennett, Robert F. "The Life-Savers: For Those in Peril on the Sea," pt. 1. U.S. Naval Institute *Proceedings* 102 (March 1976): 54–63.
Benson, Rodney J. "Romance and Story of Pea Island Station." *The U.S. Coast Guard Magazine* 6, no. 1 (November 1932): 52.
Bertholf, E. P. *Reports of Vessels on Ice Patrol in the North Atlantic Ocean. April, May, June, 1913.* Washington, D.C.: Government Printing Office, 1913.
Cantwell, John C. "Captain Healy's Reindeer." *The Marine Corps Gazette,* May 1935, 26–29, 58–60.
Gaw, Cooper. "Tilton's Walk and the Whaling Tradition." In *Capt. George Fred Tilton Tablet Dedication at the Seamen's Bethel,* 16 July 1933, New Bedford (Mass.) Port Society.
Gray, John P. "Schooldays on a Sailing Ship." *Baltimore Sun.* 5 February 1956, *The Sunday Magazine.*
Hills, Charles D. *Information Relative to Appointments to Cadetships in the Line of the United States Revenue Cutter Service, 1910.* Washington, D.C.: Government Printing Office, 1910.
Johnson, Paul H. "Portrait of Captain Michael A. Healy, Part II." U.S. Coast Guard Academy Alumni Association *Bulletin* 41, (March–April 1979): 22–23, 26–27.
————. "Portrait of Captain Michael A. Healy, Part III." U.S. Coast Guard Academy Alumni Association *Bulletin* 41, May–June 1979, 26–30.
Killey, Gwen L. "Opening the Door to Alaska: The Cruises of The Revenue Cutter *Thomas Corwin.*" *Naval History* 2, no. 4 (Fall 1988): 23–27.
MacVeagh, Franklin. *Information Relative to Appointments to Cadetships in the Line of the United States Revenue Cutter Service, 1909.* Washington, D.C.: Government Printing Office, 1909.
McAdoo, W. G. "To Create the Coast Guard." In *House Reports,* 63d Cong., 2d sess., vol. 2, 1913–1914.
McCutchenk, John T. "The Surrender of Manila." *The Century Magazine,* April 1899.
Mead, Ernest E. "The Rescue of the *Winslow.*" *Harper's New Monthly Magazine* 98 (December 1898): 123–29.
Means, Dennis R. "A Heavy Sea Running: The Formation of the U.S. Life-Saving Service, 1848–1878." *Prologue* 19, no. 4 (Winter 1987): 223–43.

Merryman, J. H., and Sumner Increase Kimball. "The United States Revenue Marine." In *Hamersly's Naval Encyclopedia, 1881*, 690–91.

Morgan, Charles S. "Coastal Shipping under Sail, 1880–1920." Thirty-Seventh Annual Newcomen Lecture presented at the U.S. Coast Guard Academy, New London, Conn., 3 November 1978.

Murphy, John F. "Portrait of Captain Michael A. Healy." U.S. Coast Guard Academy Alumni Association *Bulletin* 41 (January–February 1979): 14–18.

Nalty, Bernard C., and Truman R. Strobridge. "The Lyle Gun: A Cannon That Saved Lives." *Compass*, no. 2 (1979): 8–11.

Noble, Dennis L., and Truman R. Strobridge. "The Arctic Adventures of the *Thetis*." *Arctic Journal* of the Arctic Institute of North America 30, no. 1 (March 1977): 3–12.

Noble, Dennis L., and Truman R. Strobridge. "The Thetis in Alaskan Waters." *Alaska Journal*. no. 1 (1979): 50–57.

Noble, Dennis L., and Truman R. Strobridge. "You Have to Go Out." *Naval History* 3 (Fall 1989): 12–20.

Noble, Dennis L., and Barbara Voulgaris. "Alaska and Hawaii." Commandant's *Bulletin* (May 1991): 1–18.

Platt, Brainard. "Saving 5,896 Lives." *Courier-Journal Magazine*, 17 January 1937.

Reed, Byron L. "The Contribution of the Coast Guard to the Development of Alaska." U.S. Naval Institute *Proceedings* 55 (May 1929): 406–10.

Ridgely, Randolph. "The Coast Guard Cutter *McCulloch* at Manila." United States Naval Institute *Proceedings* 55 (May 1929): 417–26.

Ross, Worth G. "Our Coast Guard." *Harpers New Monthly Magazine* 73 (November 1886): 909–22.

Strobridge, Truman R. *The History of Blacks in the Coast Guard from 1790*. Reference Collection, U.S. Coast Guard Academy Library.

"To Create the Coast Guard." In *Senate Reports*. 63d Cong., 2d sess., vol. 1, 1914.

Treasury Department, United States Revenue Cutter Service. *Methods of Searching for Derelicts at Sea*, RCS Bulletin No. 2. Washington: Government Printing Office, 1913.

"Vessels Recently Added to the Navy." *Marine Engineering* 2, no. 7 (1898): 17.

Wilkinson, Alec. "A Reporter at Large." *The New Yorker*, 26 November 1990, 61–118.

York, Wick. "The Architecture of the U.S. Life-Saving Stations." The *Log* of Mystic Seaport 34, no. 1 (Spring 1982): 3–20.

UNPUBLISHED MANUSCRIPTS AND RECORDS

Baker, Eben. "Seamanship Notes, Boston Harbor," 9 July 1896. U.S. Coast Guard Academy Library (hereafter referred to as USCGA Library).

Barrett, John B., "Seamanship Notebook. Summer of 1909, on board the *Itasca*." USCGA Library.

Bering Sea Patrol File. USCGA Library.

Bertholf, Ellsworth P. Records and Papers. USCGA Library.

Cantwell, John C., letter to President of the United States, 8 May 1911. Cantwell collection, USCGA Library.

Carden, Godfrey L. Records and Papers. USCGA Library.

"Case, Michael A. Healy (1890)." Records of the Revenue Cutter Service. Entry 184, RG 26, National Archives and Record Service.

Communications File on loss of the *Perry*. USCGA Library.

Congdon, Joseph W. "Newspaper Clippings." USCGA Library.

"Correspondence of the Secretary of the Treasury with Collectors of Customs, 1789–1833." 39 rolls. Microcopy No. 178. National Archives Microfilm Publications.

Evans, S. H., and A. A. Lawrence. "The History and Organization of the United States Coast Guard." Manuscript. October 1938. USCGA Library.

File on cruise of the *Manning* in Bering Sea in 1910. USCGA Library.

Hall, David Allen. Records and Papers. USCGA Library.

Hamlet, Oscar C. Records and Papers. USCGA Library.

Jacobs, William V. E. Records and Papers. USCGA Library.

Jarvis, David H. Correspondence of David H. Jarvis. USCGA Library.

"Letters from Cadets at Brest, France to Friends in New Bedford," published in a New Bedford, Mass., newspaper. Collection. USCGA Library.

J. C. "Japanese Sealing Vessels," memorandum to Lt. P. H. Brereton, Seattle, Wash., 25 October 1910. USCGA Library.

Murphy, John. "Cutter Captain: The Life and Times of John C. Cantwell." Manuscript. USCGA Library.

Prout, James D. "An Investigation of Coast Guard Academy History" (June 1972). Manuscript. USCGA Library.

Record of Proceedings of Board of Inquiry, U.S. Revenue Cutter Service, on the loss of the *Perry*. USCGA Library.

Records of the United States Coast Guard. Record Group 26, National Archives.

Reynolds, William Edward. Records and Papers. USCGA Library.

Reinburg, John Ernest. Records and Papers. USCGA Library.

"Secretary of the Treasury, letters to collectors of customs at all ports, 1789–1847, and at small ports, 1847–1879." 43 Rolls. Microcopy No. 175. National Archives Microfilm Publications.

Shoemaker, C. F. "The Evolution of the Life-saving System of the United States from 1837 to June 30, 1890." Copy in USCGA Library.

Stewart, C. U. "Diary on U.S. Practice Cutter *Itasca* Cruise Summer of 1909, from Arundel Cove, Maryland, and Return." USCGA Library.

U.S. Practice Cutter *Itasca* Weekly Hull-Board Reports. USCGA Library.

Wheeler, William J., letter to A. A. Lawrence. 2 August 1938. USCGA Library.

White, James T. "Diary of Cruise of Revenue Steamer *Bear* in 1889, 10 June–28 Sept. 1889." USCGA Library.

NEWSPAPERS

Baltimore Sun

The Boston Daily Globe

The Boston Sunday Globe
Daily Eastern Argus (Portland, Maine)
The Louisville Courier-Journal
New Orleans Times-Democrat
New York Herald
New York Sun
The New York Times
Portland Evening Express
San Francisco Chronicle
Seattle Post-Intelligencer

Index

Abbey, Charles, 109
Active (USRC), 6
Acushnet (USRC), 137
Ada, British schooner, 86
Adamson, William Charles, 220, 239
Aguinaldo, Emilio, 116–17
aids to navigation, 2
Alaska: cruise reports reveal value of, 22, 25, 43–46; cutter officers' influence on public policy regarding, 22, 26, 27–28, 37–40, 46, 86, 88–89, 91–92; exploration of, 22–23, 25, 26, 34, 36, 43–46, 88, 127; fear of violence in, 28–31; firearm laws in, 28, 34–35, 36, 40, 41, 50, 84, 227; gunboat diplomacy in, 37–40; impact on RCS of purchase of, 4–5, 7; liquor laws in, 28, 34–35, 40–41, 50, 84, 227; protection of people and resources in, 22, 27–28, 34–35, 36, 40, 41, 49, 50, 51, 85, 127, 227; protection of seals in, 28, 41, 50–53, 85–86, 152; reindeer in, 86, 88, 89, 91–92; rescue of whalers in, 22, 31, 41–42, 49, 84, 86, 94–107; transportation of officials in, 22–23, 36, 42, 46; transportation of stranded Americans in, 42, 49, 106, 108
Alaska Commercial Co., 27, 49

Albert Gallatin (USRC), 14, 16, 75, 162
Albion, Black Ball liner, 193
Albion, Robert G., 82
Alert, British, 83
Alert (USRC), 15, 78
Alexander J. Dallas (USRC), 15, 122
Algonquin (USRC), 79, 80, 111
Allard, Dean C., 34
Allen, Joseph, 155
Allie Alger, American schooner, 85–86
American Missionary Association, 89, 100
Amethyst, whaling bark, 47
anchorage laws, 69–70
Andrew Jackson (USRC), 16–17
Andrew Johnson (USRC), 6
Andrews, Thomas, 145
Androscoggin (USRC), 126, 139–40, 143–44
Antietam (USRC), 6
Antinett, steamer, 109
Arabia, barkentine, 148
Arctic Ocean, 31, 34, 41–42
Arey, Ned, 102
Arthur, Chester, 83
Artisarlook, Charlie, 96, 100, 101
Artisarlook, Mary, 100
Asbury Fountain, schooner, 143
Asiatic Squadron, 111, 122–23
Ayrshire, British immigrant ship, 194

Baelena, whaler, 41
Bagley, Worth, 119, 120
Bailhache, T. H., 85
Baker, John G., 63
Baltic, 136
Bancroft, 175
Barrett, John B., 176
Bayne, E. H., 39
Bear (USRC), 23, 43, 49, 51, 73, 75, 77, 224; description of, 82; enforces sealing laws, 85–86; during gold rush, 107–8; on Greely relief expedition, 83–84; on overland expedition, 94–95, 102, 106; rescues whalers, 86; and San Francisco earthquake, 133–35; transports reindeer to Alaska, 86, 88–89, 91–92
Bearse, Maynard, 66, 69
Beda, steamer, 42
Bell, John T., 133
Belvedere, whaler, 86, 98, 102, 103, 106
Bennett, James Gordon, 33
Berg, Harold, 132
Bering Sea Patrol, 52–53, 127, 173, 180, 230, 235
Bernadou, John B., 118, 119
Berry, John C., 134
Berry, M. P., 28, 29, 30, 37
Bertholf, Ellsworth P.: and academy, 166, 168, 183; as commandant, 223–25, 230, 231, 233–36, 237; defense of service by, 233–36; and derelict destruction, 141; on doctors for cutters, 153; on illegal immigration, 151–52; and international ice patrol, 147–50; on loss of cutters, 153; on overland expedition, 94, 97–98, 101–2, 107
Berwick, U.S. schooner, 91
Beston, Henry, 206
Bibb, Albert B., 205–6
Bibb (USRC), 75

Billard, Frederick C., 166, 183, 186
bill creating U.S. Coast Guard, 236–41
Binns, Jack, 136
Black Diamond, British schooner, 50–52
Blanchard, Newton Crain, 131
Blankinship, Charles, 136
Board of Life-Saving Appliances, 207–8
Bonnett, Peter, 72
Boston, 114, 115
Boston, John, 155
Boston and Savannah Steamship Co., 64
Boutwell, George S., 5–6, 28, 196
Boutwell (USRC), 109, 110
Bowdoin College, 10, 159
Bowhead, whaler, 41
brewery workers, 85
Brower, Charles D., 103, 106
Brown, Joseph E., 155
Brumby, Thomas M., 116
Bryan, William Jennings, 169
Buhner, Albert, 84
Bureau of Marine Inspection and Navigation, 243
Bureau of Navigation, 226
Burke, Francis, 138

Cacheaux, M. Emile, 220
Caleb Eaton, schooner, 42
California, steamer, 29, 145–46
Call, Dr. Samuel J., 94, 97, 99–102, 104–5, 107
Calumet (USRC), 75, 78, 79, 111
Campbell (USRC), 15, 68
Canada's sealing policies, 50–52
Cantwell, John C., 47, 163; as candidate for commandant, 223–25; commands *Nunivak*, 127–29; explores Kowak and Noatak rivers, 43–46, 88; and San Francisco earthquake, 135
Cape Smithe Whaling and Trading Co., 103
Carden, Godfrey, 52–53, 225

Carlisle, John G., 75, 76, 78, 81, 94, 109
Carman, B. A., 175
Carpathia, 145–46
Carrie A. Buckman, schooner, 140
Cervera, Pascual, 121, 122
Chandler, William, 54–56, 59, 60, 72, 230
Chappell, John G., 200
Chase, Salmon P., 155
Chukchees, 88
City of Columbus, 64–69
City of Richmond, steamer, 110
Civil Service Act of 1883, 13
Civil War, 3, 9, 16, 75, 77, 80, 155, 159, 195
Clark, Ezra, 15, 16, 63, 72; defends independent RCS, 56–59; improves operations of RCS, 19–21; reduces RCS operating costs, 17–18; and Revenue Cutter School of Instruction, 156, 160, 164–65
Claytor, Edmond C., 131–32
Cleveland, Frederick A., 225
Cleveland, Grover, 109
Cleveland Commission, 147, 182, 225–36
Cluea Light, schooner, 84
Coast Seamen's Union, 85
Coast Survey, 23, 60
Coffin, George W., 83
Collins, John W., 76
Conant, Charles F., 28
Concord, 114, 115
Congdon, Joseph B., 70, 165
Conger, Omar D., 201
Constellation, 175, 223
Cook, John, 66
Copeland, Charles W., 5
Cortelyou, George B., 179
Coste, Napoleon L., 155
Cox, Samuel S., 200, 201
Crawford (USRC), 6, 75
Cunningham, Patrick, 213–14
Cunningham rocket, 213–14
Curtiss, W. E., 152

Dallas (USRC), 122
Daniels, George C., 217
Daniels, George M., 93, 139–40
Dauntless, tug, 110
Davidson, George, 23
Davis, Dunbar, 215
Dawn, whaler, 41, 42
DeFilippis, Attilio, 185
DeHart, William C., 63
DeLong, George Washington (USN), 32–33, 34
Dennis, I. C., 30, 39
Department of Commerce and Labor, 226, 229–30, 234, 235–36
derelict destruction, 140–44, 147, 233, 235
de Stoeckl, Edward, 22
Devereux, N. Broughton, 5, 6, 7
Dewey, George (USN), 111, 113–17, 170
Dexter (USRC), 15, 63–69, 122, 123, 124
Dimmick, Chester E., 175
Dix (USRC, ex-*Wilderness*), 16, 69
Dobbin (USRC), 5, 155, 157, 158

Earle, Bill, 171, 172, 176
E. A. Stevens (USRC, also *Naugatuck*), 16, 63, 70
Edmonds, S. P., 168
embargo, 2
Emery, Charles E., 14–15, 159, 160
Emery, Edwin, 158–59
Emory, William H., 83
English, Earl, 224
Esmeralda, British steamer, 115
E. S. Newman, schooner, 216–17
Estella, coal bark, 84–85
Etheridge, Richard, 216–17
Evans, Robley D. (USN), 31
Evans, Stephen H., 167

Fairchild, Charles S., 70–71
Faunce, John, 5, 11, 12, 196, 197

Fearless, 98, 103, 106
Fleetwing, whaler, 42
Florida, Italian liner, 136
Foley, Albert S., 37
Foley, Daniel P., 123
Folger, Charles J., 69
Forbes, R. B., 66
Forward, Walter, 58
Forward (USRC), 109, 110
Foster, Charles, 74, 75
Francis, Joseph, 192, 194
Fraser, Alexander, 2, 3, 61, 154–55
Fuller, Edwin, 64

Gabrielson, Eric, 67–69
Gage, Lyman J., 81, 94, 110, 124–25
Galveston (USRC), 74, 78, 121
Gamble, Aaron L., 147–48
Gardiner, Stephen A., 216–17
Gatchell, William F., 138
Geddis, L. N., 196
Geier, 122
George E. Starr, steamer, 150
George S. Boutwell (USRC), 15, 109, 110
Giovanni, Italian bark, 214
Glaucus, steamer, 66, 69
Globe Ironworks Co., 135
Glover, Russell, 63, 76, 150–51
Golden Fleece, 67
Golden Gate (USRC), 79, 133–35
Gold Lifesaving Medal, 216
Goldstein, Sam, 30
Gooding, George H., 110
Goodrich, C. F., 134–35
Gordon Pew Fisheries Co., 139
Grace, 131
Grant, Ulysses S., 5, 13, 28
Grant (USRC), 14, 72, 75
Gray, John P., 172, 175, 180
Great Britain's sealing policies, 50–52
Greely, Adolpheus W., 83–84
Greely relief expedition, 83–84
Gresham (USRC), 79, 80, 111, 126, 135–38, 139

Grubin, John, 89
Guard (USRC), 79
Guthrie (USRC), 72, 79, 122

Hall, David A., 40, 170–71
Hamilton, Alexander, 1, 58
Hamilton (USRC), 14, 109, 180
Hamlet, Henry G., 166
Hamlet, Oscar C., 85, 86, 134, 166, 168, 170
Hamlin, Henry P., 14
Hamlin (USRC), 14, 71
Hammond, Thomas R., 65
Hand, William H., 35, 109
Harding, Augustus, 64–65
Harland and Wolff yard, 145
Harriet Lane (USRC), 3, 6
Harrison, Benjamin, 60
Hartley (USRC), 15, 71, 133, 152
Hayes, Rutherford B., 13, 201
Healy, James Augustine, 37
Healy, Michael A., 47, 49; charged with drunkenness and cruelty, 85, 92–94; commands *Bear*, 82–94; commands *Thetis*, 94; court-martialed, 92–94; death of, 94; enforces laws in Arctic, 84; enforces liquor laws, 40–41; enforces sealing laws, 85–86; explores Alaskan rivers, 43–46; and gunboat diplomacy, 37–40; as son of a slave, 37; transports reindeer to Alaska, 86, 88–89, 91–92; transports stranded whalers, 41–42, 86
Healy, Patrick Frances, 37
Helen G. Wells, schooner, 139
Helen Mar, whaling bark, 33
Henriques, John A., 13, 37, 156, 158, 160, 165
Henry Brothers, 155
Herald Island, 33, 34
Herring, William J., 33, 110
Hinckley, Harold D., 176
Hodgsdon, Daniel B., 63, 111–12, 123, 170

Holton, J. S., 146
Hooper, Calvin L., 31, 33, 34–35, 36, 37, 52
Hottel, James F., 170
Howard, Oliver O., 25
Howard, William A., 23
Hudson (USRC), 78, 79, 117–20
Hugh McCulloch (USRC, ex-*Mosswood*), side-wheeler, 14, 16, 69, 70
Hunt, Edmund S., 213–14
Hunter, whaler, 42
Hunt gun, 213–14
Huntington, Jabez W., 58
Huron, navy steamer, 200
Hydrographic Office, 141

illegal immigration, 150–51, 243
international ice patrol, 146–50
Inuits, 23, 36, 40, 88, 89, 91; and overland expedition, 99, 100, 101, 102
Ismay, J. Bruce, 145–46
Itasca (USRC), 176, 177–79, 180, 181, 183, 186, 190

Jackson, Andrew, 2
Jackson, Sheldon, 88, 89, 91–92
Jacobs, William V. E., 180, 181, 183
Jacob Thompson (USRC), 6
James, Joshua, 219–20
James Campbell (USRC), 6
James C. Dobbin (USRC), 6
James G. Swan, sealer, 51
Jamestown, steamer, 143
Japan's sealing policies, 52
Jarvis, David, 85, 91–92; and academy, 165; during gold rush, 107–8; on overland expedition, 94–107
Jeanie, 98, 103, 106
Jeannette, steam bark, 33, 34, 173
Jefferson, Thomas, 2
Jesse H. Freeman, 98, 103, 106
Johansson, Carl, 137
John A. Dix (USRC), 6

John F. Hartley (USRC), 15
John Roach and Sons, 64
Johnson, E.V.D., 168
Johnson, Paul, 171, 172, 176
Johnson (USRC), 16
Johnston, Charles E., 147–49
Joseph Lane (USRC), 6
Juanita, British schooner, 51

Kalenin, Alexis, 96–97
Kennedy, Charles D., 68–69
Kilgore, William F., 110
Kimball, Sumner Increase: advocates retirement list for officers, 18–21; establishes centralized control of RCS, 11; establishes Revenue Cutter School of Instruction, 154–55, 158–59; as head of Revenue Marine Bureau, 9–10; improves cutters, 14–16, 18–21, 54; opposes reductions in officer corps, 19–21; promotes economy in RCS, 11, 13, 17–18; reduces size of RCS, 13, 18; reduces tonnage of cutter fleet, 13–14; retirement of, 240; revises RCS regulations, 11, 19–21, 164–65; as superintendent of LSS, 16, 194, 195, 196, 197, 198–99, 200, 201, 202–4, 206, 207, 208, 209, 212, 213, 217, 218, 219, 220, 222, 228, 236, 237
Klane, Tith, 39
Koltchoff, 94, 97
Kootznahoo Inlet, Alaska, 39
Korei Maru, 152
Kowak River, 43–46, 88, 127
Kwonchoi, 124

Lark, schooner, 109
Lawrence, Albert A., 166
Lawrence (USRC), 154–55
Leach, Frank A., 134
Leary, Edward, 65
Lee, James, 76

Leo, schooner, 35
Levi Woodbury (USRC, ex-*Mahoning*), 16, 69, 122
Lewis, Frank, 43
Lewis Cass (USRC), 77
Lincoln (USRC), 7, 14, 16, 23, 24
Loch Garry, 83
Loleta, schooner, 35
Long, John D., 123
Lopp, W. Thomas, 89, 96, 100, 101, 102, 103
Lord, Stanley, 145–46
Louisiana Naval Militia, 131
Louis McLane (USRC, ex-*Delaware*), 16, 70, 72, 75, 109, 110, 120, 173
Lutz, John E., 41
Lyle, David A., 213–14
Lyle gun, 213–14

Machias, 118
Machiavelli, Italian bark, 63
MacVeagh, Franklin, 140, 174, 179–80, 184, 225, 231–33, 236–37
Maggie Mae, sealer, 50–51
Maguire, Samuel E., 117–18
Mahoning (USRC), 6
Maine, battleship, 110
Main Street Iron Works, 135
M & S Henderson, 217
Manhattan (USRC), 15, 16, 70, 74
Mann, James Robert, 239
Mann, Philip, 106
Manning, Daniel, 70, 82
Manning (USRC), 52–53, 79, 80, 111, 122, 124, 135, 170, 180, 223
Marblehead, 117
Marconi, 138
Marine Hospital Service, 69, 76, 85, 130–31, 160, 183, 199, 208, 232
Maritime Association of the Port of New York, 140, 146
Marsh, Richmond, 105
Mary D. Hume, 106
Massachusetts Humane Society, 64, 67, 69, 192, 202, 219

Maxen, John, 194
Maynard, Washburn, 117
McAdoo, William G., 146, 149, 237–38
McCalla, Bowman H., 117
McConnell, George E., 63
McCulloch (USRC), 79, 80, 111–12, 114–16, 120, 122–24, 133–35, 170, 223
McDonald, Roderick A., 64
McGowan, John, 5, 63, 194
McIlhenney, E. A., 104
McKenney, James, 40–41
McKinley, William, 110, 111, 117, 120
McLane, Louis, 58
McLellan, Charles H., 63, 199
McLenehan, Samuel B., 43–46
McMillan, C. C., 134
Mead, Ernest E., 119
Means, Dennis, 195, 196
medical care for fishermen, 152
Meekins, Theodore, 216–17
Meihner, H., 132
merchant shipping, 4–5; during Spanish-American War, 112–13, 121
Merriman, E. C., 39
Merry, John F., 118
Merryman, James H., 13, 14–15, 63, 78, 155, 197–98, 202, 214
Metropolis, wooden steamer, 200
Mexican War, 2, 3
Meyer, George von Lengerke, 230–31
Miami (USRC), 126, 146–48, 232
Midgett, Rasmus, 216
Miller, James, 43
Minnie, British sealer, 50
Mitchell Boat Co., 158
Moccasin (USRC), 72
Mohawk (USRC), 143
Montojo, Don Patricio, 114, 115
Moore, George W., 13, 23
Moore, John C., 171
Morgan, Charles S., 140
Morning Star, 152

Morrill (USRC), 109, 110
Morris, William Gouverneur, 25, 28, 29, 30, 31, 37
Morrison, James J., 77
Mount Wollaston, whaler, 31, 33–34
Muir, John, 31, 35, 36–37
Mullett, Thomas B., 14
Munger, Frederick M., 122
Munter, William, 141

Nagel, Charles, 229–30
Nansemond (USRC), 14
Nanshan, British collier, 113, 114, 115
Napoleon, whaling bark, 86
Narwhal, whaler, 41
Nathan Esterbrook, Jr., schooner, 215
Navarch, 98, 106
Navigation Act of 1817, 4–5
Nelson, Edward W., 36
Neutrality Patrol (1895–98), 109–10, 227
Newall, William A., 193, 194, 195
Newall Act, 193, 194, 204
Newcomb, Frank, 63, 119–20
New Hampshire (USRC), 154
New Orleans Times-Democrat, 129–30
Newport, 98, 103, 106
Newport News Shipbuilding and Dry-dock Co., 140
New York Maritime Exchange, 149
Noatak River, 43–46
North Atlantic Squadron, 111, 117, 120–21
Northern Light, bark, 40–41
Noyes, Joseph, 194
Nullification Controversy, 2
Nunivak (USRC), 126–29
Nye, Ebenezer F., 33–34

O'Connor, William D., 201
Ogir, 215
Old Dominion Steamship Co., 143
O'Leary, Thomas, 65
Oliver Wolcott (USRC), 15, 26, 29, 30, 150

Olympia, 114, 115, 122
Onondaga (USRC), 79, 80, 143
opium smuggling, 150–51
Orca, 42, 98, 103, 106
Ord, E.O.C., 134
Oriole, 171
Otero, Miguel, 77
Ottinger, Douglass, 5, 193, 194
overland expedition, 92, 94–106, 224, 233

Pacific Mail Co., 134
Packer, Stanley V., 141
Pasig, 124
Pathfinder, British schooner, 51
Patterson, Carlisle T., 5–6, 11
Peckham, Henry L., 165
Pelz, John J., 205
Penrose (USRC), 69, 71, 122
Perry, Kirtland W., 135–38
Perry (USRC), 6, 75, 153
Peters, Joseph, 67
Petrel (USRC), 6, 14
Phelps, T. G., 85
Philadelphia Maritime Exchange, 146
Pierce, Franklin, 2
Poole, Fred, 67
Portland, steamer, 219
Powhattan, 195
Pratt, E. Spencer, 111
Prince, Paul C., 170
Priscilla, barkentine, 215–16
Public Health Service, 130–31, 153, 160, 183, 191, 232
Pulsifer, Frank H., 5

quarantine laws, 2
Quasi-War with France, 3

Racer (USRC), 6, 14
Rainbow, whaling bark, 33
Raleigh, 114, 115
Randall, Frank B., 115
Rath, William, 30

Red Rover, sloop, 63
Reed, Byron L., 39
Reinburg, John E., 176, 179
Reliance (USRC), 4, 7, 14, 15
Relief (USRC), 6, 14
Republic, 126, 135–38
Rescue (USRC), 6, 15
Resolute (USRC), 6
Revenue Cutter School of Instruction, 55, 57–58, 60, 72, 74, 77, 223, 224; administration of, 186–87; admission to, 156, 157, 158, 166, 167–68, 175, 183–86, 190; and cadet engineers, 174–75; cadet routine at, 158, 163, 188–89; church attendance at, 189; class distinctions at, 168, 187; class size at, 163, 172, 182–83; closing and reopening of, 165; compensation for cadets at, 166, 172, 175, 178; curriculum of, 158, 159–60, 163, 165–66, 172, 173, 174, 180, 189, 190; drill at, 190; examinations at, 190–91; facilities at, 158, 165, 171–72, 180, 181, 182; faculty of, 158–59, 160, 175; graduations at, 163–64, 191; hazing and discipline at, 172; inspections at, 188; liberty at, 158, 172, 188; locations of, 156, 167, 171, 173, 179, 180–81, 182; merit system of appointment to, 156, 157, 183–86; origins of, 154–55; professional training at, 160, 166–67, 190–91; quality of programs at, 160, 164–65, 167, 182; recreation at, 163, 167, 172; regulations of, 158, 188, 189; sail training at, 157–58, 160–61, 162–63, 166, 172; school year of, 187; ships belonging to, 155–56, 157, 160, 161–63, 164–73, 175, 176–79, 186, 190; superintendents of, 160–61, 162–63, 165, 166, 168, 170–71, 172–73, 179, 180, 181, 183, 186; third year added to program at, 174; and training at sea, 175, 176–79, 190. *See also* U.S. Coast Guard Academy; U.S. Revenue Cutter Academy
Revenue Marine Bureau, 9–10
Reynolds, William E., 120, 136, 138, 172–73, 176
Rhodes, John, 67–69
Richard F. C. Harley, schooner, 170
Richard Rush (USRC), 15, 31, 37, 72
Roath, Warrington D., 68
Roberts, William H., 110
Roosevelt, Theodore, 135
Rosario, 98, 103, 106
Rose, Earl G., 182
Ross, Worth G.: and academy, 158–61; and 1905 yellow fever epidemic, 131–32; retirement of, 223, 225
Rosse, Irving C., 36
Rostron, Arthur H., 145–46
Rush (USRC), 43, 46–52, 127
Russia, 49; sealing policies of, 52–53

Sadie C. Symner, schooner, 143
St. Christopher, French barkentine, 147
Saint George Island, 27, 28, 31, 50
Saint Lawrence Island, 35
Saint Paul Island, 27, 28, 31, 41, 50, 85
Salmon P. Chase (USRC), bark, 15, 72, 74, 78, 155–56, 158, 160–63, 165–72, 175, 176, 180
Sampson, William T., 110–11, 117, 120
Samuel Dexter (USRC), 63
San Francisco earthquake, 15, 31, 33, 35, 41, 46–47, 52, 133–35
Sargent, Aaron A., 200, 201
Sargent, Nathan, 123
Schley, Winfield Scott, 83, 120–21
Schuyler Colfax (USRC), 14, 16, 68, 109, 110, 165

Scotia, British whaler, 149–50
Scout (USRC), 79
Sealby, William Inman, 136, 137, 138
Seaman, Peter, 186
Selden, James M., 29, 30
Seminole War, 3
Seneca (USRC), 126, 136, 138, 173;
    and derelict destruction, 140–43;
    and international ice patrol,
    146–48
Seward, William H., 22
Shaw, Leslie M., 131, 134, 175
Shepard, Isabel S., 47, 49–52
Shepard, Leonard: as academy super-
    intendent, 163; advocates retire-
    ment system for officers, 73–74,
    76–77, 80–81; as commandant,
    72–81; fights for new ships,
    73–79, 80; provides technical ex-
    pertise, 76; supports move of rein-
    deer to Alaska, 92
Sherman, John, 28, 201, 220, 222
Sherman (USRC), 6
Shoemaker, Charles F., 127; and acad-
    emy, 166, 171; as commandant,
    77–81; improves cutters, 77–81;
    improves officer corps, 77, 80–81;
    and Life-Saving Service, 194, 195,
    198–99, 209–11, 217, 218–19
Shoemaker, William, 77
Slicer, George, 5, 11, 63
Small, John Humphrey, 240
Smith, Edward J., 145
Smith, Everett E., 41
Smith (USRC), 121
Spanish-American War, 78, 81, 109–
    25, 170, 173, 180, 233
S. P. Chase (USRC), side-wheeler, 6, 14,
    16
Speedwell, navy tug, 66–67
Sperry (USRC), 78
Springsteen, Benjamin E., 215–16
Springsteen, William, 215–16
S. R. Mallory, schooner, 110
Stamboul, 49

Steamboat Inspection Service, 138, 226
Stein, E. H. (USN), 11
Stevens. See E. A. Stevens
Stewart, Gustavus U., 176–79
Stika, J. E., 182
Strager, Edgar, 165
Stulzman, S. S., 39

Taft, William Howard, 182, 225, 231,
    236–37
Tahoma (USRC), 153
Taylor, Willard U., 146
Tchuktchis, 33
Teller, Henry M., 89
Teller Reindeer Station, 89, 100, 107
Templemore, steamer, 143
Tench Coxe (USRC), 15, 71
Tenyse Maru, 152
Terasto, Austrian brig, 193
Thetis (USRC), 49, 83–84, 94, 133–35,
    153, 180
Thomas Corwin (USRC), 15, 29, 30, 31,
    32, 63, 82, 88; enforces liquor
    laws, 40; explores Alaskan rivers,
    43–46; and gunboat diplomacy,
    37–40; regular cruises of Arctic
    by, 31, 33, 36; and search for *Jean-
    nette*, 33–34, 173; transports
    stranded whalers, 41–42
Thorne, Charles, 29
Thrasher, whaler, 42
Three Friends, steamer, 110
Tilton, George Fred, 98–99, 103
Tipsey, 131
Titanic, 138, 140, 144–46
Todd, Chapman C., 118, 120, 122
Tokai Maru, 152
Toucey, Isaac, 59
Toucey (USRC), 6, 59
Townsend, Charles H., 88
Tracy, Benjamin, 59, 60, 227, 230
Tununak, Alaska, 96
Tuscarora (USRC), 180
Tuttle, Francis, 51, 94–95, 106, 107
Tybee (USRC), 79

Unalga (USRC), 233

U.S. Army, 60, 83, 107, 111, 121, 122, 125, 134–35, 213–14, 239, 240

U.S. Coast Guard Academy, 13, 15, 183. *See also* Revenue Cutter School of Instruction; U.S. Revenue Cutter Academy

U.S. Life-Saving Service, 15, 16, 17, 63–64, 66–69, 78, 180, 190, 192–222, 226, 228, 230, 232, 237, 238, 239; beach patrols of, 212; communications in, 217–18; crews of, 195–97, 198, 199, 201, 204, 207, 208, 209–20, 222, 228, 237; and deaths of surfmen, 237; district superintendents of, 208, 209–11; districts of, 198, 201; keepers in, 195–200, 208, 209–12, 215–19, 222, 228; lifeboats in, 197, 199, 208, 218, 222; and lifesaving equipment, 193, 194, 196, 197, 199, 200, 201, 204, 207, 208, 212, 213–14, 215, 218; lives and property saved by, 195, 202, 203, 213, 215–17, 218, 219, 222, 238; merit system in, 209–12, 222; and ordnance, 199, 213–14; origins of, 192–93; political patronage in, 199, 209–12, 222; praised, 201, 220, 222, 239, 240; regulations of, 197–98; retirement and longevity pay in, 237, 238, 239; and Revenue Cutter Service, 199, 200, 208, 211, 218, 228, 238; signaling in, 197, 200, 207, 212, 216; stations of, 193–94, 196–207, 209, 212, 215, 217, 219, 222; superintendents of, 207–8, 209, 222; surfboats in, 199, 213, 215, 222; and use of lifecars, 194, 215

U.S. Lighthouse Service, 2, 60, 67, 193, 226, 230, 243

U.S. Naval Academy, 54–56, 58, 60, 77, 168, 175, 182, 223, 230

U.S. Navy, 3, 4, 54–61, 76, 153, 223, 226, 227, 229–32, 234, 235, 237–38, 239, 240, 243; and Greely relief expedition, 83–84; and international ice patrol, 146; and Life-Saving Service, 200, 201; and San Francisco earthquake, 133–34; in Spanish-American War, 110, 112–25

U.S. Revenue Cutter Academy, 183, 186. *See also* Revenue Cutter School of Instruction; U.S. Coast Guard Academy

U.S. Steamboat Inspection Service, 69

Vance, Sherrington, 66

Vigilant, whaler, 31, 33–34

Vigilant (USRC), 6

Vincent, J. B., 86

von Diederichs, Otto, 123

Walker, Robert J., 193

Walker, Thomas D., 63

Walton, John Q., 7, 76

Walton, Walter, 63

Wanderer, whaler, 42, 84, 106

War Department, 141

War of 1812, 3

Wasdin, Eugene, 130–32

Washington, George, 1

Washington (USRC), 16, 71, 72, 75, 78

Watts, Edward, 194

Wayanda (USRC), 6, 7, 14, 25, 26, 27, 85

Webster, John A., 155

Wheeler, Charles S., 5

Wheeler, William J., 167–70

White, Chester M., 89

White, James T., 92–93

White, John, merchant seaman, 66

White, John (RCS), 14, 25, 26–27, 29–30, 63, 85

Wilbur, Horace, 43

Wilkinson, Alex, 39–40

William Aiken (USRC), 155
William Cramp and Sons, 111
William E. Chandler (USRC), 16, 75
William F. Morrisey, schooner, 139
William H. Seward (USRC), 16
William P. Fessenden (USRC), 6
Williams, R. J., 137
Wilmington, 118, 119
Wilson, Woodrow, 150, 237, 241
Windom, William, 59–60, 70, 72, 74, 85
Windom (USRC), 79, 109, 117–18
Winona (USRC), 74, 109, 110, 122, 126, 131–32
Winslow (navy torpedo boat), 118–20
wireless, 135–38, 139–40, 143, 146, 148

Wolcott (USRC), 15, 26, 29, 30, 150
Women's Christian Temperance Union, 85
World War I, 243
World War II, 243
Wright, Schuyler E., 64–69
Wyck, Paul, 35
Wyman, Walter, 160, 161

Yeaton, Hopley, 154
yellow fever epidemic (1905), 129–31
York, Wick, 193, 204–6
Young, Lucian, 200

Zafiro, British supply ship, 113, 114, 115

About the Author

Irving H. King is a professor of history and former head of the Department of Humanities at the U.S. Coast Guard Academy in New London, Connecticut. He is the author of *George Washington's Coast Guard* and *The Coast Guard under Sail*, both published by the Naval Institute Press.

The **Naval Institute Press** is the book-publishing arm of the U.S. Naval Institute, a private, nonprofit society for sea service professionals and others who share an interest in naval and maritime affairs. Established in 1873 at the U.S. Naval Academy in Annapolis, Maryland, where its offices remain today, the Naval Institute has more than 85,000 members worldwide.

Members of the Naval Institute receive the influential monthly magazine *Proceedings* and discounts on fine nautical prints and on ship and aircraft photos. They also have access to the transcripts of the Institute's Oral History Program and get discounted admission to any of the Institute-sponsored seminars offered around the country.

The Naval Institute also publishes *Naval History* magazine. This colorful bimonthly is filled with entertaining and thought-provoking articles, first-person reminiscences, and dramatic art and photography. Members receive a discount on *Naval History* subscriptions.

The Naval Institute's book-publishing program, begun in 1898 with basic guides to naval practices, has broadened its scope in recent years to include books of more general interest. Now the Naval Institute Press publishes about 100 titles each year, ranging from how-to books on boating and navigation to battle histories, biographies, ship and aircraft guides, and novels. Institute members receive discounts of 20 to 50 percent on the Press's nearly 600 books in print.

For a free catalog describing Naval Institute Press books currently available, and for further information about subscribing to *Naval History* magazine or about joining the U.S. Naval Institute, please write to:

Membership & Communications Department
U.S. Naval Institute
118 Maryland Avenue
Annapolis, Maryland 21402-5035
Telephone: (800) 233-8764
Fax: (410) 269-7940